Communists and Perverts under the Palms

UNIVERSITY PRESS OF FLORIDA

Florida A&M University, Tallahassee
Florida Atlantic University, Boca Raton
Florida Gulf Coast University, Ft. Myers
Florida International University, Miami
Florida State University, Tallahassee
New College of Florida, Sarasota
University of Central Florida, Orlando
University of Florida, Gainesville
University of North Florida, Jacksonville
University of South Florida, Tampa
University of West Florida, Pensacola

Communists and Perverts under the Palms

The Johns Committee in Florida, 1956–1965

STACY BRAUKMAN

University Press of Florida

Gainesville · Tallahassee · Tampa · Boca Raton
Pensacola · Orlando · Miami · Jacksonville · Ft. Myers · Sarasota

Printed in the United States of America. This book is printed on Glatfelter
Natures Book, a paper certified under the standards of the Forestry
Stewardship Council (FSC). It is a recycled stock that contains 30 percent
post-consumer waste and is acid-free.

17 16 15 14 13 12   6 5 4 3 2 1

Library of Congress Cataloging-in-Publication Data
Braukman, Stacy Lorraine.
Communists and perverts under the palms : the Johns Committee in
Florida, 1956–1965 / Stacy Braukman.
p. cm.
Includes bibliographical references and index.
ISBN 978-0-8130-3982-4 (alk. paper)
1. Florida. Legislature. Legislative Investigation Committee. 2. Florida—
Politics and government—1951– 3. Culture conflict—Florida—History.
4. Communism—Florida—History. 5. Homosexuality—Florida—
History. 6. Civil rights—Florida—History. 7. National Association for the
Advancement of Colored People. I. Title.
F316.2.B68 2012
975.9'063—dc23
2011037505

The University Press of Florida is the scholarly publishing agency for the
State University System of Florida, comprising Florida A&M University,
Florida Atlantic University, Florida Gulf Coast University, Florida
International University, Florida State University, New College of Florida,
University of Central Florida, University of Florida, University of North
Florida, University of South Florida, and University of West Florida.

University Press of Florida
15 Northwest 15th Street
Gainesville, FL 32611-2079
http://www.upf.com

Contents

Figures

Acknowledgments

This book would not have been possible without the support of many people, to whom I owe an enormous debt of gratitude. My editor, Meredith Morris-Babb at the University Press of Florida, belongs at the top of the list, thanks to her endless patience and unwavering belief in the project. The librarians and archivists at the George A. Smathers Libraries and Special Collections at the University of Florida, the Special Collections of the Otto G. Richter Library at the University of Miami, the Mississippi State Archives, and the Arthur and Elizabeth Schlesinger Library on the History of Women in America at Harvard University were unfailingly helpful. I am especially grateful to Paul Camp at the University of South Florida's Special Collections, as well as David Coles and Jody Norman at the State Archives of Florida in Tallahassee, who always had a friendly word and a wealth of knowledge to share.

In Chapel Hill, I was fortunate to be surrounded by enormously talented colleagues and friends. Kirsten Delegard, Eve Duffy, Natalie Fousekis, Kathy Newfont, and Ginny Noble are extraordinary women whose humor, intellect, and appreciation for good food and drink sustained and inspired me, as did their meticulous reading and thoughtful comments on draft after draft of this book. Gavin Campbell, Tom Devine, Gary Frost, John Hepp, Molly Rozum, Robert Tinkler, and Michael Trotti made the act of sharing my writing more fun than it probably should have been. I know they made my writing better and my thinking sharper, and I thank them.

I am grateful to UNC for institutional support in the form of research and writing grants. I also deeply appreciate the friendship of the people who made Chapel Hill so special and so hard to leave for the better part of a decade: Eric Carrig, Spencer Downing, Lars Golumbic, Elizabeth Horst, Ethan Kytle, Kelly Manno, Hans and Jennifer Muller, Jennifer Ritterhouse,

Blain Roberts, David Sartorius, Mike Snyder, Adam and Jennifer Tuchinsky, David and Kathy Walbert, and LeNaye Willis.

I began writing this book during an unforgettable four years in Boston, the only time I've lived north of the Mason-Dixon Line. As the assistant editor for the latest volume of the venerable *Notable American Women*, I joined the staff of the Schlesinger Library at Harvard University, which I can only describe as a dream come true. My colleagues were exceptional in every way. Three notable women in particular, Diane Hamer, Sylvia McDowell, and Debbie Richards, shared with me their knowledge and love of Boston and showed me the ropes at Harvard—no easy task. I am proud to call them my friends. Annie Bergen, Amanda Bird, Jennifer Cote, Kathryn Losavio, and David Wagner demonstrated grace under fire and a supportiveness that seemed to know no bounds. Melissa Carlson, Kirsten Condry, Shayne Goldberg, Lisa Hurlbutt, Matt Kaliner, Meredith Leigh, Deborah Levine, Heather Malkani, Dan Miller, Robin Morris, Jessica Shroder, and Chris Timmerman were there for me in ways that I will never be able to sufficiently thank them for. My life is all the richer for their friendship.

It has been my greatest privilege—and still, after all these years, hard to believe my good fortune—to work with some truly remarkable historians. The depth of my gratitude to John D'Emilio, Jacquelyn Dowd Hall, Nancy Hewitt, and Steven Lawson is immeasurable. Since our days together at the University of South Florida more than twenty years ago, Nancy and Steven have encouraged my writing and supported me through good times and bad. John was patient and skillful in guiding me through every stage of research and writing, and his deft blending of scholarship with activism continues to awe. And I thank Jacquelyn for challenging me to take myself seriously as a writer and as a person. I have taken every word to heart, and I consider myself lucky to have her as a mentor and a friend.

Countless other scholars have been indispensable to this project. George Lewis read and reread the manuscript through two rounds of revisions, and each time he made the work vastly better with his suggestions and queries. Steven Niven didn't hesitate when I asked him to read it. His skills as a historian and a writer are humbling, and his generosity exceeds anything I could have hoped for. I have never met James Schnur in person, but our e-mail exchanges over the past two years inspired me to forge ahead with the book when my spirits were flagging and my faith in people dimming. I will always be grateful to him for reminding me that academic integrity and hard, honest work still have meaning. Wesley Chenault has kept me sane and been a phenomenal cheerleader and partner in crime for the past six years. He also tracked down sources for my book even while he was researching and writing one of his own. I eagerly await future collaborations and adventures with him.

A special thank you goes to Maria Tonelli, my lifelong friend, who put me up during my research trips to Gainesville and has shared sound advice, a friendly ear, and a gift for making me laugh for more than three decades—which more than makes up for the unfortunate poison oak episode of 1978. I am also grateful to Mike Ross, who for many years has unselfishly dispensed advice about work, writing, and publishing. It is not an exaggeration to say that the deadlines of the past two years simply would not have been met without Ashley Ross holding me accountable to them, and I thank her. Finally, I am indebted to Amy Hurd, who has taught me more about compassion and forgiveness than anyone I know. Her love and encouragement changed the way I see the world. I wish I could leave a copy of this book on the counter for her.

During the years it took to complete this project, my family underwent some dramatic changes, as all families do. My brother, Howard Braukman, and his wife Claudia welcomed three daughters into the world. I hope that when Angela, Rebeca, and Camilla are old enough to read this, the content will truly seem like the distant past, unrecognizable to them. Even if I don't always make it apparent, I appreciate all of their love as well as their tolerance for my imperfect phone habits.

This book is dedicated to my parents, Ernie and Mary Alice Braukman, who never lost faith in my abilities. My mother has been cheering me on from the beginning, and I couldn't have seen this through without her. I wish my father had lived to see the book, hold it in his hands, chuckle at the raunchy parts, and convey in his usual quiet, easy way his pride in the finished product. I'd like to think he would have believed that the long and rambling journey was worth it in the end. I also wish that my uncle and aunt, Reymer and Betty Gaventa, could be here for me to thank them. A college professor and an elementary school teacher, they were passionate educators and fiercely proud to call themselves liberals. They set a lasting example of what it means to care about fairness, justice, and taking a stand when it really matters. I miss them, and my dad, every day.

Introduction

Where the Sunbelt Meets the Old South

It is when communists (or any other group) are outlawed, cast into outer darkness, and set apart from the rest of the human race that they take on the unearthly quality of witches. They become, in the public mind, shadowy and ill defined, the personification of evil and wrong. And people, in all their frailty, identify such proclaimed demons with anyone or any idea they fear and hate.

> Anne Braden, "House Un-American Activities Committee:
> Bulwark of Segregation," 1963

In 2002 in the pages of the *New York Times*, the poet Campbell McGrath asked of Florida, "Why here? Why psychopaths and terrorists, upside-down elections and general weirdness? Is it the unrootedness of people, the extraordinariness of the landscape, the lack of seasons that untether you from the past?"[1] It might have been all of those things. Florida's history is replete with the unrooted, the fugitive, the quixotic. The landscape is extraordinary, though not by the usual measures. It is extraordinary in its flatness, drenching heat, and, before the advent of air conditioning and mosquito repellent, its general inhospitableness. The state's saving grace, and indeed its main draw since Henry Flagler's palatial hotels and railroads appeared in the 1880s to cater to well-to-do visitors, has always been its sparkling beaches and abounding sunshine. At first a tropical vacation land for the wealthy, Florida became an increasingly affordable and popular destination, a place where growing numbers of Americans went to the beach, looked to make a fresh start, or retired.

But by the twentieth century's end, many had begun to wonder, What happened to Florida? Less a successor to the postwar California dream than a modern Sunbelt nightmare, Florida had come to be known for bizarre characters, outlandish crimes, and sensationalized spectacles.

Breathless media coverage of the murderous spree and execution of Aileen Wuornos, the televised manhunt for the gay murderer of Gianni Versace in South Beach, the international custody battle over little Elián González, and September 11 ringleader Mohammad Atta's purported pre-attack strip-club binge—to name only a very few—left many wondering if Carl Hiaasen had been too generous to the Sunshine State in his fictional portrayals of political graft and nutty residents. In 2000, round-the-clock cable news channels even managed to make "hanging chads" in Florida a national punch line out of alleged malfeasance by Republican officials, including secretary of state Katherine Harris, which tipped the balance in a close and acrimonious presidential election. It bears mentioning that Harris is the granddaughter of citrus baron and politician Ben Hill Griffin Jr., who in the early 1960s served on the Florida Legislative Investigation Committee (FLIC), a body forged in the heat of the South's resistance against integration, a forerunner in the modern culture wars, and the subject of this book.[2]

Until the summer of 1993, few people, in Florida or anywhere else, knew about the committee. But with the release of thousands of pages of FLIC documents on July 1, Floridians discovered a chapter in the state's history that most saw as appalling. The opening of the records itself became a sensation, as journalists flocked to the state archives in Tallahassee to comb through documents, find the most eye-popping quotes from interrogation transcripts, and tell the stories of those most egregiously victimized by the committee. Their reporting focused on the FLIC's most outrageous and unconstitutional practices, as well as what looked to modern eyes like brazen racism and homophobia. Labeled "notorious," "infamous," and "evil," as having been engaged in "witch hunts" and "Gestapo" and "police state" tactics, the committee's existence, removed though it was by nearly thirty years, became yet another damning piece of evidence of Florida's dark underbelly.[3]

* * *

From frontier outpost to prepackaged paradise, Florida has always been buffeted by demographic tumult—colonial conquest by vying European powers, Seminole Indian expulsion, speculative land and real estate schemes, influxes and exoduses that left an ever-shrinking proportion of native-born residents—and this undercurrent of transience has led to Florida's marginalized status in U.S. and southern history. Generally speaking, Florida has tended to appear fleetingly and tangentially in both national and regional narratives. Yet if we want to understand the political culture of the United States in the second half of the twentieth century, we ignore or underestimate Florida at our own risk. By 1945 the state had begun showing signs of the economic changes that would eventually transform the rest of the South. War industries brought new wealth and new workers to the state, GIs poured into its colleges and filled its towns and suburbs, and low taxes, minimal regulation, and wanton growth ruled the day.[4] Few but the most visionary politicians and real estate developers could have predicted Florida's full-scale transformation in the years following World War II, the unrelenting waves of new residents, the explosion of tourism, rapid urbanization, and suburban spread. Several states, particularly those in the South and West, witnessed similar patterns. But in Florida, many people, especially native-born whites, clung to the state's Confederate past and its old racial attitudes. Alongside all of the signs of modernization, there existed a powerful strain of small-town traditionalism, conservatism, and resistance to change—in V. O. Key's words, a "faintly tropical rebel yell."[5]

In 1956, the tension between these two forces was evident in the creation of the Florida Legislative Investigation Committee, whose name became synonymous with its founder, state senator Charley Eugene Johns. The committee set out, as did many of its southern counterparts, to tarnish the reputation and hamper the efforts of the National Association for the Advancement of Colored People (NAACP), the force behind the litigation that culminated in the U.S. Supreme Court's 1954 *Brown v. Board of Education of Topeka* decision. In Florida, as in Alabama, Louisiana, Mississippi, South Carolina, and Virginia, legislators sought to expose what they believed to be the criminal activities and subversive ties of the NAACP and other groups advocating racial equality.[6] Unlike the other states, however, Florida, by means of the FLIC, commonly known as the Johns Committee, expanded its antisubversive mission over a period of nine years to include homosexual teachers, indecent literature and pornography, liberal professors, and student peace and civil rights groups. As a state-sponsored agency, it was unique in moving so far beyond its original anti-NAACP objective, but at the same time it was not alone on the right in critiquing these cultural and political articulations of liberalism.

What follows is a study of the Johns Committee's efforts to defend Florida's schools and universities on all of these fronts. By tracing the committee's evolution from an agent of massive resistance to a conservative cultural watchdog, we can see not only changing strategies for defending segregation and white supremacy in the South but also changing concerns in the wider culture and among conservatives over social issues—particularly those relating to race, sexuality, youth, and education. Before Anita Bryant's Save Our Children campaign, before Jerry Falwell's Moral Majority, southern segregationists, including the Johns Committee, were making claims about protecting children and educational institutions from subversive incursions of racialized, sexualized, contaminating threats and protecting parents' right to send their children to schools that reinforced their own racial, religious, and political values. In this way, the FLIC prefigured conservative attacks on liberalism and its 1960s' unleashing of corrosive forces (nonmarital sex, abortion, pornography, homosexuality, welfare, the banning of school prayer, and so on) that later became a fixture of the New Right, the evangelical Christian Right, and the Republican Party. As historian K. A. Cuordileone puts it, McCarthyism, of which the Johns Committee must be viewed as a southern offshoot, "greatly accelerated the association between liberals and moral laxity, and that association would endure on the right. The repudiation of liberal tolerance and moral relativism would become, with varying degrees of intensity, a defining element of conservative politics for the rest of the century."[7]

The committee's trajectory serves as an important reminder that anti-Communism as a political tool was often about more than just communism. In the words of historian Robert Dean, earlier scholars "stressed anti-Communism as the central ideology of the Red Scare. But this focus has neglected the extent to which 'McCarthyism' was also driven by related and equally deep-rooted concerns about sexual and gender order. In this conservative vision of politics and society, effective resistance to communism or other threats to '100 percent Americanism' demanded that citizens adhere to a traditional, patriarchal sexual order."[8] My purpose is not to unravel the "true" central ideology of McCarthyism, but to argue that anti-Communism shaped ways of thinking about other forms of subversion and allowed southern conservatives to construct other enemies in those terms: homosexuals as secret infiltrators, polluters, and corrupters, and integrationists as secret race mixers and statists.

The Johns Committee also can be viewed as a litmus test of changing southern conservative values in the postwar era. Its wide-ranging activities help illuminate the extent to which national discussions about race, sexuality, education, and communism shaped political concerns on the local and state levels and intersected with the desire to maintain racial segregation. In the late 1950s and early 1960s, conservative white Floridians taking stock of the changing social and cultural landscape, including school desegregation, new forms of mass-produced popular culture that seemed to flout earlier standards, and a stream of liberal Supreme Court decisions, were alarmed by what they saw as a fraying moral fabric, and in addition to voicing their concerns at PTA meetings or joining local decent literature groups and patriotic societies, they found a champion for their beliefs in the FLIC. The committee began as a vehicle for resisting racial integration, a self-professed law-and-order, anti-Communist investigating body dedicated to exposing the Communist penetration and perversion of the civil rights movement and other left-wing causes and organizations. It ended as something different, a sounding board for conservative complaints in Florida and a politically powerful group catering to segregationists and social conservatives by simultaneously perpetuating and mollifying fears of social and moral decay.

*   *   *

The period in which the FLIC operated, from 1956 to 1965, saw the unleashing of a vast arsenal of antisubversive, anti-integration, and anti-intellectual weaponry in the South, from loyalty oaths and spying to book banning and school closures, from the Senate Internal Subversion Subcommittee to the Citizens' Councils. In his 1969 pathbreaking work, *The Rise of Massive Resistance*, Numan Bartley credited elites with setting the tone and the agenda of resisting integration and finding a receptive audience among the white southern grass roots. It was the most influential among a wave of studies detailing the ideologies and tactics of white supremacist organizations and politicians as well as flashpoints in the larger conflict over school desegregation in places such as Little Rock, the University of Mississippi, and Virginia.[9] Bartley concluded his study on an optimistic note, confident that the election of John F. Kennedy and the growing militancy of black protest beginning in 1960 "further doomed neobourbon dreams of defeating the principle of the *Brown* decision." Massive resistance, he wrote, "passed into history."[10]

By the 1990s, historians were revisiting massive resistance and asking whether its passing had in fact occurred much later, and after many iterations. At the same time, the burgeoning literature on the origins of modern conservatism, its intellectual underpinnings, and the conservative capture of the GOP led scholars to consider the connections between massive resistance in the South and the rising national tide of conservatism.[11] Dan Carter's portrait of George Wallace as "the alchemist of the new social conservatism" suggested that the politics of massive resistance were foundational to the "conservative counterrevolution that reshaped American politics in the 1970s and 1980s." Carter argued that the Alabama governor's influence upon national politics was the result of his uncanny ability to meld "racial fear, anti-Communism, cultural nostalgia and traditional right-wing economics" in appealing to working-class whites both within and outside of the South amid the turmoil of the late 1960s and early 1970s. In this way, white resistance to mandated racial equality did not slip quietly away with what appeared to be the triumph of liberalism in the 1960s.[12]

Perhaps no one has done more to expand the terms of debate over massive resistance than Kevin Kruse in his work on a new, subtler brand of resistance in Atlanta articulated through the rhetoric of individual rights. An explicit rebuttal to situating modern conservatism's roots in Sunbelt suburbia, *White Flight* traces "new conservative causes, such as tuition vouchers, the tax revolt, and the privatization of public services"—issues emanating from white resistance to the integration of schools, neighborhoods, and public accommodations—to Atlanta and other southern cities and argues that it was only later exported to the suburbs.[13] Similarly, Joseph Crespino has shown how massive resistance was reconfigured in "ways that would come to resonate with white Americans far outside of the Deep South." Segregationists, he argues, constructed their fight as a national struggle to "preserve fundamental American freedoms"—freedom of association, freedom from federal intrusions, and so on.[14] These studies, along with Matthew Lassiter's exploration of suburban Sunbelt politics, while illuminating the economic and political changes that redrew racial and class lines of power and created a self-proclaimed colorblind "suburban ethos of middle-class entitlement," undervalue the significance of social issues, particularly those related to sexuality, in the battles over integration and the ascendancy of conservatism.[15] This study on the Johns Committee refocuses attention on how the fight to maintain segregated schools intersected with and helped shape a wider war against sexualized subversive forces that were considered threatening to children.

The past decade and a half has seen a proliferation of scholarship on anti-Communism and segregation. One strand emphasizes the upside of the United States' global war against communism in heightening international awareness of the contradictions of a superpower claiming to defend freedom in far-flung lands while failing to live up to its own constitutional promises of equality at home.[16] The other explores the debilitating effects of Red baiting on liberal and leftist politics, including civil rights. In her work on anti-Communism, southern liberalism, and the cooperative efforts of the federal government and southern states to investigate subversive integrationists, Sarah Hart Brown concludes that "most southern politicians found it logical, convincing, and profitable to combine red-baiting with race-baiting." The idea that betrayal of one's race was a sign of disloyalty to one's nation became cemented as a commonsense assumption among segregationists, and it was employed against progressives, both black and white, who challenged the orthodoxy of segregation.[17]

Recent studies of James Eastland and Jesse Helms use individual politicians as a lens for viewing the intersections of race, anti-Communism, and politics. Much like Dan Carter before them, historians have shown how two powerful southern senators' racial views and antipathy to communism mingled with and shaped their attacks on liberalism in many forms over many decades.[18] Others have examined the deployment of state institutions against school integration, again with an eye toward the manipulation of Cold War fears of political subversion. In his monograph on the Mississippi State Sovereignty Commission and "homegrown McCarthyism," Yasuhiro Katagiri traces the history of the group, its ties to the Citizens' Council, and efforts to build a regional network of like-minded state agencies.[19] M. J. Heale's work on state-level anti-Communism documents the pervasiveness of anti-Communist political structures beginning in the 1930s in the South and across the country. Heale missed the mark, however, when he claimed that by 1949, "enthusiasm for the politics of exposure had peaked." The State Department's decades-long purges of gay men and women employees in the name of national security began the following year, and state and federal investigating committees were scouring the southern countryside just a few years after that. Whether uncovering Communists within the NAACP or homosexuals in the military, civil service, or Florida schools, the politics of exposure was central to the conservative, segregationist, and antisubversive ethos well into the 1960s. Heale also reduced the southern Red scare of the 1950s and 1960s to a "disturbing postscript to the history of the little HUACs," writing that "the South remained relatively unmoved by the prospect of Communist subversion."[20]

Rather than seeing anti-Communism as an uninspiring afterthought, however, subsequent scholars explored the breadth of its appeal and the flexibility of its uses. Harking back to Bartley, Jeff Woods maintained that elite conservatives planned and carried out this southern strategy, bolstered by widespread popular support. "White working-class southerners needed little convincing from elites that Communism and integration were part of a unified threat to the region and the nation," he wrote, concluding that the Red baiting of civil rights activists failed to stop integration and voting rights protections, and it failed to prove any actual link between communism and civil rights.[21] It is true that "southern nationalists disrupted the struggle for black equality, but they could not prevent desegregation or the rise of black voters as a political force in the South." These southern nationalists did, however, popularize ideas that later were central to the New Right about the relationship between the power of the federal government and the forcing of "special rights" for minorities down the proverbial throats of white (and heterosexual and Christian and conservative) Americans. They also created new strategies and a new vocabulary for resisting integration that set the tone for later conservative invectives against everything from busing and welfare to open housing and affirmative action.[22]

In *The White South and the Red Menace: Segregationists, Anticommunism, and Massive Resistance, 1945–1965* and *Massive Resistance: The White Response to the Civil Rights Movement*, George Lewis rejects Bartley's top-down thesis and focuses on the interplay between grass-roots and elite support for massive resistance, as well as the diverse methods used to fight integration. His is an expansive view, calling it a "multilayered and multifaceted campaign" against individuals, groups, and the federal government who sought black equality.[23] He is careful to note that a great deal of variation existed even among those segregationists who employed anti-Communism. The story of the Johns Committee helps to reveal the full range of massive resistance, and the particular state and local exigencies that resulted in such diversity among segregationists.[24] In Florida, massive resistance became intertwined with other social issues, in part because of Charley Johns's personal agenda and in part because of committee members' attentiveness to constituents' complaints.

As tensions arose around civil rights and the Cold War, they were exacerbated by many factors: Florida's proximity to Cuba, faint yet visible signs of urban gay culture in places such as Miami and Tampa–St. Petersburg, pressing demands on the school and university systems to keep pace with the growing population, and the widening gulf not only between rural and urban dwellers but also between natives and newcomers, southerners and nonsoutherners.

Contrary to Jeff Woods's assertion that the South lacked "social and political turmoil" until the 1950s and 1960s, when the "status quo was challenged amid the racial struggles" and the region finally "experienced the upheaval necessary to sustain its own brand of McCarthyism," southern radicalism—and antiradicalism—and its attendant turmoil had existed for many decades leading up to what some have called the classical phase of the civil rights movement.[25] By the mid-1950s, as the United States' global struggle against communism came to shape both foreign and domestic policymaking, southern white fears of black subversion had been building, thanks to, in historian Glenda Gilmore's words, "the radical edges of a human rights movement" in the South—a progressive labor and civil rights coalition that included Communists, whose "small numbers mattered less than their very existence. It was Communists who stood up to say that black and white people should organize together, eat together, go to school together, and marry each other if they chose."[26] White southerners would not forget the Communist Party's involvement in the 1929 Gastonia, North Carolina, textile strikes and the Scottsboro case two years later, or its presence in the steel mills of Birmingham, the cotton fields of Arkansas, and the cigarette factories of Winston-Salem. The Dixiecrat revolt of 1948, followed by vitriolic Red-baiting and race-baiting Senate campaigns in Florida and North Carolina in 1950, also demonstrated the efficacy of smearing progressives as integration-minded subversives. The Dixiecrats, in the words of Kari Frederickson, "inaugurated a highly experimental era" when conservative southern whites began to "experiment with new political institutions and new alliances in their desperate attempt to stymie racial progress and preserve power."[27] The Johns Committee was one product of that experimentation.

*   *   *

A major component of the attack on racial progressives was the implication of sexual deviance. Given the postwar political landscape, in which sexual nonconformity was both equated with and linked to un-Americanism and communism, this is hardly surprising. John D'Emilio and Allan Bérubé were among the first to explore Cold War fears of the homosexual menace and the resulting political and legal repression, in the State Department and other federal agencies, in the military, and as a spark for early homophile groups.[28] Recent work examines more closely the State Department purges, federal investigations of homosexual employees, postwar anxieties about gender and sexuality and their expression in foreign policy and electoral politics, and the extent to which homophobia was integral to domestic anti-Communism during the postwar Red scare. Robert Dean, in his study of the gendered culture of the State Department and Cold War policymaking, observed historians' tendency to discuss the "Lavender Scare" of the 1950s in passing, many treating it, if at all, as a "peripheral absurdity" of the fringe Right.[29] He sought to remedy that, as do I, by showing that Cold War ideological and rhetorical linkages between political subversion and sexual perversion were sufficiently powerful to shape policy and discourse at both the state and national levels, and to influence thinking about other social issues, such as juvenile delinquency, obscenity, and civil rights. David K. Johnson has done the most to advance this argument, writing that the Lavender Scare "permeated 1950s political culture" and "sparked a moral panic within mainstream American culture."[30] Homophobia was used as a political tool and at times a blunt political weapon, and the ability of the Johns Committee to conjure up a familiar Cold war enemy, this time in the context of the dangers presented by homosexual teachers, speaks to both its efficacy and its adaptability—much like massive resistance itself.

The committee worked from this popular assumption, its members using homosexuality to rally support among conservative constituents and to attack liberals, especially educators who tampered with tradition, whether it be integrating the University of Florida (UF) law school or assigning J. D. Salinger in an English class at the University of South Florida (USF). K. A. Cuordileone, in *Manhood and American Political Culture in the Cold War*, explored this confluence of fears of communism, liberalism, and sexuality, arguing that although "the rhetoric that vilified 'pinks,' 'lavenders,' and 'reds' was strategically and opportunistically employed as a weapon with which to stigmatize political opponents," the rhetoric itself "relied on (and mobilized) real anxieties about both Communism and sexual disorder in American life."[31] Similarly, *Communists and Perverts under the Palms* demonstrates that Red baiting civil rights activists was an effective political tactic, just as claims of protecting youth from homosexual predators, eradicating smut from newsstands and classrooms, or defending the rights of Christian college students also proved useful, but these tactics were based on more than mere political expediency. They were carried out by a group of people who believed that their values were, at best, being undermined through modernization and, at worst, being threatened with extinction through the liberal subversion of American institutions.

Race and sexuality, then, are central rather than peripheral to our understanding of domestic anti-Communism, particularly as southern segregationists employed it. This book adds sexuality to Clive Webb's litany of forces that shaped massive resistance politics—"race but also religion, class, gender, and global politics."[32] It reminds us that sexuality has been invoked as a signifier of un-Americanness in many different contexts and toward many different political ends. In a recent collection on the ideologies and uses of Americanism, Michael Kazin and Joseph A. McCartin explored such topics as race, ethnicity, immigration, nationalism, anti-Communism, and religious diversity.[33] But what is missing is the subject of sexual identity and definitions of American and un-American, and this book on the Johns Committee helps to redress that oversight. Moreover, it suggests rethinking the origins of the social conservatism that became central to the New Right and the Republican Party. Rather than focusing solely on the role of Christian conservatives in bringing social issues to the forefront of the conservative agenda in the 1970s, we must also look closely at the ideas invoked to marginalize and silence those who opposed segregation as well as the imagined links between sexual and political nonconformity earlier in the postwar period.

While the literature on anti-Communism and modern conservatism is extensive and ever expanding, scholarship on the Johns Committee remains sparse. In "The Florida Legislative Investigation Committee and the Constitutional Readjustment of Race Relations," which appeared in 1989, Steven F. Lawson examined the FLIC's legal skirmishes with the NAACP and measured the short-term success of the committee in delaying school desegregation. Bonnie Stark, a graduate student of Lawson's at the University of South Florida, was the first to study the committee in her 1985 master's thesis. Although access to primary sources was limited by the fact that the FLIC records were still under seal, Stark interviewed

several key figures connected to the committee, including chief investigator R. J. Strickland.[34] A 1993 state constitutional amendment designed to
improve public access to legislative, judicial, and executive records resulted in the release of FLIC files, and James A. Schnur was the first to
make use of them. His meticulously researched 1995 master's thesis provided invaluable details about the political context and day-to-day activities of the Johns Committee. Schnur also contributed an article to John
Howard's groundbreaking collection, *Carryin' On in the Lesbian and Gay
South*, in which he addressed the committee's antihomosexual campaigns
as both an extremist outgrowth of McCarthyism and a "microcosm for
cold war crackdowns throughout the nation."[35] The committee has been
mentioned in several studies of massive resistance as well as postwar gay
and lesbian history, including James Sears's *Lonely Hunters: An Oral History of Lesbian and Gay Southern Life, 1948–1968*, published in 1997. More
recently, historians have examined specific areas of committee activities
in articles ranging from the USF investigation to the investigation of gay
public school teachers and the wider harassment of homosexuals in Florida in the 1950s and 1960s. The first full-length work appeared in 2009.
Karen L. Graves's *And They Were Wonderful Teachers: Florida's Purge of
Gay and Lesbian Teachers* focused on the Johns Committee as a product
and a tool of Cold War containment and measured its impact on education in Florida.[36]

Much of this scholarship has tended to treat committee members and
tactics in one-dimensional terms, as buffoonish, reactionary bigots and
homophobes. There is near-consensus as well that the FLIC simply chose
homosexuals as targets because they were easy marks or because committee members were desperately grasping to find some enemy in order
to maintain their power. Homosexuals could be used as scapegoats and
diversions or to whip up fear and anxiety. By today's standards, the Johns
Committee seems hopelessly homophobic and extreme and thus lends
itself to oversimplification and ahistorical value judgments. But by the
standards of the late 1950s and early 1960s, it is best understood as an
instrument of state power that was at once aggressive in its attacks on integrationists and responsive to the concerns of those Floridians nervously
watching the exploding civil rights movement, the escalating Cold War,
and the emergence of an urban gay subculture.

To a certain extent we must take the committee at its word. Members
claimed to believe that the Communist Party had infiltrated or influenced

civil rights groups in Florida, that mixed schools would lead to mixed blood, and that gay teachers and liberal professors threatened the normal, healthy development of Florida's youth. We can decry the unconstitutional and morally objectionable lengths to which the committee went during its investigations or speculate about the degree of committee members' personal or psychosexual stake in the proceedings. The motives of the committee, however, ultimately tell us less about massive resistance and social conservatism than do the terms by which committee members articulated their mission, formulated their reports to the legislature and the press, and went about the daily business of identifying threats, pursuing subversives, and framing and publicizing their own work. If the United States military, the federal government, and the police and courts, from Boise, Idaho, to Atlanta, Georgia, to Northampton, Massachusetts, all agreed that homosexuals were untrustworthy, morally degenerate, and a threat to children, it matters little whether Charley Johns's adherence to these beliefs was sincere. In fact, he likely used the committee to raise his own political profile, in addition to trying to stanch civil rights activism, halt the rapid changes that were occurring in the society in which he lived, and simply—and more nebulously—trying to defend conservative values. But it matters a great deal that these ideas could be put into practice and accepted, even applauded, by many Floridians for almost a decade.[37]

Johns and his colleagues were playing to an audience, and while there is no evidence that they actively tailored their investigations to appeal to previously identified constituencies, in most cases committee members claimed to be responding to specific complaints related to schools and universities. This served to make the FLIC appear attentive to voters and to make the committee's work seem more relevant, more attuned to changing times, and thus more likely to be voted future appropriations. The FLIC may have been the only anti-integration legislative committee to branch out into investigating other forms of subversion during this period, but it was by no means alone in the South in casting aspersions on the sexual behavior and moral values of African Americans, college students, liberals, and homosexuals. George Wallace remarked on the 1963 March on Washington that he had better things to do than "waste my time" on "communists and sex perverts."[38] The Cold War had helped solidify the belief that political subversion and sexual deviance were dangerously related to each other. In the South, this notion converged with whites' ideas about black sexuality to create a discourse on deviance through which they articulated their opposition to integration as well as to communism, liberalism, or progressivism in virtually any form. Understanding how these enemies came to be constructed illuminates postwar regional and national political culture in a new way, forcing us to consider the intersections of race and sexuality with southern resistance against integration and the transformation of the South during the peak years of the Cold War.

*   *   *

Communists and Perverts under the Palms explores the Johns Committee from its launch during a special session of the Florida legislature in the summer of 1956 to its quiet demise nine years later. Chapter 1 focuses on the committee's founding in a tumultuous year in Florida politics, a year that witnessed a heated gubernatorial election, skirmishes between a segregationist-dominated legislature and a moderate governor, and bus boycotts in Tallahassee and Miami. Subsequent chapters, organized chronologically, examine the committee's investigations and hearings during each legislative biennium. Generally speaking, as the FLIC's membership and leadership changed every two years, its agenda often shifted to varying degrees as well, though it could also change according to the particular exigencies of a community, city, university, or school district. Chapter 2, covering 1957–58, analyzes the committee's tactics against the NAACP, as well as initial forays into the existence of homosexual teachers in Tampa and Gainesville. In chapter 3, I examine the 1959 purge of homosexual professors at the University of Florida and its aftershocks, and the changing approach by the Johns Committee toward civil rights activists following the wave of sit-ins in 1960. Chapter 4 covers 1961–62, when the FLIC found an ally in a newly elected segregationist governor and received his stamp of approval to sponsor a statewide educational campaign about the related dangers of homosexuality and obscene literature, and when the committee began hearing murmurs of discontent from conservative parents of University of South Florida students. The final chapter, covering 1963–65, looks at the USF investigation, which began in secret and ended up bitterly dividing critics of liberal education and supporters of academic freedom. It recounts later missteps that undercut the committee's legitimacy and led many to question its mission, particularly in light of the triumphs of civil rights on the federal level and the changing face of massive resistance. Finally, in the epilogue I examine Anita Bryant's

1977 Save Our Children crusade, showing how many of the ideas about the corrupting influence of homosexual teachers articulated by members of the Johns Committee echoed in Bryant's campaign to overturn a gay rights ordinance, this time through an evangelical narrative of morality.

∗   ∗   ∗

As Victor Navasky wrote of the Hollywood blacklist, "What the hunters were doing was pronouncing a tribal judgment—you're not our kind; get out of town. The classic way to make such judgments stick is to label the hunted person as 'foreign' and then to identify him as conspiratorial, unclean, and immoral."[39] By understanding that the Johns Committee's anti-Communist critique of sexual and racial perversion bound them together under the rubric of subversion and the rhetoric of defending children, we can see more clearly how the South and the Sunbelt reaped their own Red scare from what McCarthy and others had sown in the late 1940s and early 1950s. Members of the Johns Committee might be easily dismissed as mean-spirited, anti-intellectual homophobes and racists if we dwell on the ease with which they sacrificed civil liberties to the mission of eradicating homosexuality, obscene literature, race mixing, and liberalism from public schools and universities. Instead, I seek to understand the committee's agenda and its supporters' views of a changing world in order to explain why its mission resonated during and beyond its lifetime and to help remedy the misconception that the conservatism of the New Right sprung up in a fully formed backlash during the 1970s against the perceived excesses and failures of liberalism from the decade before.

1

The NAACP and the Origins of the Johns Committee, 1956

Since the NAACP elected to fight with the weapons of pressure instead of persuasion, it should not now complain when similar weapons are turned against it.

William D. Workman, *The Case for the South*, 1960

In 1956, the Florida legislature established an investigating committee charged with identifying legal infractions by the NAACP. Florida joined other southern states that were creating sovereignty commissions, education commissions, and committees on un-American activities. All of them shared a single goal: to keep white schools white. Florida's committee was the product of a wildly unrepresentative state legislature in which elected officials from small rural counties held political power beyond their numbers. Employing any tactic that would help in the cause of maintaining segregated schools, including passing an interposition resolution, a bloc of segregationist legislators argued that an investigating committee was necessary to expose the state's NAACP chapters as lawbreakers bent on creating chaos and attaining social equality, duped by national leaders in New York City. Opposing them stood the moderate governor, LeRoy Collins, who faced reelection in 1956. Collins had defeated state senator Charley Johns in the governor's race of 1954, and now Johns was leading the fight to preserve segregation. The investigating committee that came to bear his name was part of one strand of massive resistance in the region, but it also represented the tensions between old Florida and new, between traditional expressions of white supremacy and an approach to segregationist resistance that tied it to America's global battle against communism.

*   *   *

At midcentury, Florida was growing faster than almost any state in the nation. Between 1940 and 1950 the population increased from two million people to three million. By the end of the 1950s, that figure had jumped to nearly five million. Florida's rate of urban growth also outpaced all of its regional counterparts. Between 1950 and 1960, the number of Floridians living in cities doubled, from 1.8 million to 3.7 million.[1] Many of the new residents came from the Northeast and Midwest. While towns in the Panhandle and the northeastern section of Florida remained largely populated by white, southern, and Protestant residents, central and south Florida cities drew new inhabitants from a variety of ethnic and religious groups, including Cubans, Italians, Spanish, and Jews. For most of the century Florida had boasted a higher rate of urbanization than any other state in the South, but the differences between city and countryside became even more pronounced in the decades after World War II as cities and suburbs grew.[2]

Other major transformations were underway in Florida as well. At the beginning of the twentieth century, over half of the state's population worked in agriculture, raising cattle and growing cotton, tobacco, and citrus. Industries included phosphate mining, lumber, and shipping. During and after the war, construction, finance, insurance, and real estate boomed. Computers, the space program, and trade with Latin America catapulted the state into a position of importance in the national and global economies by the early 1960s.[3]

These rapid changes occurred in the context of an outmoded political system characterized by one-party politics, a governor who could not serve two consecutive terms and who shared power with an elected six-person cabinet, and an undemocratically apportioned legislature. The "Pork Chop Gang," or porkchoppers, were a group of conservative white Democrats from rural counties who controlled state government during the middle decades of the twentieth century. The editor of the *Tampa Tribune* introduced the moniker in 1955 in an attack on their extravagant pork-barrel spending on their own constituents at the expense of Florida's growing urban areas.[4] The state constitution enabled the president of the

Florida Senate to appoint all committee members and chairmen, to determine the order in which legislative business was conducted, and to recognize members during senate debates, all of which solidified porkchoppers' power during the postwar period.[5] In 1950, the state's seven largest districts were home to half the population but elected only 20 percent of Florida's representatives. By the early 1960s, legislators representing less than 15 percent of Floridians controlled state government.[6]

Still, moderates were gaining a foothold after World War II, particularly those who stressed economic and educational reform. Dan McCarty was just such a gubernatorial candidate in 1952. A cattle rancher and citrus grower from Ft. Pierce, sixty miles north of West Palm Beach, McCarty had served as a state representative before World War II. After running unsuccessfully for governor in 1948, he was elected four years later, promising industrial expansion, improved roads and infrastructure, and more effective law enforcement. McCarty enjoyed significant support from metropolitan areas, particularly in south Florida.[7] But on February 25, 1953, one month after taking office, he suffered a debilitating heart attack and died seven months later at the age of forty-one. According to the state constitution, the president of the senate was to assume the role of acting governor, and in 1953 that was Charley Johns.

Born in 1905 in Starke, Florida, in rural northeastern Bradford County, Johns attended the University of Florida without graduating, worked for the Seaboard Air-Line Railroad, and started his own life insurance company. While working the Tampa to Jacksonville route for Seaboard, he met and later married Thelma Brinson, also a native of Starke. Johns first held office as a state representative beginning in 1934, and in 1936 he was elected to the Florida Senate. In 1947, Johns supported a white primary bill as well as legalized slot machines. He voted against increased school construction and opposed a bill that would unmask the Ku Klux Klan.[8] He was serving his third term when called to take over as acting governor in 1953. A self-proclaimed champion of the working man, Johns practiced the brand of personal politics common to the rural South, and his constituents returned him to the senate every six years until his retirement in 1966.[9]

One of Johns's first moves as acting governor was to ask for the resignation of several of McCarty's appointees, including the heads of the Turnpike Commission, the Racing Commission, and the State Road Department. When they refused, Johns suspended them. Moderate Democrats, including Dan McCarty's brother John, were livid. On December 11, 1953, the Florida Supreme Court mandated that an election to complete Mc-Carty's term be held in 1954. In its follow-up ruling in *Ervin v. Collins*, the court held that the winner of that election would be eligible to run for a full term in 1956.[10] In the primary, after considerable debate about the merits of a John McCarty candidacy, the business progressives threw their support behind LeRoy Collins, an attorney and state legislator representing Tallahassee.[11] Collins advocated reapportionment and sought to modernize Florida's economy, bolster tourism, and bring new industries and corporations to the state. In the 1954 primary, Johns faced Collins and another candidate, the liberal Democrat Brailey Oldham, a former state senator from Sanford.

On May 4, Johns won the primary by a margin of nearly thirty-three thousand votes but did not gain a majority. Collins came in second, and third-place finisher Oldham promised his votes to Collins in the runoff.[12] Johns and Collins squared off in a debate in the television studios of Miami's WTVJ on May 13. Broadcast on Florida radio stations and south Florida TV stations, the occasion helped make LeRoy Collins, if not a household name, at least a rising star in state politics. He scored points with his opening remarks, as he smiled into the camera, eyes twinkling mischievously, and in a casual southern drawl thanked acting governor Johns for "finally" agreeing to "participate in a joint meeting of this kind. I regret that he was unwilling to participate in many offers" to debate during the primary. "I've been reading the last few days some of the rather vicious, scurrilous advertising that's been taking place in the *Miami Herald* here in regard to this approaching meeting. And I was amazed when I came into the studio tonight, out on the street to pick up a copy of tomorrow morning's *Miami Herald*, to find that the meeting had already been held."

Now Collins broke into a wide grin, pulled out a newspaper, and put on his reading glasses. He scanned the paper. "I just wanted to ask the acting governor something about this. . . . It's an official advertisement by Acting Governor Johns." After quoting the mock headline in the ad declaring Johns the clear winner in the debate, Collins went on reading: "Well Senator Collins, wherever you are, we told you what would happen. You asked for it on television last night, and you got it. You didn't look so good, Senator, did you? . . . You wanted to get on television. Well, you got your wish, didn't you? We hope you're satisfied now, Senator."

Johns sat, stunned. Claiming to have known nothing about the advertisement, he quickly shifted attention to his lifelong concern for the "little man," the "man that has to make his living by the sweat of his brow. And that's my legislative record." He stumbled through promises to reapportion the legislature in 1955. He denied charges of payroll padding, machine politics, and patronage. Johns also had a habit of leafing through a large stack of documents as each panelist posed a question, which gave him the appearance of being unprepared and occasionally flustered. Furthermore, he called his opponent by his first name, while Collins respectfully referred to Johns as "Governor" or "Acting Governor." Collins ended the evening by criticizing Johns's opposition to a bill that would have forced the unmasking of the Ku Klux Klan. As time ran out and the moderator sped through his closing remarks, Johns was left sputtering unconvincingly about his vote.[13] The acting governor won thirty-four out of thirty-six counties in north Florida. Collins won a majority of south Florida counties, eleven of them with more than 60 percent of the vote. All told, Collins won the primary by sixty-six thousand votes and went on to capture the governor's seat in the general election.[14]

*　　*　　*

Four days after the debate, the U.S. Supreme Court declared school segregation unconstitutional. In Florida and across the South, the initial reaction ranged from stunned silence and uncertain wariness to pledges of defiance and, among some, disappointed acceptance. With the waning of sharecropping and the growth of industrialization, the mechanization of agriculture, and black migration out of the South, African Americans' lives were changing inexorably, and so was their threshold for enduring racism. World War II brought greater economic opportunities to black Americans through war work, and their military service instilled a fierce pride.[15] Yet with every inch of ground gained—the end of the all-white primary in 1944, the desegregation of the armed forces in 1948, the entrance of the first black graduate and professional students into southern universities in 1950—African Americans regularly bore the consequences of white wrath through harassment and humiliation, economic reprisals and violence.[16]

For its part, Florida had a mixed record on race. On the one hand, it was the site of some of the most horrific violence in the South. Marianna, near the Alabama-Florida line, witnessed in 1934 the ghastly sexualized mutilation and lynching of Claude Neal, a black farmworker accused of molesting and murdering a white girl. This familiar scene was avoided in Groveland, Florida, in 1949, after four black men, two of them military veterans, were charged with raping and kidnapping a white woman and assaulting her husband. While frenzied white mobs destroyed blacks' property and homes in Groveland, the men were actually protected from would-be lynchers—only to suffer at the hands of Sheriff Willis McCall, who shot two of the suspects while transporting them from the state prison to a pretrial hearing, killing one. In the midst of a series of appeals, on Christmas Eve 1951 in Mims, a small town near Cape Canaveral, a bomb planted under his front porch killed civil rights leader Harry T. Moore and his wife Harriette. Between 1941 and 1951, Moore had served as the first president of the Florida State Conference of NAACP Branches. He had cofounded the Progressive Voters' League in 1945, encouraging black Floridians to register as Democrats and investigating charges of election officials' interference. His reputation already well established, Moore had further angered segregationists with his outspoken criticism of Willis McCall and the "little Scottsboro" episode in Groveland. Then, in the early 1950s, a string of synagogue bombings shook Miami, the Klan's response to the token integration of an apartment complex on the western outskirts of the city.[17]

In spite of this violence, and though their opportunities were severely constrained, black Floridians often fared better economically than their counterparts elsewhere in the South. Higher paying service jobs were plentiful, particularly during and after World War II, and were open to African Americans, who still received the least lucrative and palatable of them. Urban areas contained enclaves of black middle- and upper-class professionals. And two universities, the public Florida A&M University (FAMU) in Tallahassee and the private Bethune-Cookman College in Daytona Beach, enrolled African Americans exclusively. In electoral politics, blacks had greater access to the ballot than most of their counterparts in the region. The state's poll tax had been abolished in 1937 and Florida required no literacy tests for would-be voters. As a result, more than forty-eight thousand African Americans had registered to vote by 1946. Six years later, they made up 15 percent of the voting-age population in Florida and 10 percent of the voters.[18]

Nevertheless, segregation remained fixed in custom and law. The U.S. Supreme Court's ruling in *Brown* on May 17, 1954, reviled as "Black

Monday" by opponents, and the implementation ruling a year later, spurred the white South into action. Membership in the Ku Klux Klan soared. The Citizens' Council, the less violent but no less vituperative cousin to the Klan, was established in 1954 in Mississippi and soon began counting members in every southern state and beyond. Newspaper editors and politicians railed against the Supreme Court, and some, such as Mississippi's U.S. senator James Eastland, charged that it had been tainted by communism. Antiblack violence increased. And legislation resisting or rejecting *Brown* poured forth from across the South, while southern senators and representatives promised to defend segregated schools.[19]

One means of resisting the Supreme Court was the state legislative investigating committee, designed to dredge up the criminal activities and Communist ties of civil rights advocates. These "little HUACs" followed on the heels of committees that had flourished in the 1940s, largely outside of the South, from California, Washington, and Illinois to Ohio and Massachusetts. They were expressions of the prevailing Cold War belief, in the words of historian M. J. Heale, that "exposure was the most effective answer to the red menace."[20] This public display of rooting out Communists from American institutions—labor unions, government, churches, and universities—became a ritualized spectacle, political theater that served both to frighten and reassure audiences. If the West and the Midwest were no longer hotbeds of state-level committees by the time of McCarthy's 1954 censure, the House Un-American Activities Committee (HUAC) as well as James Eastland's Senate Internal Subversion Subcommittee (SISS) remained active and at times assisted the committees in the South that formed in response to the growing civil rights movement. In 1953, the Georgia legislature established the Commission on Education, which quickly became, in one historian's words, a "fixture in Georgia's campaign against integration." The following year, Louisiana's Joint Legislative Committee on Segregation was created, and members used information and allegations compiled by federal investigators, including HUAC and the Senate Internal Security Subcommittee, to link Communists to the NAACP and other progressive reform groups such as the Southern Conference for Human Welfare and the Southern Regional Council. In 1956, both Florida and Mississippi founded similar committees. Other southern states would follow.[21]

These committees rarely tried to conceal the identity of their target, the NAACP, the nation's oldest civil rights organization and the driving force behind the lawsuits that had led to *Brown*. Southern lawmakers believed that sullying the group's reputation and associating it in the public mind with lawlessness, violence, un-Americanism, and communism would make Americans, both black and white, less sympathetic to its efforts. More practically, it would deflect the NAACP's resources and time away from school desegregation cases. Segregationists argued that Negroes, being childlike and indolent, were easily duped and especially susceptible to outside agitators and subversive influences. They also claimed that the NAACP sought to violate laws and create chaos and was ultimately intent on achieving social equality—a euphemism for interracial sex—which would sap the nation's strength by weakening the white race. Underlying all of these assumptions was the paternalistic argument that African Americans were intellectually incapable of organizing complex civil rights activities independently and that some other entity, namely, the Communist Party, had to be behind the movement. In 1956, Congressman E. C. Gathings of Arkansas recommended a federal investigation of the NAACP to "protect the southern Negro and others who have been duped, victimized, and exploited" by the civil rights group.[22] Florida's investigating committee at various times operated under all of these assumptions, its members speaking a language familiar to segregationists, charging the NAACP with lawlessness, Communist involvement, and supporting intermarriage.

Race and sexuality had been interwoven in an intricate web of power and symbolism since the first African slaves arrived on American shores. Miscegenation was an incontrovertible reality in a slaveholding society and, as such, took on a range of meanings and uses as diverse as the young nation itself. Some historians have argued that the tenor and degree of antimiscegenation sentiment intensified following emancipation, when white southerners sought to control newly freed people. During Reconstruction and beyond, a "new language of sexualized politics" took shape in which the political rights of black men were equated with sexual access to white women. Now, even more so than during the antebellum period, the "political and sexual perils of racial equality" became central to white supremacist thought.[23] Beginning in the late nineteenth century and persisting into the first decades of the twentieth, whites maintained political and economic control in part through endless repetition of the mantra that black men's predatory sexuality and their desire for white women threatened the purity of the white race and the integrity of the nation and that granting black Americans certain freedoms would jeopardize those of white Americans. Whether it took the form of antimiscegenation laws or the lynching epidemic that came to scar the southern landscape with a grotesque mundane regularity, white fear of race mixing was a powerful political narrative in the South and became a fundamental ingredient of the invective against integration in the 1950s.[24]

It is not surprising that the target of segregationist rage was the NAACP. Former Georgia governor Herman Talmadge imputed immense power to the civil rights group, arguing in his 1955 book *You and Segregation* that "our Federal Government and Supreme Court are both being dictated to and dominated by" the NAACP "and its satellites."[25] As a writer in the *Nation* saw it, many whites seemed to believe that the group was "guilty of the outrageous sin of being effective in its fight for racial equality and integration. This is why they're out to get it."[26] The moderate Atlanta editor Ralph McGill observed in 1956 that the "angry South" thought "a proper government would put [the NAACP] in jail or order it to go away, and then everything would again be as it was."[27] Another writer claimed that the "fear that mixed schools in the South would open the way for racial amalgamation is not a bogey or a smoke screen or a pretense of any kind but the basic animating motive of the white South in resisting the drive of the NAACP and its supporters." In addition to miscegenation, integrated schools would also expose the white "adolescent and therefore defenseless mind" to "brain-washing." It would result, he wrote, in the "wholesale impregnation" of white children "by a propaganda persuasive and by them unanswerable."[28]

Beginning in 1956, state legislatures across the region responded to the Supreme Court's 1955 *Brown II* decision by enacting laws to impede the civil rights organization. Florida, Georgia, Mississippi, South Carolina, Tennessee, and Virginia redefined and strengthened existing laws against the incitement of litigation and paying a litigant in a case in which one had no stake. Virginia, Tennessee, Texas, and Arkansas required groups that solicited money for racial litigation or legislation to register with the state, including submitting membership lists. Other laws targeted teachers but were clearly connected to their participation in the NAACP. Mississippi required public school teachers to file an affidavit with the state listing every organization they had belonged to for the previous five years. Louisiana prohibited teachers from joining any group that had been banned from operating in the state, which, thanks to a recent injunction against it, meant the NAACP. The Bayou State also stipulated by law that any teacher who advocated integration could be fired.[29] The most common form of pressure exerted by the barrage of anti-NAACP laws was the mandate that state and local branches turn over membership lists, financial statements, and other documents so that state officials could determine whether they were operating legally. Strictly portrayed as a tough law-and-order stance by southern state legislators, the legislation led NAACP officials to believe that members would be subjected to economic and physical reprisals if their names were made public.

Alabama proved especially adept at this brand of intimidation. In 1956, a circuit court judge enjoined the association from doing any business in the state on the grounds that it had not properly registered as a "foreign corporation." At the same time, the judge prohibited the NAACP from going through the process of registering and thereby effectively criminalized it. Alabama attorney general John Patterson asked the judge to force the group to submit its records, documents, and membership lists, and he did so. The NAACP refused and was cited for contempt and fined one hundred thousand dollars. According to one legal scholar, the association "could not legally operate in Alabama, qualify to operate in Alabama, or obtain a hearing on whether it should be covered by the registration statute, until it divulged its membership lists."[30] It could, and did, appeal to the U.S. Supreme Court. In 1958 the court ruled in *NAACP v. Alabama* that demanding access to membership lists violated NAACP members' First Amendment rights of free speech and association.[31] But when the justices remanded the case to the Alabama Supreme Court, they ensured that the battle would not be resolved swiftly. Indeed, the legal wrangling did not conclude until 1964, a crucial eight-year span in the history of the civil rights movement during which the NAACP was effectively silenced in Alabama.[32]

Florida, under the comparatively moderate leadership of Governor LeRoy Collins, opted to resist quietly and, as much as possible, pleasantly. The state had almost 650,000 public school students, of whom approximately 142,000 were African American.[33] Collins and many lawmakers recognized the economic need to maintain the state's positive national image for the sake of attracting tourists, residents, and business. Most of Florida's newspapers took a similarly cautious and pragmatic, if not to say resigned, tone while simultaneously echoing Collins's warning that such a sea change in southern law and tradition would take years to carry out.[34] At the same time, segregationists, including the Johns Commit-tee, the porkchoppers, and rank-and-file conservative white Democrats, pressured the governor to oppose school integration, which he did. This tension between placating segregationists and avoiding blatant race bait-ing would preoccupy Collins and other moderates after *Brown*. It helped shape policies that combined resistance and lip service to cooperation with federal power, giving Florida an air of moderation absent in other parts of the Deep South. But it also helped to conceal the real influence of segregationists within state government.

*   *   *

The issue of segregation dominated Florida politics in 1956. Florida's at-torney general, Richard Ervin, representing the Board of Control (BOC), the governing body of Florida's university system, petitioned the state su-preme court to allow the board to devise a questionnaire that would mea-sure statewide opinion about admitting African Americans into white schools. In response to the original *Brown* decision, Ervin had implored the high court in an amicus brief to remember the "need for reasonable time and planning by state and local authorities in any revision of the existing legal structure of the State of Florida."[35] Florida, he intimated, would not submit easily. In his appeal to the state supreme court two years later, he made a similar plea. The court agreed, and the survey went forward. The deadline was set for May 1956. The attorney general's office mailed fifty-six thousand copies of the questionnaire to students, parents, faculty, alumni, and health service employees at the University of Florida, Florida State University (FSU), and Florida A&M University.

On March 12, 1956, in the middle of the primary season, the U.S. Su-preme Court ruled that the University of Florida must open its doors to Virgil Hawkins, who had first attempted to enroll in the law school there in 1949.[36] It overrode the Florida high court's decision to postpone any action until the statewide survey had been completed. Attorney General Ervin condemned the decision as "precipitous, unreasonable and arbi-trary." Less diplomatically, the commissioner of agriculture fumed that this was just another instance of the Supreme Court "ramming it down our throats." LeRoy Collins vowed to find a way to resist the decision le-gally. But Hawkins's lawyer, Horace Hill, who would soon find himself a target of the Johns Committee, saw their reactions as little more than folly. "It is expensive, un-American as well as morally wrong to circumvent the law," he declared.[37] Two days later, Collins appointed an advisory commission headed by Judge L. L. Fabisinski to devise a plan for resisting school desegregation within the bounds of the law. Collins too had seen the ugly mob violence that greeted black library science graduate student Autherine Lucy just a month earlier, when she stepped onto the campus of the University of Alabama.

Collins advocated strengthening the existing pupil assignment law, which had originally been sponsored by Charley Johns, Senator John Rawls, and conservative Panhandle representatives Prentice Pruitt, Hugh Dukes, and John Shipp, and signed into law in 1955.[38] As it stood, the law allowed county school board officials to assign students to certain schools based on such criteria as their academic backgrounds and qualifications, the facilities available at each school, broadly defined "psychological characteristics" of students, and the potential for a student's enrollment at a particular school causing any disruption.[39] Race was never explicitly mentioned, but the law kept black children out of white schools. During the very month that Collins announced the creation of the Fabisinski commission, dozens of southern senators and representatives signed the "Southern Manifesto" condemning the Supreme Court for trampling on states' rights. The statement resounded with themes that would echo continuously in the public discourse on race and federal power after *Brown*, such as the charge that parents were being "deprived by Government of the right to direct the lives and education of their own children" or the Court was "destroying the amicable relations between the white and Negro races that have been created through 90 years of patient effort by the good people of both races" and "outside mediators are threatening immediate and revolutionary changes in our public schools [sic] system."[40] Florida's senators, George Smathers and Spessard Holland, signed the statement, as did six Florida representatives. In the next two years, beginning with Virginia and including Florida, eight states in the South passed interposition resolutions, in which legislators stood between federal power and state sovereignty and refused to accede to the Court's ruling.[41]

Late that spring, the Board of Control studied the results of the survey of parents, teachers, and students. The final report advised against integration but also revealed an emerging generation gap in racial attitudes among whites. Close to 59 percent of the recipients filled out and returned the forms.[42] In its summary of the findings, the BOC distilled the answers to a wide range of questions into a single conclusion: The "main fear expressed was that of intermarriage between the white and Negro races." The questions themselves helped shape this interpretation. Respondents were asked, among other things, what they would do if Negroes were allowed in classrooms, school cafeterias, swimming pools, parties and dances, and dormitory rooms with whites.

By focusing on the social aspects of desegregation, the questions played on the prejudices of parents. Among white parents, 8 percent stated that they would admit black students immediately, 22 percent would admit them after an unspecified length of preparation, 24 percent would delay admission as long as possible, and 44 percent would not admit them under any circumstances. White students appeared less averse. A third of them claimed indifference to fellow students' race. Forty-one percent of the men claimed they would treat their black counterparts as they would any other students, as did 46 percent of the women. The unavoidable and glaring fact emerged from the polling that white parents were far more resistant to integration at the university level than were their children; those who selected "let's not allow negroes to come into the white universities under any circumstances" included 64 percent of white parents of high school seniors, 44 percent of white parents of college students, and only 21 percent of white university students themselves.[43] Attorney General Ervin conveyed the results to Florida's high court, arguing for the need to maintain segregated schools.

At the same time, three Democratic hopefuls were vying for the governor's office during the spring and summer of 1956. The gubernatorial election hinged on segregation, and the candidates seemed determined to out-race bait one another. Collins's Democratic primary opponents ran the ideological gamut, but all shared a commitment to preserving segregated schools. Fuller Warren had served as Florida's governor from 1949 to 1953, and in his bid for the nomination in 1956 he used campaign posters featuring his signed affidavit, swearing that "no Negroes will be admitted to White schools and colleges of this state if Fuller Warren is governor."[44] Conservative state representative Farris Bryant from Ocala emphasized the threat of contamination by blacks if they were to attend school and socialize with whites. In a stump speech he told the Tampa League of Women Voters, "In the homes of Negroes we find different intellectual levels, and moral and sanitary standards. . . . I feel that it would not be good for two groups with such different standards to be drawn into direct contact."[45] Bryant would have to wait until 1960 before that line of reasoning won him the governor's seat.

The third challenger, Sumter L. Lowry, a Tampa businessman, anti-Communist, and states' rights enthusiast, adopted the most extreme position on race. Lowry had never held political office but existed as an ever-present voice from the far Right during the 1950s and 1960s in Florida. His twin obsessions were interracial marriage and Communist influence within civil rights groups. Lowry was a member of the National Guard and the American Legion, served as chairman of the board of Gulf Life Insurance Company, and after the 1956 primaries founded the Florida Coalition of Patriotic Societies. A pamphlet supporting Lowry blared, "Vote for Lowry and keep white schools white!" and criticized LeRoy Collins for appointing a black man, Henry H. Arrington, as assistant state's attorney, suggestively describing Harrington's white secretaries taking dictation from him. In fact, in March, Lowry had already made news with a campaign appearance in Ft. Lauderdale in which he described Arrington "chortling to the Communist-inspired NAACP that 'I have a white secretary and the office is fully integrated.'"[46] Lowry also accused Collins of having "the most livid record of friendship with the NAACP-Communist coalition" of any of the candidates.[47] Though he was viewed by most as a fringe candidate, one small-town newspaper in central Florida cheered him on: "He will lead the fight against the NAACP—the insidious, communist-dominated organization which is poisoning the minds of Southern negroes and leading them down the road to self-destruction."[48] Many white voters may have agreed with Lowry and the other candidates on some issues, but Collins's fence sitting found a more receptive audience in Florida.

In June 1956, one state representative appealed to Governor Collins to sign off on a proposed investigating committee. A. J. Musselman, representing Pompano Beach, a small town just north of Ft. Lauderdale, was a friend of Johns's who later became a member of the FLIC. He envisioned the committee gathering information "as to the extent of activities in the NAACP and other pro-integration groups of Communist paid employees, sympathizers or agitators." It would be made up, he maintained, of "persons generally classified as moderates."[49] The legislator couched his plea in terms of a patriotic national defense against an enemy dedicated to fomenting racial animosity as part of its larger mission of world domination. He argued that the race problem was national and international, not confined to the South. In his mind it was "natural" for racial groups everywhere to want to associate with their own "peoples." Communists and other rabble-rousers had convinced blacks and people of color around the world that what they really wanted was unfettered access to all things white. Musselman further claimed that Communists were fully aware of global racial and ethnic tensions and would "with greater force . . . exploit this field of human discontent in an all out effort to turn persons other than the White man, who harbor resentment against the White man, to the Communist cause."[50]

Collins was lukewarm, concerned instead with convening the legislature in July 1956 to devise a plan for maintaining segregated schools based on the recommendations of the Fabisinski commission. Normally the state legislature met biannually, in odd-numbered years. The sessions began on the first Tuesday in April and lasted no longer than sixty consecutive days.[51] But given the urgency Collins felt to come up with a solid legislative plan, the assembly came together in the summer and generated dozens of bills, many of them written by Charley Johns and the porkchoppers. One would give the governor emergency powers to use state military forces and law enforcement agencies to keep order in the face of any "overt threat of violence."[52] Another reaffirmed the principle of local control over school admissions policies, and a third was little more than an echo of the Southern Manifesto, an extended diatribe against the Supreme Court for denying states "the power to regulate public education by the use of practices first declared constitutional by the state of Massachusetts, adopted by the Congress, approved by the executive, . . . and practiced by states for more than a century." This resolution not only parroted the manifesto by deflecting blame for segregated schools onto a liberal northeastern state but also warned that the Court's "usurpation" of power, "if condoned by the people and allowed to continue, will destroy the American system of government."[53]

Senate bill 38, introduced by Johns and three other porkchoppers, called for the creation of an investigating committee to look into "the activities in this State of organizations advocating violence or a cause of conduct which would constitute a violation of the laws of Florida." In the senate, it passed by a vote of thirty-five to one.[54] House speaker Thomas E. "Ted" David sat on the bill, claiming that it was unrelated to the business of the extraordinary legislative session. David was a moderate Democrat first elected in 1949 from Hollywood, a small but rapidly growing city nestled between Miami and Ft. Lauderdale. He, like Collins, advocated a measured resistance to forced desegregation while criticizing inflammatory tactics such as interposition and school closures.[55] One representative kept it alive, however, and after the Committee on Appropriations and Committee Resolutions recommended its passage, the bill went back to the house for a full vote and was approved seventy-three to fourteen.[56] Johns had been pushing for this since 1953, when as president of the senate he introduced legislation creating a committee to investigate gambling and other crime in Florida. He tried again two years later, but it was not until the summer of 1956, when the issue dominated state politics, that Johns's colleagues recognized the value of a committee in stopping or slowing down the group they considered the masterminds of integration, the NAACP.[57]

After reviewing the bills, Governor Collins allowed Senate bill 38 to become law without his signature, but in August he sent a copy of all of the laws passed during the special session to the incoming director of the Mississippi State Sovereignty Commission.[58] Collins was wary, given the porkchoppers' foundational role in the committee and the as-yet-untested constitutional parameters of its operation, but to the press he cleverly deemed the law expansive enough to allow for future investigations of groups such as the Ku Klux Klan, about which he claimed to have received "many inquiries." Above all, the governor wanted to avoid sanctioning even the appearance of a witch hunt against the NAACP. He expressed confidence that "the members of the committee will recognize their responsibilities to all the people of Florida and not abuse the broad powers granted them."[59] In response, porkchopper Dewey Johnson remarked that the FLIC was obviously "aimed at the NAACP" and that he knew of "nothing the KKK is doing to violate the law."[60]

*   *   *

The committee was made up of three senators and four representatives and had the power to hold hearings and subpoena witnesses. Senate president Turner Davis had appointed the Florida Senate members by the end of July: Johnson, Charley Johns, and John Rawls from Marianna, a small Panhandle town. Just a year earlier, Rawls had warned his fellow senators that school integration would "encourage the reprehensible, unnatural, abominable, abhorrent, execrable and revolting practice of miscegenation which is recognized, both in conscience and by the law of the state of Florida as a criminal offense."[61] House speaker Ted David chose representatives from metropolitan areas, including A. J. Musselman, a Broward County lawyer; J. B. Hopkins, an attorney from the Panhandle; W. C. "Cliff" Herrell from Miami; and Henry Land, a farmer and county commissioner from Tangerine, a small town outside of Orlando.[62]

LeRoy Collins, it seemed, had been true to his word in seeing to it that segregated schools remained untouched while keeping a lid on white extremism. One critic was furious with the results of the special legislative session, including the governor's abrupt adjournment in the middle of a debate over an interposition bill that had been drafted by the state's attorney general. "Interposition is the keystone of the people's defense to preserve their constitutional rights and to preserve segregation in Florida," Sumter Lowry seethed to Collins. "You killed the Interposition resolution. . . . You had your chance to stand up for the sovereignty of your state. But you failed."[63] If Lowry and other segregationists believed that Collins had not done enough, NAACP members knew that their organization was under siege even in the ostensibly moderate state of Florida. Executive Secretary Roy Wilkins and Chief Counsel Thurgood Marshall contacted branches across the South and asked that they send all records, including membership lists, to the national offices in New York. In Florida, NAACP attorney Francisco Rodriguez collected the materials and shipped them north. According to the treasurer of the Tallahassee branch, Rodriguez came into his office one day in August and, without a word, gathered up "all correspondence and all other written records . . . except the checkbook."[64] At the same time, however, Marshall struck a defiantly optimistic tone in his keynote address at the NAACP's forty-seventh annual convention in San Francisco when he decried Mississippi's "setting up a Gestapo of paid informers to infiltrate the NAACP branches." Across the South, he predicted, "We will keep these stooges out, just as we have kept the Communists out."[65]

Between the creation of the committee in July 1956 and its first hearings the following February, newspaper editors commented on the battle between the FLIC and the NAACP. Even those who questioned the hazy parameters of the committee's legal powers tended to support the overall mission of investigating the association. In August 1956, for instance, the *Tallahassee Democrat* expressed reservations about turning "a committee of House and Senate members loose with $50,000 in cash and broad subpoena power to investigate almost anything they want to for the next

10 or 11 months." The only reason the bill passed in the first place was because legislators had made it very clear that the NAACP would be the only target of inquiry. In the next breath, the editorial stated, "Now, we have no sympathy for the NAACP. We do not like its methods. We think it has followed a philosophy and a policy of agitation and sensationalism that has brought an unwholesome situation in the nation—both North and South. We are suspicious of the motives of its national leaders and organizers." Still, it argued that the bill was "dangerous" because it left ample room for the committee, unchecked, to "decide whose principles and activities it wants to investigate."[66]

The committee's inaugural meeting took place on September 11, 1956, and featured six of the seven members. Johns himself was absent. From the mundane, such as choosing the group's name and voting on procedures for hiring support staff, to the urgent—planning to "immediately secure all information" from other states about their dealings with civil rights activists—the newly christened Florida Legislative Investigation Committee prepared to do battle with the NAACP. Senator Dewey Johnson told the *St. Petersburg Times* that he and his colleagues envisioned running it "somewhat like the Un-American Activities Committee of the American Congress."[67]

The following month, with the assistance of the state attorney's office and with the use of the Mississippi Sovereignty Commission's rules and procedures as a guide, the FLIC set down the legal guidelines by which it would operate.[68] In part, they were modeled after the rules of procedure of the House Committee on Un-American Activities, which committee chair Henry Land claimed to have obtained from HUAC personally.[69] Witnesses who appeared before the committee would be compelled to answer all questions, under threat of contempt charges. They could also be held in contempt of the legislature if they refused committee requests to produce documents related to the investigation. Witnesses could have counsel present during any questioning. The FLIC's attorney was responsible for examining investigation reports and advising committee members about what information was appropriate to include in hearings and reports to the legislature, preparing interrogation briefs, conducting the questioning of witnesses before all public sessions, and assisting in the preparation of interim and final reports to the legislature. The FLIC's chief investigator was to conduct and oversee all investigations, which included taking depositions and written statements under oath, hiring informants, and interrogating "any person in the State of Florida or elsewhere relating to the business of the Committee."[70] He was also to screen outside requests for investigations and recommend action, to establish ties with other like-minded states' committees, and to examine records and documents supplied by witnesses.

As the committee prepared its agenda, it revealed porkchoppers' bitter resentment against LeRoy Collins, both for his crushing defeat of Johns in 1954 and his relative caution on the question of school desegregation, or at least for his refusal to strongly condemn the Supreme Court. In truth, Collins's record on race was mixed and changed during his years in office.[71] The executive secretary of the Florida State Teachers Association, the black teachers' union, noted in 1956 that the gubernatorial campaign seemed to have thrust Collins into a more openly segregationist position. He concluded that for Florida under his leadership, "there is reason to believe that there will be no spectacular or unusual rush into the waiting arms of integration."[72] A writer for the *Nation* was even less sanguine: "In Florida, nothing has been done. Not even the most gradual plan for Negro school attendance at any level has been suggested by the Governor. And yet Collins leads the moderates." Collins was such a persuasive salesman of the "New Florida"—racially moderate, business and industry friendly—that he made hardliners like Johns suspicious of his integrationist intentions, despite all evidence to the contrary.[73]

The state of Mississippi had established the Mississippi Sovereignty Commission in March 1956. It consisted of individuals from both the state house and senate and held broad subpoena powers. Yet unlike the Johns Committee, the Sovereignty Commission started out as primarily a propaganda agent. Its membership included the governor, attorney general, president of the senate, and speaker of the state house, as well as three private citizens appointed by the governor. Moreover, rather than a sweeping sanction to investigate groups or individuals who violated laws or advocated the overthrow of the government, the power of the Mississippi commission set the U.S. government squarely in its sights and stretched its purview beyond state lines: "to do and perform any and all acts and things deemed necessary and proper to protect the sovereignty of the State of Mississippi, and her sister states, from encroachment thereon by the Federal Government or any branch, department or agency thereof." The commission could receive financial donations and gifts from other government agencies, public and private organizations, corporations, and individuals, with no limits. And finally, the law compelled Mississippi's government employees and universities to cooperate with the commission "and render such aid and assistance as may be requested of them."[74]

One nongovernmental organization founded in 1954, the Association of Citizens' Councils of Mississippi, did not need to be coerced. Secretary Robert B. Patterson offered his group's services, reminding commission director Ney Gore that he had "contacts in every one of the forty-eight states and eight foreign countries, which may be of value to you at some future date." He added, "Of course you have noted that a number of the members of your States [sic] Sovereignty Commission are Citizens' Council members."[75]

*   *   *

The Florida Legislative Investigation Committee chose Tallahassee as the site of its first investigation because, according to Chairman Henry Land, that city's officials' "request came in first."[76] They were alarmed by African Americans' recent efforts to desegregate city buses. On May 26, 1956, in a moment that recalled Rosa Parks's heroics in Montgomery, Alabama, the previous December, Tallahassee police arrested two female students from Florida A&M University when they refused to leave their seats near the front of a Cities Transit bus. Inspired by the Montgomery bus boycott, which had followed Parks's arrest and was at that point in its sixth month, FAMU students quickly called on black Tallahasseans to launch a boycott of their own.[77] Rev. Charles Kenzie "C. K." Steele, president of the local NAACP, followed the students' lead by bringing together a group of black ministers to organize African Americans. Born in 1914 and raised in West Virginia, the grandson of slaves, Steele received his calling to the ministry at the age of fifteen. In the mid-1930s he attended Morehouse College, and in 1939 he became a pastor at the Hall Street Baptist Church in Montgomery. These experiences, especially his college years, shaped his thinking about Christianity, race, and social justice. Accepting a position at Bethel Baptist Church, Steele moved with his wife and children to Tallahassee in 1952. He soon began networking with local black activists, and within two years he was elected president of the Tallahassee branch of the NAACP.[78]

Steele spearheaded the transformation of a single incident into a burgeoning movement that spilled over the university's borders into the community. Days after the students' arrest, he called for a mass meeting at Bethel Baptist to gauge attitudes about a citywide bus boycott.

The overflow crowd voted to support it, and from this pivotal meeting emerged a new organization, the Inter-Civic Council (ICC), to plan and run the boycott. Like its model, the Montgomery Improvement Association, the ICC was headed by black clergymen and community leaders and guided by the principle of nonviolent resistance.[79] The boycott began on Memorial Day. Participants demanded first-come, first-served seating on all city buses, courtesy from drivers to all passengers, and the employment of black drivers. Stretching throughout the summer, the boycott was punctuated by occasional and unsuccessful meetings between ICC leaders, city commissioners, and representatives of the bus company. The impasse inspired frustration from all sides as well as familiar white claims about black civil rights supporters. The president of Cities Transit told the *Tallahassee Democrat* that the boycott was "a put up job, an un-American activity." Governor Collins disparaged boycott leaders as "outsiders."[80] Meanwhile, the ICC formed a carpool system to provide transportation for the city's black residents who were refusing to ride. The Tallahassee Police Department in turn initiated a campaign of harassment and surveillance to suppress these efforts.

Directed by Remus J. Strickland, who in a matter of months would be named chief investigator for the Johns Committee, the police operation against the boycott consisted of two elements: arresting carpool drivers for minor traffic violations and spying on boycott leaders and participants. The police, including Chief Frank Stoutamire and Officer Burl Peacock, who also later assisted in the Johns Committee's interrogations of suspected homosexuals, concentrated on the former, arresting Steele within the first days of the boycott, while Strickland tackled the latter.[81] His work on behalf of the city foreshadowed the methods he would later bring to his work with the investigating committee. First, Strickland traveled to Montgomery to investigate the ties between Steele and the minister's longtime friend, Martin Luther King Jr. Here he determined that "Communist influence is felt in the Alabama boycott. It is clear, however, that the boycott is not Communist in its present personnel nor in its appeal to Negroes. Certain Communists have been active in it without assuming dominant leadership and these are known to Alabama authorities."[82] Thus he leveled vague, unspecified charges of Communist influence without naming names and planted the seeds of doubt about the loyalty of boycotters in Montgomery, which would implicate by association the black activists in Florida's capital city.

In Tallahassee, Strickland made lists of the leaders of the Inter-Civic Council and boycotters who were affiliated with Florida A&M University and drew up extensive recommendations for crushing the boycott. His plan included classifying cars used for transporting boycotters as common carriers and charging drivers the appropriate operators' fees, ensuring that all drivers met strict insurance requirements, and fingerprinting all drivers. Strickland also urged rigid police enforcement, so that "after the first warning the second time may result in detention for complete investigation."[83] But the Tallahassee Police Department had already begun taking boycotters and carpoolers into custody and grilling them about their activities in the ICC. In a confidential memo to the police, Strickland also suggested influencing news coverage: "Have conservative releases slanted to show concern for public in the operation of unsafe and uninspected vehicles, not paying their proper taxes."[84] Law and order had long been and would continue to be a rallying cry for conservatives to stifle racial dissent in the United States. The investigating committee itself was founded on the argument that the state simply wanted to keep the peace by protecting its citizens from lawbreakers. Just as spying, infiltrating, and spreading propaganda were integral to the nation's Cold War against the Soviets, so too were they used by the Johns Committee to expose hidden enemies within the Inter-Civic Council and the Tallahassee branch of the NAACP.

The boycott persisted into the fall of 1956. In October, eleven ICC members were found guilty of operating an illegal commercial transportation service, fined five hundred dollars, and sentenced to sixty days in jail. The sentence was suspended, but the carpoolers were required to pay the fines. Though the group disbanded the carpool soon after the arrests, C. K. Steele urged black Tallahasseans to persevere. As he told a local newspaper, "The war is not over; we are still walking."[85] Whites fumed. On behalf of a group of white Baptist ministers, Rev. W. E. Hall implored the Johns Committee to investigate the "outside element" behind the Tallahassee boycott. Hall, who hailed from Johns's hometown of Starke, had served as chaplain of the Florida Senate in 1953, when Johns was senate president.[86] Despite the pressure, the boycott received a boost from the federal judiciary in November 1956, when the U.S. Supreme Court ruled in *Gayle v. Browder* that Montgomery's segregated buses were unconstitutional.[87] That month, LeRoy Collins was reelected, this time to a full term as governor. In spite of his promises to uphold school segregation through all legal means, this might have given civil rights advocates hope that the governor, no longer burdened by having to prove his segregationist credentials on the campaign trail, would demonstrate some degree of equanimity in dealing with the boycott and the grievances behind it. Roused by the latest Supreme Court decision, within days Steele was leading groups of African Americans on bus rides around town to challenge Tallahassee's segregation law. During the week between Christmas and New Year's Day, 1956, several incidents and threats of violence occurred. First, protesters called off a planned ride on December 27 when a mob of hundreds stood around a bus that Steele and sixteen others were about to board. Then gunfire blew out several windows in a grocery store owned by an African American, and a few days later whites threw bricks and rocks through the living room windows of Steele's home.[88]

In late 1956 and into the early months of 1957, Mark R. Hawes, once described as a "barrel-chested, gravel-voiced ex-Marine," directed the NAACP investigation.[89] A Tampa attorney, he was the former assistant attorney general under segregationist Richard Ervin, a prosecutor in the Tallahassee carpoolers' trial, and now chief counsel of the FLIC. Hawes was joined by investigator John Cye Cheasty, himself an attorney, who had also spent years in the U.S. Secret Service and the New York Crime Commission, and R. J. Strickland, an assistant investigator for the committee. In addition to questioning NAACP members, the team hired informants and traveled to Texas to confer with the attorney general about his state's investigation of the civil rights group. Cheasty told the *Tampa Tribune* that the three men had also met with the chief counsel for James Eastland's Senate Internal Security Subcommittee and with associates of Florida's U.S. senators, Spessard Holland and George Smathers.[90]

Hawes compiled their findings to present to the committee in anticipation of a public hearing planned for the spring of 1957. He carefully outlined the national and regional structure of the NAACP and inserted statistics on the number of branches and members within each region as of 1955. Hawes stated that the "national office maintains a very rigid and strict discipline over all of the paid employees of the NAACP and likewise over all of the local and state offices." He warned that the civil rights group had "promulgated very concrete and highly effective plans for concerted action by all of its various branches and members," who followed "directives" sent down by the national headquarters. Along with being suspiciously doctrinaire, the organization, observed Hawes, engaged in criminal activities such as soliciting and pressuring black parents to try to enroll their children in white schools, covering the legal costs of such cases, and offering other forms of financial assistance to plaintiffs. Hawes rightly concluded, "If the colored people are stripped of this legal machine and left to their own individual initiative and financial resources," then "the integration movement could be slowed down."[91]

*   *   *

Opposition to segregated busing had also become a public issue in Miami in 1956, when the local NAACP branch threatened to launch its own boycott of Miami Transit Company buses. In three separate incidents, police arrested black riders for refusing to relinquish their seats. A municipal judge found one man guilty of disorderly conduct and fined him fifty dollars. The prosecutor blamed the NAACP for provoking his actions, arguing that they were intended to stir up racial animosity in Miami. The man was indeed a member of the local NAACP youth council, but his attorney denied his role in any planned test of the city's segregation laws.[92] Ultimately, the Miami branch opted against a boycott and instead pursued integration through lawsuits, and the Miami Transit Company desegregated its buses the following year. The city had avoided the demonstrations and mass meetings that were still going on in Tallahassee as 1956 drew to a close. The Inter-Civic Council and the NAACP were poised to test the Supreme Court case declaring Alabama's segregated bus system unconstitutional. In Montgomery, the year-long boycott was reaching its end and the young, charismatic Martin Luther King Jr. had become a national civil rights leader almost overnight. King and Ralph Abernathy, among others, boarded an integrated bus on the morning of December 21, 1956, riding triumphantly through the streets of the cradle of the Confederacy.[93]

Although there were no mass meetings, no demonstrations, and no boycotts in Miami in 1956, the city later became the site of countless legal actions on behalf of African Americans who wanted equal access to schools, public accommodations, neighborhoods, and beaches. Local chapters of progressive and civil rights groups, including the NAACP, Congress of Racial Equality (CORE), Southern Regional Council, and the Dade County Council on Community Relations, led the way.[94] The Johns Committee was just beginning its fight against the NAACP, but the very formation of the FLIC sounded a warning to civil rights activists. In the coming biennium, the committee would journey to Miami twice, accusing NAACP leaders of harboring current and former Communists and pressuring them to surrender membership lists and other vital documents. NAACP resistance in Miami ultimately drove the committee to search elsewhere for targets and led to the U.S. Supreme Court. As these events unfolded, activists continued the struggle for racial justice in Miami and across the state, undaunted if not unencumbered by political intimidation.

2

Racial and Sexual Perversion, 1957–1958

The law of nature is on our side. After all, the average American is not a racial pervert.

James O. Eastland, state convention of the Association of
Citizens' Councils of Mississippi, 1955

The Florida Legislative Investigation Committee's first full two-year term began in the spring of 1957. FLIC members spent this time, as did many other southern state committees, dedicated to forestalling integration by harassing the NAACP. Under the chairmanship of Charley Johns, the FLIC aggressively subpoenaed members of civil rights groups, bus boycotters, and college students, questioning them in a series of high-profile public hearings. The Johns Committee proved resilient in changing tactics and accusations in response to NAACP resistance, by turns charging criminal malfeasance, inciting racial discord, and cooperating with Communists. The NAACP proved equally steadfast. Most witnesses called before the committee defended their right to freedom of assembly, association, and speech, refusing to accede to the FLIC's framing of their activities as illegal or un-American.

During this biennium, the Johns Committee also received reports from other legislators and from law enforcement agents in central Florida that homosexuals were becoming a problem in state institutions—in hospitals but also, more disconcertingly, in public schools. Charley Johns had dealt with homosexuality as a civic problem when, as acting governor in 1954, he intervened in a debate over how to deal with the growing public presence of homosexuals in Miami Beach. By the end of 1958, the committee began investigating alleged homosexual professors at the University of Florida, which marked a turning point not only in terms of a target but also in the fact of the investigation being conducted in secret. Now committee members used the threat of public hearings to gather confessions and names rather than using the hearings themselves as political theater in which charges could be aired, only to linger and take hold within the public imagination and the political discourse. The Johns Committee remained focused on Florida's educational system and its children, but now a familiar Cold War enemy, the homosexual, joined the integrationist as a subversive threat to the state.

* * *

On the morning of January 19, 1957, a group of Florida State University and Florida A&M University students met at Dan Speed's grocery store and boarded a Cities Transit bus at the corner of Park and Monroe streets. They were testing Tallahassee's new seat assignment law, the city's response to a federal court decision outlawing segregated buses. When the driver instructed the white students to sit up front and the black students to find seats in the back, they obliged at first, but after a few minutes they traded places. Within the hour, three of the boys found themselves in police custody. They were convicted of violating the city bus ordinance, and Judge John Rudd sentenced them to sixty days in jail.[1] Many white Tallahasseans were alarmed to learn that white college students, even if only a small number of them, had been attending Inter-Civic Council meetings and were now publicly supporting integration.

The city commission had defied the federal ruling with the seat assignment law, which allowed drivers to assign riders to particular seats, ostensibly in the interest of passenger safety, using criteria like "weight distribution" and "possibilities of violence."[2] Just as disingenuously as the pupil assignment law, the bus plan made no mention of race but was an obvious means of allowing white drivers, bus by bus, rider by rider, to defend the line separating black from white. NAACP attorney Francisco Rodriguez immediately filed a federal lawsuit to overturn the seat assignment ordinance, dismissing it as "a subterfuge designed to circumvent what is now the established law of the land."[3]

Amid this ongoing tension surrounding bus segregation, the Johns Committee began its first public hearings in Tallahassee on February 4, 1957. Virgil Hawkins, a forty-seven-year-old African American man who had been trying to enter the University of Florida law school since 1949, was the first to testify in the Capitol Building. He insisted that it was entirely his idea to apply and, when he was refused entrance, his idea to hire a lawyer and sue the university.[4] FLIC attorney Mark Hawes spent the rest of the day trying to show that Hawkins was lying, that he had been solicited by the NAACP to apply to the all-white law school, and that the organization had financially supported his lawsuit.

One of Hawes's main strategies was to drive home the point that state and local branches did not make their own decisions or act independently of the national leadership. From the beginning of the hearings, the attorney latched on to a directive from Roy Wilkins, the executive secretary of the NAACP, to prove that the group was merely following the party line in its school desegregation efforts. In a context in which such behavior was seen as a sign of a Soviet-style, antidemocratic political organization, neither Hawes nor committee members had to accuse witnesses directly of un-American activities. Instead, they could imply it by repeating the claim that Florida Negroes were not acting on their own but were being guided by outside forces. Days after the Supreme Court's second *Brown* decision of May 31, 1955, mandating undefined yet reasonably swift implementation of school desegregation, the NAACP had convened an "Emergency Regional Conference" in Atlanta to establish guidelines for African Americans to pressure their local schools to integrate. These included petitioning school boards to comply with *Brown*, following up regularly with inquiries into each district's compliance, and holding "meetings, forums, debates, conferences" to explain the court's decision and to emphasize that school desegregation lay "not in the hands of the politicians or the School Board officials, but in the hands of the Federal Courts."[5]

Participants were to go back to their neighborhoods and "organize and prepare the community so that as many as possible will be familiar with the procedure when and if lawsuits are begun."[6] During the FLIC hearings, without comment, Mark Hawes asked one witness to read this quote from the Atlanta report twice, making certain that its self-incriminating meaning could sink in. He then grilled NAACP attorney Rodriguez about the extent to which he had followed the 1955 Atlanta directive in a recent desegregation case in Dade County, inquiring whether the petition he filed "is a verbatim, word-for-word, comma-for-comma, period-for-period copy of the sample petition set out in this directive." When Rodriguez cheekily answered that he had not "made an etymological analysis of that petition" and that he believed the two petitions were only similar "in spirit," Hawes produced a copy of the Atlanta directive and compelled Rodriguez to admit that his petition was indeed an exact copy of Roy Wilkins's, as were later petitions he filed in Pinellas and Hillsborough Counties.[7]

In another instance, while questioning civil rights attorney Horace Hill, Hawes cast doubt on how much control Hill actually had in the Virgil Hawkins case and the degree to which he had looked for direction from Thurgood Marshall and Robert L. Carter, Marshall's assistant and, after 1957, chief counsel for the NAACP. Hill claimed to have discussed the case with these and other national officers but flatly denied that he had been "representing the NAACP." When he did that, Hawes pulled out a letter from Hill to Carter dated September 22, 1954, in which he had enclosed a "redrafted form" of a petition to be filed with the Florida Supreme Court. It was, Hill had written, submitted for Carter's "modification in whatever way you may deem feasible." Hawes asked if he had written the letter. Hill demurred, "I don't know specifically whether I did or not. I would assume that I did. It has my typewritten name at the end of it." But, he noted, "it isn't signed by me," and he then suggested the possibility that his secretary had actually composed the letter.[8] The evidence demonstrated little more than one attorney deferring to another. In Rodriguez's case, it showed how one attorney expediently used a blueprint devised by the NAACP leadership as the most effective and convenient way of testing segregation laws rather than reinventing the wheel with each case. But Hill's unwillingness to admit that he had followed the orders of high-ranking NAACP lawyers, along with his denial of any connection to the organization, gave him an air of duplicity.

Frustrations mounted for the Johns Committee during the hearings, as Hawes managed only to draw out circumstantial evidence and as witnesses met him with vague answers and faulty memories. The *St. Petersburg Times* described committee members as "obviously nettled by repeated answers of 'I don't remember' from these witnesses."[9] Virgil Hawkins, his attorneys, and his supporters all claimed not to remember certain meetings or conversations, not to have been directed to take certain actions by the NAACP brass, not knowingly to have been paid by the organization, and so on. Tempers flared. After one particularly circuitous exchange, Representative A. J. Musselman interjected to warn a witness that his slipperiness was "prolonging these proceedings unduly, and the

Committee has to draw some conclusions from all of this testimony when it gets through, and by acting in the fashion you are, I am afraid one of the conclusions that we are going to draw is that you have hedged on these questions." In another instance, Senator John Rawls upbraided NAACP attorney William A. Fordham: "I would like to remind this witness he is a member of the Florida bar. He is testifying under oath and seemingly his memory can be a little better than he is testifying to."[10]

John Boardman, a twenty-four-year-old white graduate student at Florida State University, was less evasive but just as irksome to committee members. He had received a bachelor of arts degree at the University of Chicago and a master's degree at Iowa State College and was now working on a doctorate in theoretical physics. His academic credentials and mid-western origins, which identified him as a liberal intellectual and an out-sider, did not work in his favor at the hearing. Boardman testified that he had joined the Tallahassee NAACP in 1956 and become more engaged in the local civil rights struggle since he began attending Inter-Civic Council meetings in September. He also acknowledged that FSU administrators had informed him he was no longer welcome there because his extracur-ricular activities had heaped negative publicity on the university. After establishing the student's dubious reputation, Hawes asked him to explain as specifically as possible his understanding of the NAACP's mission. Boardman responded, "The elimination of any legal distinction between the races."

"That applies to every phase of American life, does it?"

The student answered yes. Hawes asked, "Including the prohibition against intermarriage between the races?"[11] Boardman denied any spe-cific knowledge of the NAACP's stand on interracial marriage, but the insinuation had become a part of the public record, the suspicion that FLIC members shared with many southern whites, that somehow sex was really at the center of the quest for integration.

Florida State University president Doak Campbell wanted to rid his school of the young rabble-rouser. At a meeting of educational and politi-cal leaders at the governor's office in January, Campbell had confided his concern about a "little group of ten who regard themselves as the 'saviors of the world'" under the "leadership of a man who is a very confused young fellow." Campbell called Boardman a brilliant math student but "unstable otherwise, . . . very erratic and incoherent," with a "dramatic, evangelistic sort of bearing."[12] Then, without mentioning Boardman by name, he expressed his unhappiness with the amount of social interaction occurring between black and white college students in Tallahassee. Campbell reported that boys from Florida State "have been getting a good many telephone calls from women students at A&M indicating that they were giving a party" and that "some of the FSU people have been going over there attending 'Jazz Parties,' whatever they may be." This reflected a common anxiety among older observers regarding the newly emergent teen culture that centered, among other things, on rock and roll and R&B music. It was also an important ideological tenet of segregationists: Youth culture and music were encouraging moral degradation and creating a permissive environment in which interracial sex would become commonplace.[13] Finally, with regard to another of the young men involved in the bus case, Campbell noted with disgust a recent back-page article about student Jon Folsom in the *Tallahassee Democrat* describing his feud with his landlord over the fact that he "has been entertaining Negroes in his apartment at night—until around 3 o'clock."[14]

The *Democrat*, which ran the story of Boardman's testimony under the doggerel headline "Mix Student Mix Campaign Boardman Aim," focused on his NAACP membership and his advocacy of interracial cooperation, recasting his words and intentions: "Asked whether the NAACP is working toward abolishing the legal prohibition against interracial marriage, Boardman countered, 'To the best of my knowledge this would be a target of any group working against racial discrimination.'"[15] Even the more liberal *St. Petersburg Times* titled its story "FSU Student 'Presumes' NAACP Desires Change in Marriage Law" and explained more accurately the context in which the comment was made. The article included an excerpt from the testimony that quoted both Hawes and Boardman, and quoted Boardman's rejoinder that he was unaware of the NAACP specifically pursuing interracial marriage cases.[16]

This first group of witnesses understood that they were viewed as propagandists and brainwashers devoted to race mixing. Although that language was rarely used directly by Hawes or other committee members during the questioning, its coded meanings pervaded the proceedings. For those who testified, any strategy other than denial and avoidance was unthinkable. The downside of this approach, as many other victims of the government's antisubversive machinery had discovered, was that it rarely allayed suspicions and more often fanned them. Charley Johns's admonition to Virgil Hawkins's lawyer that he was "fast perjuring himself" as well as Mark Hawes's sardonic observation that the truth had been "a mighty scarce commodity up here at times," for example, were both widely reported.[17] As the targets of McCarthyism, and those who had appeared before HUAC or similar state committees, well knew, telling the truth could be construed as confession, yet evasiveness often only heightened mistrust. The *Tampa Tribune* concluded that the NAACP was defying the government and had been discredited by members' appearance before the Johns Committee.[18]

To add to the suspicion of NAACP wrongdoing in Florida, Charley Johns issued a press release on February 7 at the conclusion of the Tallahassee hearings, giving a tantalizing glimpse of what was still to come. "One of the aims of the Communist Party in Florida, as elsewhere in the South, is to agitate racial conflict and unrest. This phase of the Communist party activities in Florida," he promised, "will be thoroughly developed."[19]

*   *   *

The hearings ended on February 8 and resumed ten days later. This time, the focus was on the role of Florida A&M University in the bus boycott. Hawes called the school's president, George W. Gore, along with several professors and students, all of whom were active in the ICC and the NAACP, as witnesses. Gore insisted that he had warned his faculty not to become involved in the Inter-Civic Council or the boycott, but one professor in particular, Emmett Bashful, testified: "I thought that he [Gore] meant to be as careful as possible and not involve the school too much, but that's all. I didn't think that he meant don't participate."[20] Furthermore, he added, "To tell me I can't take part in a meeting held in a church of my God which might advance my benefits appears to me to violate my Constitutional rights."[21]

If the adult witnesses vexed Hawes and the committee, the teenagers who testified made them downright apoplectic. Their lighthearted attitude seemed to mock the proceedings, as did the young men's unwillingness to admit they had ridden on Tallahassee's buses back in January with the express purpose of being arrested and becoming a test case in the courts. With one notable exception, the witnesses stuck to their story that they had merely been sightseeing, even when the story rang patently false. Their calm demeanor confounded and irritated committee members. When asked why he and his white friends drove over to Dan Speed's grocery store in Frenchtown, the black section of Tallahassee, to meet up with Negro students, Joe Spagna, a white FSU student, coolly replied, "We were just going over there—a Saturday morning jaunt, college boys." His bravado soon faded, however, when Hawes asked pointed questions about who had planned and organized the excursion and what their intentions were. Spagna retreated, invoking the Fifth Amendment, though he did respond when the attorney asked if he had any idea why Leonard Speed, a young man born and raised in Tallahassee who had lived there all his life, would need to go on a sightseeing tour: "No." Some committee members chafed at the perceived impudence of the student witnesses. Representative J. B. Hopkins broke in and admonished Spagna, "I would appreciate your showing some proper respect to counsel and to this Committee, and I would appreciate it also if you wouldn't have so many 'yep' and 'yips' and 'nopes' and that sort of thing."[22]

Leonard Speed proved equally elusive, if more polite. Because his father was a respected community leader, Hawes believed that Leonard must have played an important part in organizing and planning the group ride. Speed admitted under oath that he had given each of his fellow riders a dollar, but he insisted it had come out of his own pocket. Since they would be sightseeing, he claimed, he wanted to make sure that everyone had some cash on hand. Meanwhile, Spagna had already testified that he never received any money from Speed, while another participant, Johnny Herndon, recalled asking to borrow the dollar. "Didn't nobody say anything about borrowing anything," Speed corrected.[23] To the extent that such testimony could be damaging, since no criminal behavior was proven, it was damaging in the same way the NAACP lawyers' testimony had been: by implication, and by giving the appearance of wrongdoing and prevarication.

This became even more apparent when Harold Owens, a Florida A&M student, was called before the committee. Hawes asked Owens if Dan Speed had offered the free legal services of the ICC if the boys were arrested, and Owens confirmed it:

Owens: He said that if we was going sightseeing and if we was arrested that he would pay.
Hawes: He told you that?
Owens: That's right.
Hawes: Well, you didn't think you could get arrested without sitting integrated on those buses, did you?

Owens: Well, that's the way we went. We knowed—I guess we figure we wanted to be arrested.

Hawes: You figured you wanted to be arrested?

Owens: That's right.

Hawes: What?

Owens: That's right.

Hawes: Now, that's the real truth about it, isn't it?

Owens: That's right.[24]

Owens's admission cast new light on what previous witnesses had denied. In spite of failing to prove that any of the witnesses had broken the law, at the very least the FLIC succeeded in making them hedge and provide conflicting testimony. For the witnesses, however, denying accusations and evading questions about their associations had only to do with survival at a time when the NAACP was under siege and when almost any activity on behalf of desegregation was seen by segregationists as criminal. The Tallahassee hearings ended on an anticlimactic note when Francisco Rodriguez appeared voluntarily before the committee to confirm that the NAACP had indeed had a hand in every lawsuit filed in Florida since *Brown* to desegregate buses, schools, swimming pools, golf courses, and beaches—or, as the *Democrat* paraphrased him, "The NAACP is masterminding desegregation lawsuits." Rodriguez stressed, however, that "contrary to popular belief, we don't go out looking for plaintiffs. In fact, we have more volunteers than we ever think of using." With that, Mark Hawes announced that no further hearings were necessary for this phase of the FLIC's work. But he and other committee members promised that new legislation would result from this inquiry that would be aimed at "slowing down" the "paid agitation" so that "advocates of overthrowing established law and custom may be almost entirely suppressed."[25]

* * *

At the end of February, the committee traveled to Miami to question local NAACP activists. On the first day of hearings, February 25, 1957, attorney Grattan Graves spent the morning explaining that the national headquarters of the NAACP had requested that local branches initiate legal action against schools and school boards that showed no signs of complying with *Brown*. Later that day, Miami NAACP secretary Ruth Perry, a white woman, testified that she had handed over all organizational records and membership lists to Graves, who in turn shipped them to New York headquarters "under orders" from Thurgood Marshall.[26] The events were cut short after only one day, when Dade County representative and FLIC member Cliff Herrell sponsored a resolution to immediately begin an investigation of the Seaboard White Citizens' Council. The group's leader had just been arrested for attempting to burn a cross in a black neighborhood in Miami. The Johns Committee seized the chance to prove it was not targeting only the NAACP and that it was serious about protecting Floridians against social disorder. But in truth, this was a convenient moment for the FLIC to back out of a potentially embarrassing experience—the utter inability to compel NAACP members to divulge records and information related to their political beliefs and associations. The committee continued the Miami hearings but shifted entirely to the white supremacist group. The FLIC was set to expire in mid-April. Herrell announced that the legislature would likely renew it and that the committee's work, yet unfinished, would continue.

As the FLIC conducted the business of slowing integration in Florida in February 1957, Congress was poised to launch its own hearings on President Eisenhower's civil rights bill. His proposals included the creation of a bipartisan committee to investigate charges of civil rights violations, the establishment of a civil rights division within the Department of Justice, new laws to protect voting rights, and greater involvement of the federal government in civil cases.[27] While some critics charged that the legislation would be ineffectual and largely symbolic, southern conservatives were outraged. Georgia attorney general Eugene Cook predicted without irony that the legislation would lead to the creation of "a federal Gestapo which would hold needless investigations, pry into the affairs of the states and their citizens, and intimidate a majority of our citizens solely to appease the politically powerful minority pressure groups inspired by the communistic ideologies of the police state."[28] In Florida, U.S. senator George Smathers took a moderate approach in Senate debates, arguing against the use of troops to enforce federal law and that black claims of disenfranchisement were exaggerated. In the end, however, he and his Florida counterpart, Senator Spessard Holland, voted for the diluted bill.[29]

The FLIC submitted its first report to the legislature in April 1957. On the NAACP's illegal activities and dubious motives in Florida, the report stated, "The NAACP has formulated a plan calling for the full, complete and absolute integration of the races in this country in every phase of life by 1963. This includes the removal of all legal prohibitions against intermarriage of the races."[30] It also pointed out that the committee could have uncovered more proof of wrongdoing had the civil rights group not "secretly removed" all state branch records at the direction of the "rigid and strict" national leadership.[31] Finally, FLIC members pleaded their case for renewal by noting that within "the last few days" investigators had discovered the "Communist Party and certain other subversive organizations have made plans to use the racial tensions in the South to set one segment of the population against the other in this country and to thereby help accomplish their aim of world domination."[32]

How could Florida lawmakers say no to battling Communist world domination? They could not, despite the fact that in the words of the *St. Petersburg Times*, the FLIC had really only demonstrated, "beyond the shadow of a doubt, that the NAACP is trying to advance colored people."[33] The intentional mention of international Cold War concerns reflected a running theme and a common segregationist strategy in the years of massive resistance. In this instance, the committee recast local and sectional problems in terms of national security, knowing that it would resonate with the legislators who would decide the committee's fate when the vote for renewal came up. It also signaled a new direction for the FLIC, alerting the assembly that another two years would mean continued investigations of the group that was doing the most to integrate Florida's schools, as well as the continued smearing of the group, this time under the rubric of Communist subversion. That month, when the legislature met, Charley Johns, Dewey Johnson, and John Rawls sponsored a series of NAACP-related bills, including measures against the unauthorized practice of law and in favor of stricter definitions and enforcement of antibarratry laws, the renewal of the investigating committee, strengthening the law against soliciting and funding litigation, limiting citizens' ability to initiate legal proceedings against the state, and requiring the NAACP to file membership lists and statements of expenditures with the secretary of state. This last passed in the senate unanimously but was defeated in the house judiciary committee. Of these, only one passed, the law to reinstate the FLIC for another two years. Once again, Governor Collins allowed the bill to become law without his signature.[34]

On May 2, 1957, the day the Florida House voted eighty-three to zero to extend the life of the Florida Legislative Investigation Committee, the house and senate passed a joint resolution supporting interposition. The legislature also considered other bills, including the closing of the public school system under certain conditions. Governor Collins wrote an impassioned two-paragraph critique of interposition. Because the resolution was simply an expression of opinion and not a bill, Collins could not veto it, nor did it have any actual impact on Florida's schools. He called it "anarchy and rebellion against the nation which must remain 'indivisible under God' if it is to survive. Not only will I not condone 'interposition' as so many have sought me to do, I decry it as an evil thing, whipped up by the demagogues and carried on the hot and erratic winds of passion, prejudice, and hysteria."[35] That same day, Senator Joe McCarthy died of complications from alcoholism at the Naval Medical Center in Bethesda, Maryland.[36] But the ideas and tactics to which his name had become attached long outlived the senator, and perhaps no region continued his fight with more urgency than the South. As legislative committees continued battling integration in Mississippi, Georgia, Alabama, South Carolina, and Arkansas, outgoing FLIC chairman Henry Land told the press about the committee's recent discovery of evidence "strongly" indicating "the Communist Party has sought to, and to some degree may have actually, infiltrated the NAACP."[37] Having demonstrated its commitment to revealing the "truth" about integrationists in Florida through a series of damning hearings, the committee was now alerting the public that it would take the Communist threat seriously.

The results of the committee's early efforts were mixed. On the one hand, with the help of largely uncritical press coverage—the notable exception being the *St. Petersburg Times*—the committee sent its message to the public and the legislature that NAACP members had something to hide and they were trying to further their goal of race mixing. Moreover, Florida branches were at the beck and call of national leaders working from their integrated Manhattan offices. The committee attempted to demonstrate fair-mindedness by briefly investigating a white supremacist group, the Seaboard White Citizens' Council, though it is just as likely that by targeting this group, the committee was in fact comparing it to the extremism of the NAACP. FLIC members' smartest move was to raise the specter of Communist influence in the report to the state house and senate. This investigation would require more time and resources, and it would resonate with the public by playing on Cold War anxieties. The committee also succeeded in tying up a number of active NAACP lawyers, who otherwise would have been working on school desegregation cases. What the FLIC failed to do, however, was to convict any NAACP lawyer of criminal conduct or get them disbarred, stop African Americans from continuing the fight against segregation, or pass any meaningful laws that would outlaw or ban the NAACP from operating in the state of Florida.

*　*　*

The newly minted lineup of the Johns Committee in the late spring of 1957 included six porkchoppers: Chairman Johns, Senator Randolph Hodges from Cedar Key in central Florida, Senator Marion B. Knight from Blountstown in the Panhandle, and Representatives Ben Hill Griffin Jr. from Frostproof, J. B. Hopkins from Pensacola, and William G. O'Neill from Ocala. The lone voice from south Florida remained Miami representative Cliff Herrell. The new speaker of the house, Doyle E. Conner, who at twenty-nine had already served three terms, appointed the latter group. Conner hailed from Starke, hometown of Charley Johns. His approach to legislative procedures and committee appointments reflected an emerging trend within the legislature to gradually modernize and reform the lower body.[38] At the same time, however, it is likely that Johns had the junior legislator's ear when it came to naming new members to the investigating committee.

As the FLIC prepared to expose Communist influence within the NAACP, the issue of homosexuality arose in January 1957, when two young men, ages eighteen and twenty, part of a "teen-age gang which made a business of 'rolling' sex perverts," were apprehended in Tampa and charged with robbery. They had stolen fifteen dollars at knife point from a man who the police promptly charged with a crime against nature. The two also claimed responsibility for as many as a dozen other incidents of luring homosexual men into what the victims assumed would be a sexual liaison and then stealing their money. They listed three well-known public spaces in downtown Tampa (which the *Tampa Tribune* published) where they regularly targeted homosexuals: the Knotty Pine Bar, the men's restroom at the Hillsboro Hotel, and Plant Park. The judge in the case commented, "These men they robbed were no good but that doesn't give them a license to hunt them. The bad part of the juvenile law is that it gives youngsters the idea they can get away with what they think is good clean fun."[39]

In February, Julian C. Davis, director of the Florida State Hospital, publicly criticized the state's sex crime laws at a conference on corrections in Tallahassee. In 1957, Florida's laws related to sexual offenses included a sodomy statute criminalizing "the abominable and detestable crime against nature" as well as child molester and sexual psychopath statutes.[40] After providing an overview of the more than one hundred people institutionalized under these laws at the state hospital since 1951, Davis concluded that in Florida "our sex offender statutes are ineffective and are being used inconsistently." He was referring to the Child Molester Act of 1951 and the Sexual Psychopath Act of 1955, both the result of the nationwide panic over child molesters and juvenile delinquency during the early 1950s. The problem, according to Davis and many others, was the absence of a clear definition of a sex offender and a standardized set of screening procedures to differentiate the criminal, the homosexual, and the sexual psychopath.[41]

Reports of perverts on the loose in public spaces and a deficient statewide apparatus for addressing the problem alarmed the public as well as the Johns Committee, which received a series of reports from the Criminal Bureau of Investigation of the Dade County Police Department in January and February 1957. The reports detailed a house in Miami Beach that had been the source of great concern to neighbors. The original complainant, whose identity has been blotted out in the police report, stated that the house in question was "being used to promote homosexual activities," that "for the past year there has been cars in and out of this house during all hours of the night and day," and that "about a month ago there was a large party given at this address and was attended by about 100 males attired in costumes of large plum [sic] hats and feathers protruding from there [sic] shorts in the rear." Police spent weeks running background checks and copying the license plate numbers of every car they saw in the driveway.[42] After hearing reports of a "negro house boy" with a habit of propositioning "each and all delivery men, postman, the Orkin man and others" and paintings "of lewd nature" adorning the walls, one Dade County officer went undercover as a Florida Power and Light technician. He entered the house, snapped half a dozen pictures, and concluded that the artwork was inoffensive and the houseboy evidently uninterested in him.[43]

A few months later, the Hillsborough County Sheriff's Department began investigating charges of homosexual employees at the Southwest Florida Tuberculosis Hospital in Tampa. Agents performed what they called "discreet surveillance" at the hospital for four days before being detected. After that, using information provided by one disgruntled former employee and "after clearance with the Chairman of the Senate Committee [to Investigate State Tuberculosis Hospitals] and with the Attorney General's office," they began questioning other former staff members. Within the week, the sheriff's office had uncovered nearly a dozen confirmed homosexuals, including a male nurse at nearby St. Joseph's Hospital, a male orderly at Tampa General Hospital, and the dean of boys at Tampa's Plant High School.[44] It is unclear when or how these files reached the committee's hands, but Johns likely knew about the investigation as it was happening or soon afterward, given his personal and political ties to Attorney General Richard Ervin as well as Fletcher Morgan, a porkchopper and chair of the committee investigating tuberculosis hospitals.

Beginning in June 1957, law enforcement officials in the Tampa Bay area began "spot surveillance" of sites "believed to be frequented by homosexuals." In addition, "a general search was initiated to develop informants among known homosexuals in the Clearwater, St. Petersburg, and Tampa areas. Numerous contacts were made and considerable information amassed."[45] The investigation had far-reaching consequences. It laid the groundwork for future inquiries into the homosexual "problem" in the Tampa Bay area and the entire state, provided a model for spying on suspects in their homes and places of work as well as public meeting places, and established a pool of informants from which investigators could later draw upon. One investigator and former Hillsborough County sheriff later explained to the Johns Committee how the successful TB hospital investigations allowed for further inquiry:

Having already secured informers on the previous investigation in the State Hospital, I again contacted the informers, and again at night, working solely at night, going around to the bars that are frequented by the homosexuals, both men and women, and getting the information from the informers, getting the names of people, which began turning up various men and women, and the different locations, such as the Knotty Pine Bar, here in Tampa, which was the headquarters for the men; Jimmy White's Tavern . . . seemed to be the headquarters for the women.[46]

The hospital investigation turned up the names of alleged homosexuals employed in Tampa's public schools. The most prominent among them was the dean of boys at Plant High School. He in turn identified sixteen males with whom he had been sexually involved. Hillsborough sheriffs notified the county superintendent of education, who demanded further action. By the end of July 1957, nearly thirty male and female teachers had been accused of homosexual activity, and thirty more suspects' names were given to investigators. State senator Fletcher Morgan received the reports and the lists from Tampa. There is no evidence that Morgan passed them along to Charley Johns, but it is very likely that the two friends and colleagues would have discussed the issue.[47]

*　*　*

The Johns Committee began 1958 with hearings in Miami, the scene of African Americans' litigation and protests aimed at segregated public accommodations and schools and itself no stranger to antisubversive inquests. Frustrated by the committee's inability to pin guilt on NAACP lawyers in the Virgil Hawkins case and the Tallahassee bus boycott, Charley Johns chose a hardline approach to exposing the Communist connections of the NAACP in Miami—a city with a longer tradition of labor activism and more racial violence in the postwar years than any other Florida city.[48] As 1958 dawned, Americans were still reeling from the violent white mobs of Little Rock, Arkansas, and debating the role of the federal government in protecting minority rights. Many had been troubled by President Eisenhower federalizing the National Guard to escort black students into Central High School while holding off the jeering crowds of white men, women, and children at gunpoint. Professional informer J. B. Matthews would later testify before the Arkansas Legislative Council's Special Education Committee that the entire Central High debacle was stirred up by Communists who had penetrated civil rights groups there.[49]

The "Negro question" first became linked to communism with the founding of the Communist Party in the United States in 1919. Party leaders grappled with the question of organizing blacks in the South and they blamed capitalism for sharecropping, segregation, and lynching, as well as unemployment, residential segregation, and exclusion from unions in northern cities. In 1928, at the Sixth Comintern Congress, the CP included ending racial discrimination in its official platform and passed a resolution calling for "self-determination" and "social equality" for African Americans in the Black Belt—a move that alarmed white southerners and took on almost mythical proportions among segregationists for decades.[50] In 1929, the party began organizing in the Deep South, including textile mills in North Carolina, and established headquarters in Birmingham, Alabama. For the next five years it is estimated to have attracted between six and seven thousand black members, from iron and steel workers and miners to laundry workers and farmers. It offered legal defense to the Scottsboro Boys in 1931, fought for equitable unemployment relief for African Americans, organized sharecroppers and demanded fair payment of benefits by the Agricultural Adjustment Administration, and led strikes in the factories and the cotton fields.[51] For many black Communists, theirs was a brief flirtation that began to fade by the middle of the 1930s, but some former members went on to become activists in leftist and radical organizations. This "invisible army" also left its imprint on ongoing struggles for economic and racial justice in the South.[52]

On January 7, 1958, Charley Johns and fellow committee members Hodges and O'Neill deposed Sylvia Crouch, a white woman who had been married to Paul Crouch, the famed ex-Communist informant, in Johns's hometown of Starke. She began by describing her own journey in and out of the Communist Party, starting with the Textile Workers' Union in Gastonia, North Carolina, in 1929. She answered questions about her husband, who had been a party leader and organizer around the country, including Virginia, North and South Carolina, Alabama, Florida, Georgia, and Tennessee. The couple settled in Miami in 1947, the same year they openly renounced communism. Once Johns had established these facts, he proceeded to the civil rights question:

Q. Can you tell me whether or not it was an official aim of the Communist Party of the United States to agitate the race issue in the South?
A. Yes sir, it was.
Q. Is there any question at all about that?
A. There is no question about that at all.

Crouch confirmed that the party created several front organizations, including the Southern Conference for Human Welfare (SCHW), in which she and her husband had been active. Johns followed up:

> Q. Can you tell me the names of some of the organizations that were set up by other people, other than Communists, which the Communist Party instructed its members to infiltrate into and to use in this agitation?
>
> A. Well, the Communist Party members were instructed to infiltrate the existing trade unions, the NAACP—
>
> Q. Right there: Is that the National Association for the Advancement of Colored People that you are referring to?
>
> A. Yes sir; that being the strongest organization among the Negro people, the Communists emphasized the necessity for infiltrating that organization.
>
> Q. Do you know whether any of them did so?
>
> A. Yes sir, they did. In districts where they were working a number of the Communist Party members did join, and that was true all over, according to the reports that were made to the National Committee of the Communist Party. That was carried out.

Next Johns read a list of groups and asked Crouch to confirm or deny Communist infiltration into them. According to her, CP members had successfully penetrated the American Civil Liberties Union, the Abraham Lincoln Brigade, the Cigar Workers' Union of Florida, the Civil Rights Congress, SCHW, the Highlander Folk School, and the League of Women Voters. The witness then identified more than two dozen members of the Communist Party who lived in Miami, and the deposition concluded with an exchange about another aim of the Communist agenda, which was, as Johns understood it, "to break down the family as a unit" and "discourage, under this Manifesto, permanent marriage relations between men and women." Crouch confirmed even worse fears, however, when she described how "white girls would be instructed to have close relations with Negro boys."[53]

The Southern Conference for Human Welfare proved to be a long-lived bogeyman for anti-Communist segregationists, enduring for years in the southern imagination after quietly disbanding in 1948. Inspired by the National Emergency Council's July 1938 characterization of the South as "the nation's number one economic problem," the organization held its inaugural meeting in Birmingham, Alabama, later that year. It drew participants from across the spectrum of southern liberalism, from moderates such as Alabama senator Lister Hill, Alabama governor Bibb Graves, and journalists Ralph McGill and John Temple Graves II, to black educators Benjamin Mays and Mary McLeod Bethune, to a handful of Communist Party members and every imaginable brand of progressive: representatives from the CIO, the Southern Tenant Farmers' Union, the Socialist Party, the American Youth Congress, and countless others. The group sought better housing and health care, increased funding for education, and other economic improvements in the region, for blacks and whites alike.[54]

Almost immediately, SCHW provoked the wrath of southern opponents of the New Deal and the Popular Front. Newspapers dutifully repeated accusations of Communist infiltration of the organization. This was enough to drive most of the prominent early members away, notably, liberal stalwarts in the U.S. Senate Claude Pepper from Florida and North Carolinian Frank Porter Graham. Their reluctance to affiliate with radicals later proved well founded, as both suffered crushing electoral defeats in 1950, the result of both race baiting and Red baiting, which included dredging up their past membership in SCHW. Despite adopting a strict anti-Communist policy in 1942 and witnessing modest fund-raising and membership increases during the war years, SCHW could not withstand the political onslaught and ultimately failed to shake its reputation as a haven for Reds. In 1947, a HUAC report called it a "deviously camouflaged Communist-front organization" that "displayed consistent anti-American bias and pro-Soviet bias."[55]

One month after Sylvia Crouch's deposition with Charley Johns, another well-known informant, the leftist-turned-anti-Communist and former director of research for HUAC, J. B. Matthews, appeared before the Johns Committee at the state Capitol Building. His statements under oath became a powerful piece of propaganda, not only for the committee in laying the foundation for the case against Communist race mixers in Florida but also for other southern states and antisubversive groups. The Georgia Commission on Education, a counterpart to the FLIC, reprinted Matthews's testimony in full and packaged it in a pamphlet titled *Communism and the NAACP*. The Mississippi Sovereignty Commission, the Citizens' Council, and other organizations across the region distributed copies to members. Billy James Hargis, founder of the Tulsa-based anti-Communist Christian Crusade, cited Matthews in the pamphlet *Unmasking the Deceiver,* which promised to expose Martin Luther King's alleged Communist ties. And as late as 1963, while speaking before the Senate Commerce Committee against the Civil Rights Act, Mississippi senator John McLaurin quoted J. B. Matthews's FLIC testimony. McLaurin read aloud from *Communism and the NAACP* and then declared that Matthews's words "definitely established the fact that the NAACP has been a prime objective of the Communist penetration and, in numerous instances, prominent individuals connected with the NAACP have succumbed to the appeals of the Communist front apparatus. The indisputable truth of the matter is that the leaders of the NAACP, taken as a whole, have been extraordinarily soft towards the Communist conspiracy."[56] Matthews himself had been among the first informers to appear before the Dies committee in 1938. From there he went on to work for HUAC and served as an assistant to Joe McCarthy.[57] For the Johns Committee, he was a friendly witness, an expert who could enlighten Floridians about the true nature of Communists and the history of their attempts to influence Negroes. He offered a stamp of legitimacy to the committee's anti-Communist crusade.

Matthews's appearance also set the tone for the committee's upcoming hearings that would focus on the overlapping membership between the NAACP and organizations that had been labeled subversive by the U.S. attorney general. In March 1947, President Truman had signed Executive Order 9835, establishing a screening program for all federal employees to ensure their loyalty to the U.S. government. Among the criteria used to determine one's loyalty was membership, past or present, in any organization deemed by the Subversive Activities Control Board "totalitarian, Fascist, Communist or subversive." State and local governments began using the attorney general's list, as did many other institutions, including other federal government agencies and the military, often against political enemies. It became a widely publicized blacklist, and by 1958 a familiar reality of life in Cold War America.[58]

Federal and state investigations of civil rights and progressive groups were commonplace during this period. In the words of the historian Jeff Woods, HUAC was "a principal contributor to the southern red scare. With the help of his chief investigator, J. B. Matthews, [Texas congressman Martin] Dies steered the committee to probe the labor, Jewish, popular-front, and black allies of Roosevelt's New Deal coalition." In 1949, HUAC, under the direction of Georgia Congressman John Wood, conducted "Hearings Regarding Communist Infiltration of Minority Groups." As the chairman of the Senate Internal Security Subcommittee, James Eastland spent years exploring, and exploiting, the subversive ties of racially progressive groups. In 1954, SISS held hearings on Communists in the Southern Conference Educational Fund (SCEF). Among those questioned was Leo Sheiner, a Miami attorney and colleague of SCEF executive director James Dombrowski. In Louisiana, Leander Perez, the demagogic judge and Citizens' Council leader, maintained close ties to fellow segregationists across the South, among them state senator Willie Rainach, the head of Louisiana's Joint Legislative Committee on Segregation, and Georgia's attorney general Eugene Cook and state politician Roy V. Harris. In 1956, Arkansas representative E. C. Gathings entered dozens of HUAC reports on the NAACP's Communist affiliations into the record and urged further congressional inquiries into the problem.[59]

J. B. Matthews's testimony before the Johns Committee parroted the party line adopted by conservative southern whites. He held forth on various individuals and organizations with alleged Communist ties, as well as reviewing the pertinent literature related to African Americans and the Communist Party. Much of it covered the late 1920s through World War II, the period before the NAACP adopted an explicitly anti-Communist policy. Matthews recited the litany of charges against Communists in the South that had been heard for years: They were "stirring up trouble" in southern schools, they had been at work for three decades "in the field of agitation among Negroes with the ultimate goal of violent revolution," and they "favor racial amalgamation." He also conjured up the myth, which had circulated since the late 1920s and stemmed from CPUSA policy sanctioning black self-determination, of Negroes wanting to carve out their own separate "republic" from the Black Belt.[60] Matthews paid special attention to the party's agenda of "penetrating" non-Communist liberal or progressive groups. As he explained it, Communist penetration was intended for "control," to "disseminate" the views of the Communist Party, or, in some cases, to "destroy the organization which is penetrated."[61]

*　　*　　*

To make the case that Communists had contaminated the Miami branch, the FLIC demanded the state NAACP's membership lists, which would allow for comparison with the membership rolls of organizations on the attorney general's list. Further, the FLIC demanded that the NAACP answer questions about the political affiliations of certain members, another version of naming names. They would also ask witnesses if they knew women and men who had been in the Communist Party. In Tallahassee, FLIC members had not brought up the specter of Communist influence. But in Miami, thanks to a state attorney's grand jury inquests between 1946 and 1948, as well as HUAC's appearance there in 1954, FLIC investigators had the names of Communists who had also been affiliated with a host of liberal reform groups. As historian Raymond Mohl has documented, many of those in Miami who were harassed for their progressive activism were northeastern Jews, who brought to south Florida a "leftist political culture—trade unionist, progressive, socialist, and communist," which "informed, inspired, and motivated Miami's early Jewish civil rights activists."[62] Among their allies was the unabashedly liberal state representative Jack Orr, the lone voice of support for school desegregation in the legislature at the time. He was also a member of the Miami branch of the NAACP, the Florida Council on Human Relations, and the state chapter of the American Civil Liberties Union. His affiliations, coupled with his defense of Miami Communists who had been jailed after the HUAC inquiry, led to his failed reelection bid in 1958.[63]

Charley Johns knew the committee could trot out the old familiar players, the Reds who had testified years before, and resuscitate old memories of Communists infiltrating labor unions, reform organizations, and the local Miami Jewish Cultural Center. At the beginning of the Miami hearings on the morning of Wednesday, February 26, 1958, he reiterated that the sessions were intended to determine "the degree, if any, to which Communists and Communistic influence has been successful in penetrating, infiltrating, and influencing" organizations related to "race relations," labor, education, and "other vital phases of life in this State."[64] Attorney Mark Hawes read a statement declaring that being subpoenaed neither proved nor implied membership in the Communist Party, knowing that was often precisely what it implied.

The first witness was Bertha Teplow. She was Jewish, Russian born, and raised in Massachusetts. Teplow belonged to the Communist Party, had been an organizer in the South, and served on the party's National Committee. According to the FLIC's dossier on those who had been called to testify, she was the "present day State Organizer for the Communist Party of the State of Florida."[65] She gave her name and address. Hawes asked where she was born and Teplow replied, "I refuse to answer that question because it is not pertinent to any competent subject of legislative inquiry," because it violated her constitutional rights, and because "this Committee is illegally constituted and is functioning illegally." Despite Hawes's assurance that he was not trying to "coercize" her, she said nothing more.[66] Those who followed were equally steadfast in their silence, and in their demands for protection from the inquiry based on their First and Fourteenth Amendment rights. Witness after witness argued that the FLIC had no legal right to compel them to answer questions about their involvement with SCHW or the Civil Rights Congress, the Hungarian-American Cultural Club or the NAACP. They refused to say whether they had known individuals questioned by HUAC, people such as Jose Carbonell, Samuel Hirsch, or James Nimmo, all Communists in Florida who were also active in progressive racial causes. They read prepared statements about their right to freedom of association. They articulated their dedication to nonviolent, non-Communist organizations. The Reverend Edward T. Graham, longtime NAACP and ACLU member, proudly stated that he had not brought any of the "records, books and documents" of the NAACP and the Florida Council on Human Relations "called for by the subpoena." He then read a scathing statement in which he called the committee "a kind of roving Grand Jury," which is "not a proper or legitimate legislative function but, rather, constitutes an invasion by the Legislature into the provinces constitutionally reserved to the judicial and executive branches of our Government." He continued: "All my life I have worked for the betterment of my fellow man, and particularly for the improvement—"

"Wait a minute," Hawes interrupted. "I don't think that it is part of any proper objection to any questions that have been propounded to you." He warned, "We cannot permit the witnesses to read endlessly irrelevant and immaterial statements into the record." Hawes and Johns conferred briefly, then allowed Graham to continue reading:

In my opinion, the Florida Legislature has no right to make me divulge the names of persons with whom I have worked and associated on the basis of common beliefs and ideas. To do so would soon make it impossible to dissent or peaceably to assemble and seek a redress of grievance, since men exposed to the glare of an investigation such as this merely for forming opinions and beliefs, would

soon choose conformity or inactivity, rather than be placed in a position such as I am in today.

Not to be outdone, Hawes got Graham to admit that he had made notes
about the subpoena when he first received it and that he had taken it
to his attorney, who actually prepared the statement. The attorney then
prompted Graham, in a variety of fashions, dozens of times, to admit
that he belonged to the NAACP, served as vice president, knowingly associated with Communists, or had himself been a Communist. Wearily,
Hawes asked, "Do you decline on the same ground, Reverend? If you are,
we can save some time."

"Well, I want to save all of the time possible, Counsel," Graham replied,
"but I don't want the saving of time to be a noose into which somebody
has placed my neck; so, I want to make it very clear what my position is.
At the outset it was agreed that—according to the record, that I took the
position that the Committee is not legally constituted to go into my associations, and I must, therefore, decline on that basis."[67]

The committee cited Graham, along with earlier witnesses, for contempt. Graham's attorney protested, "If you feel that a man who is a
witness before this Committee, relying upon what he believes to be his
constitutional rights can be cited for contempt of the Committee without having his counsel argue the point before the Committee . . . then I
believe, sir, that I have been mistaken in the several years I have practiced
and studied law."[68] His plea fell on deaf ears.

The committee proceeded to the next witness. Vernell Albury, an African American woman active in the Miami NAACP in the late 1940s
and 1950s, had served as treasurer and board member in 1955–56 and
had joined the Communist Party. Albury identified a handful of known
Communists she had seen at various liberal meetings over the years, from
anti-Klan protests to gatherings of the American Veterans Committee to
NAACP functions. When asked for a specific count of overlapping membership between the NAACP and the Communist Party, however, her answer must have been disappointing to the committee: "Oh, about two or
three."[69]

Albury was first introduced to the party while working at Pan American Airways. In 1949, nearly two thousand Pan Am workers belonged
to Local 500 of the Transport Workers Union (TWU), a CIO affiliate.
That year, Paul Crouch wrote a series of exposés in the *Miami Daily News*

claiming among other things that Communists controlled Local 500. Since the local's founding in 1945, Communists had constituted one segment of the rank and file as well as part of the leadership. Charles Smolikoff, CP organizer and regional director of the International Union of Marine and Shipbuilding Workers of America (IUMSWU), had helped unionize Pan Am in 1943. By the end of 1948, however, the new TWU president, perhaps inspired by a recent HUAC investigation in Miami, had publicly broken with the Communist Party and directed an anti-Communist purge within the union.[70]

Many Communists in Miami were also active in liberal causes, including civil rights. Smolikoff was the best known, but other targets of state attorney George Brautigam's grand jury in the late 1940s and early 1950s, and of HUAC in 1954, included James Nimmo, a Bahamian activist in Miami since his days in the local chapter of Marcus Garvey's Universal Negro Improvement Association in the 1920s. He also organized laundry workers in the 1940s and later joined the TWU.[71] Nimmo, Smolikoff, and other labor activists joined groups such as SCHW, SCEF, and the Civil Rights Congress (CRC), a national organization devoted to civil liberties as well as civil rights that maintained close ties to the Communist Party until it was crushed under the weight of Red baiting in 1956. The Miami chapter of CRC was established in 1948 and survived just three years. During that time, the FBI kept the group under surveillance and paid particular attention to one of the leaders, Matilda "Bobbi" Graff. She, along with Smolikoff and Nimmo, also experienced harassment at the hands of local grand juries as well as HUAC, and all three had left the state by the time Charley Johns and his committee arrived. In 1954, James Eastland's committee hounded two other former Miami CRC members, Leo Sheiner and Max Schlafrock, who were also SCEF members. This veritable who's who of Miami leftists had been absent or inactive for several years when the Johns Committee arrived in February 1958. That did not stop the committee from dredging up familiar characters once again and compelling witnesses to admit that they had known these people, they had joined some of the same groups, and they had sought racial equality and economic justice. As the victims of the earlier investigations and the FLIC's latest version well knew, and as one white activist recalled, their "biggest crime was bringing blacks and whites together."[72]

*　　*　　*

The next morning, Thursday, February 27, 1958, the committee recon-
vened at 9:30 in the North Court Room of the Dade County Court House.
Among those who testified was Howard Dixon, a member of both the
ACLU and the Florida Council on Human Relations and an attorney who
had represented the NAACP until 1954. He had voluntarily resigned after the *Miami Daily News* approached him for an interview and Dixon
quickly saw that the questions focused on the leftist affiliations of Miami
NAACP members. He read his letter of resignation into the record for
the FLIC: "In order to forestall the implied accusation of alleged 'guilt
by association,' as contained in those [*Daily News*] questions, I herewith
notify you that, being dedicated to the best interests of my clients, no
matter who or what they are, recognizing my duty as an attorney, I am
withdrawing as your counsel." That was all Dixon would discuss. During
the rest of his testimony, he followed the precedent set the day before, and
frequently interjected with critiques of Hawes's questioning. Hawes asked
him, for instance, if he had belonged to the Peoples Progressive Party
of Dade County in support of Henry Wallace's 1948 presidential candidacy, which, according to "information in this Committee's files indicates
conclusively" that the group was "Communist organized and Communist
controlled and dominated." In response, Dixon said sternly, "Mr. Hawes,
you are really striking at the heart of our democratic system in asking me
which party I registered for in 1948, sir."[73]

Another outspoken witness on the second day was Ruth Perry, a white
librarian who had moved to Miami in 1945 with her husband and daughter, taken a job at the Miami Beach Public Library, and joined the NAACP,
where she served as secretary of the Miami branch as well as secretary
of the Florida State Conference of Branches. She also hosted a weekly
radio program about the organization and penned a column titled *Along
Freedom's Road* for the *Miami Times*, the city's black newspaper.[74] As had
some previous witnesses, she read a statement questioning "the right of
this Committee to compel my appearance and testimony" and informing
the committee that she had not brought any NAACP records or membership lists to the courthouse that day, as required by subpoena: "I consider
the Committee's demand for such records and memberships invalid, and
an invasion of my rights to due process of law and freedom of speech and
association." Perry's stubborn opposition got the better of the legislators
that morning. Cliff Herrell, representative from Miami, interrupted the
proceedings to make a statement of his own: "I think that any witness

that sits in this chair and cries for the right to make a statement and reads a report that is prepared for them by counsel, and yet refuses to answer questions that would allow this Committee to render a service to the State of Florida . . . is not fit to be a citizen of the State of Florida. I think this is a disgrace." With that, he recommended contempt charges against Perry. When he did, a smattering of applause echoed in the courtroom. Perry later recalled that it came from jeering Citizens' Council members in attendance.[75]

Theodore Gibson dealt the most dramatic blow to the committee that day. Gibson, rector of Christ Episcopal Church and president of the local chapter of the NAACP, had been born and raised in Miami, the son of Bahamian immigrants. He graduated from St. Augustine College in Raleigh, North Carolina, completed divinity school in Virginia, and made his way back to Miami, where by the early 1950s he had become an important spiritual leader of a growing movement to end segregation there.[76] He had already resisted the committee in 1957 and was not about to concede any ground this time. When asked about the records and lists he had been subpoenaed to bring, Gibson ignored Hawes entirely and began to speak. "There can be no question in anybody's mind in Dade County as to my citizenship," he asserted. "I am an American citizen. I believe in the heritage of America. I believe in the Constitution of the United States." He continued, "I would not permit this Committee or any other Committee to intimidate me nor to deny me my lawful Constitutional rights. . . . I have not been a Communist; I am not a Communist; I am not a Communist sympathizer." Gibson concluded, "I refuse, as of now, to answer any questions and I, therefore, consider myself no longer obligated to the Committee."[77]

The courtroom erupted with applause as Gibson stood up and stepped down from the witness stand. Hawes could scarcely believe his eyes. "And you are now leaving the hearing room?" he asked.

"I am, sir."

Before all seven committee members could cast their votes citing him for contempt, Gibson had walked out.[78]

The next morning, committee members returned to the courthouse. Rather than continuing to call witnesses from the NAACP, however, Representative Herrell made an about-face, motioning to have the committee investigate the Ku Klux Klan and other white supremacist groups in Florida. It seemed an obvious ploy to deflect attention away from what several NAACP witnesses had criticized, that the Johns Committee was singling out their organization solely on the basis of racial ideology. But the FLIC's critics, Herrell charged, had never "at any time shown, regardless of the accusations that have been made, that we're one-sided, and we're biased. Our prime responsibility to the Legislature is to maintain peace and tranquility in the State of Florida."[79] The motion passed. Just as in 1957, civil rights activists and liberal reformers demonstrated surprising mettle in the face of overt political harassment, and their noncooperation once again forced the committee to change course in the middle of the hearings. Nevertheless, Charley Johns had the satisfaction of pursuing contempt charges against Vernell Albury, Theodore Gibson, Grattan Graves, and Ruth Perry. The four appealed. In December 1958, the Florida Supreme Court ruled unanimously in favor of the FLIC. NAACP members would be compelled to answer questions. They would not have to produce membership rolls, but they were required to bring them to the hearings in order to consult them during questioning. In 1959, the witnesses appeared again before the committee but failed to bring the lists with them. Again, legal action ensued, and it was not resolved until 1963.[80]

*   *   *

The FLIC's first foray into homosexuality came while at loggerheads with the NAACP, in the fall of 1958, in a full-scale investigation of the state's flagship school, the University of Florida in Gainesville. Historian John D'Emilio has suggested that faculty support for desegregation initially attracted the committee's attention to UF, where investigators inadvertently stumbled upon gay professors.[81] The university did have a reputation for racially liberal views among some of the faculty, particularly since the UF chapter of the American Association of University Professors (AAUP) expressed support of immediate integration at the university in 1956 and argued that "no serious conflicts, incidents, or disturbances would occur and that no public harm or mischief would be done as a result of the admission of qualified students of all races."[82] In the winter of 1957, a group of UF students traveled to Chapel Hill to "study the effects of integration" at the University of North Carolina, presumably to emulate it in Gainesville.[83] Sociologists William C. Havard and Loren P. Beth argued in 1962 that the UF investigation was nothing more than a "Keystone cops tragi-comedy, ending in an investigation of homosexuality."[84] Others have speculated that Charley Johns's son, a student at the university, repeated to his father the campus gossip swirling around several male professors considered suspiciously effeminate. Some have also argued that "rumors and innuendo offered the FLIC a long-awaited opportunity to create a conspiracy that linked homosexuality, subversion, and integration" to justify its continued existence.[85] At the time, Johns explained investigators' presence in Gainesville as the result of "numerous complaints" from unnamed sources of unspecified wrongs. In an interview years later, R. J. Strickland recalled that the committee had received "a report of two homosexual professors" at the University of Florida. "We were concerned with the possible influence the professors would have on the student body. . . . So I went down there and I found it was really, really strong."[86]

All of these explanations are plausible, yet it is doubtful that committee members were self-consciously seeking an excuse to create any conspiracy. More likely, they seized upon an issue that few would criticize. Even if only a handful of Floridians were complaining about gay professors, the committee quickly found that homosexuals' often hidden identities left them extremely vulnerable, and thus valuable, as witnesses and informants. Moreover, Johns and his committee shared the wider cultural belief, circulating since the 1940s, that homosexuals posed a threat to national security. They, like other Americans, had watched Republicans successfully employ the issue of gays in the State Department to discredit the Truman administration's softness not only against communism but also against sexual perverts. The senator from Starke recognized that he could use the investigation of gay professors at the University of Florida to save face and redeem his committee's name at a time when the NAACP investigations were flagging. He also very likely considered homosexual professors a genuine menace to students and calculated that his committee's work in Gainesville would not only generate support for the FLIC but also address a grave social problem.

The issue had arisen on campus before. In 1954, a University of Florida student was "forced to resign because of insanity, and it appeared from the psychiatrist's testimony that the boy had been involved in some homosexual relations at a chicken ranch" outside the Gainesville city limits.[87] The property, a site of numerous gay parties and get-togethers, later became a surveillance and infiltration target of the committee. In the spring of 1955, the editor of the student newspaper, the Florida Alligator, notified an Alachua County sheriff that he had heard of plans for a homosexual party at the infamous ranch and he intended to carry out his own undercover investigation for a feature story. Nothing came of either episode. By the fall of 1957, however, Charley Johns declared that he had, "on the recommendation of the Chief Counsel, engaged R. J. Strickland for a period of approximately two weeks to investigate a matter in the Gainesville area."[88] The matter in question was likely homosexuality, since Strickland's two-week trip followed on the heels of the Tampa public school investigations.

On August 19, 1958, the chief investigator and a twenty-eight-year-old employee of the UF library sat down in room 202 of the Hotel Thomas for a "conversation." John Tileston, a young member of the university police department who had arrested the witness the night before, accompanied Strickland. Originally from Boston, Tileston had moved to Cedar Key, Florida, as a young man. He served in Korea, was discharged from the military in 1956, and attended the University of Florida. To help pay the bills, Tileston worked part time at the university police department and at the Alachua County Sheriff's Department. After two years, he was promoted to investigator at UF. "The next thing I know I'm called in and I'm introduced to R. J. Strickland . . . and I was told to work with him and show him the campus and around town," he remembered.[89] The investigators' primary objective was to gather names and confessions, and they started at the county courthouse in Gainesville, which was known as a site of homosexual meetings for anonymous sex. This location had been an open secret in town for years. One suspect told committee investigators that he had frequented the men's room there when he was in high school, in the early 1930s. He joked that it was "a damn good place to get jock itch."[90]

During the next few weeks, Strickland questioned several other men who had been apprehended by Tileston, working undercover. By September the Johns Committee had enough testimony to alert members of the Board of Control, the state's university governing board, about the problem afflicting the University of Florida. On September 27, 1958, the FLIC met with the BOC at the Alachua County Court House. Strickland briefed them on his findings, including a list of suspects and his own critique of UF administrators for failing to keep records on "faculty members proven to be homosexuals and dismissed for that reason." Just as unsettling and potentially embarrassing, they "were allowed to go to other positions with recommendations from the University." The board agreed to instruct UF president J. Wayne Reitz to see to it that university police cooperated with

Strickland. Johns promised to keep the upcoming investigation secret and warned the BOC that "failure to act would result in a public hearing."[91]

Many witnesses found themselves eager to agree with questioners who talked about homosexuality as a bad habit. Almost ten years later, sociologist Laud Humphreys uncovered the same pattern among patrons of "tearooms," or public bathrooms, in his observation of fifty encounters between March and August 1967. Humphreys questioned a dozen of the men and noted that most of them were married, did not consider themselves homosexuals, and were "quite secretive" about what they were doing.[92] He also documented the wide range of backgrounds, ages, and vocations of the men, which is precisely what R. J. Strickland had discovered in Gainesville. Mingling his own terminology with gay slang, Humphreys identified several types of men frequenting the restroom: "trade," or men who did not perform sexual acts on other men but received them; self-identified gay men; and "closet queens." About 38 percent fell into the first category. Many of them worked as truck drivers, machine operators, and manual laborers. The closeted men were more likely to work as teachers, salesmen, and clerks. Humphreys claimed that they "regularly cruise the streets where boys thumb rides each afternoon when school is over," and he speculated that they were the ones who most feared "exposure, arrest, the stigmatization that might result from participation in the homosexual subculture."[93]

To different ends but much like Humphreys's sociological study, the Johns Committee's men's room stakeouts revealed similar diversity among those who frequented public bathrooms in search of sex. Strickland, Tileston, and their associates apprehended students and faculty from the University of Florida, truckers, teachers, traveling salesmen, local businessmen, and day laborers. All were vulnerable to detection and unmasking, whether at work or in their married lives. Virtually none was openly gay or even comfortable in acknowledging under duress his homosexual behavior. Indeed, the very nature of the furtive, anonymous bathroom encounter meant that the committee often ended up interrogating men who were deeply conflicted about their sexual desires. And because they had everything to lose, it is not surprising that they confirmed many of the contemporary psychological explanations as well as crude stereotypes of homosexuality. Just as the postwar Red scare fostered, in one historian's words, "guilt by association, threat of punitive exposure, ritual confession, the naming of names, and blacklisting," so too did it engender, in the case of the Johns Committee, ritual contrition.[94] Suspects questioned by the committee routinely confessed self-loathing, personal and moral weakness, and promises to overcome the overpowering and debilitating urge to seek out same-sex encounters. This ritual, much like the others, reinforced the assumptions of investigators. It fueled their belief that homosexuality was a bad habit that demanded regular, and escalating, attention and that left victims feeling remorseful in the knowledge of their sickness.

Surveillance of the courthouse, the UF library, a local bar with a reputation as a hangout for homosexuals, and a wooded area behind the auditorium on campus netted dozens of men. The committee's chief investigator spent most of October 1958 taking more testimony from those caught in the stings.[95] He also gathered extensive information about their sexual practices and paid special attention to whether they were "active" or "passive" participants in homosexual acts. As the transcripts make clear, during the questioning Strickland rarely hesitated to interject with commentary on their behavior. A twenty-four-year-old marketing major spoke candidly of his desire for both giving and receiving sexual pleasure from men:

> Q. Have you ever, at the same time the other boy was giving you a blow job, have you given him one at the same time?
> A. That's correct, I have.
> Q. But you do not prefer it that way?
> A. I do prefer it that way.
> Q. Then you are sure of getting what's coming to you. Is that right?
> A. That's correct.[96]

To a thirty-two year old who had left UF after the 1957–58 academic year, Strickland said, "If it offends you, I am sorry, but it is a question I have to have an answer to, either one way or another. In your participation in the homosexual activity, from a personal standpoint, have you ever administered what is known as a blow job?" Nonplussed, the witnessed answered yes. "Would you, at this point," the investigator continued, "tell me whether or not you received the most pleasure out of giving a blow job or receiving one." Again, the man did not hesitate to answer: "If there is a feeling between two people more than animal lust to be satisfied then it's quite possible that someone could receive pleasure from both giving and receiving in this operation."[97]

Although Tileston had spent weeks in various restrooms around town and campus and had observed the patterns and rituals of sexual encounters, Strickland nonetheless insisted that witnesses explain exactly how they went about picking up men. A twenty-three-year-old freshman, recalling his disastrous encounter with Tileston, described entering the bathroom and making it known that he was interested in sex:

> Q. What did you say specifically?
> A. "I think you are having the same trouble as I am," or something to that effect, and more or less mentioned or told him to stand on the other side of the petition [sic].
> Q. Did you tell him to put his penis through the hole in the partition?
> A. Yes, I did.
> Q. And that you would suck it. Is that right?
> A. I don't know whether it was verbal but at least it was understood that I would.
> Q. Is there any specific or certain sign that is given you know of?
> A. Well, yes, if you call a sign being an erection. You look to see if the other person is having an erection is about the only thing I know.
> Q. If you can't see, then what?
> A. Well, I mean the usual is the foot tapping.[98]

Strickland and Tileston learned quickly how easy it was to catch men, even as word spread that campus and city police were cracking down on local restrooms and meeting places. One December day in 1958, well into the University of Florida investigation, Tileston arrested two men from out of state in the courthouse bathroom. One was a Merchant Marine from Los Angeles visiting relatives in nearby Lake City. The other was a traveling salesman from New Jersey who had been caught in the very same men's room the year before when he was in Gainesville for business. When Tileston enlisted him to act as a lure, the salesman "readily agreed." He started his new undercover assignment on the spot. By the end of the first day, he had entrapped a University of Florida freshman and a graduate of Florida State University who was employed as an elementary school teacher.[99]

The investigation was not made public immediately, but students and professors were aware of the committee's presence in Gainesville. One English instructor and aspiring writer, Clyde Miller, wrote to Gene Baro, his friend and former housemate at Marjorie Kinnan Rawlings's home in

Cross Creek who was teaching in Vermont at Bennington College in the fall of 1958, "The general atmosphere in Gainesville is harried and ugly with rumors, alarms and constant quizzing of students by the Johns Committee."[100] Within a matter of months, Miller had resigned, explaining, "I could not continue to teach, write a novel, and live under the pressure of charges of sexual perversion." He continued, "But—a terrible uncertainty hangs over me as long as I remain in Florida—the Committee can still issue subpoena's, and it can turn its information over to the public prosecutor of Florida—the lawyer says this is a most remote contingency—but it exists. Should subpoenas be issued, I would leave here immediately. *You must not come down here under any circumstances.*"[101]

* * *

The use of homosexuals as a political target in Florida had ominous consequences for gay teachers and students during the years that followed. It also helped to bolster the committee's antisubversive credentials among conservative supporters, who were suddenly made aware of a familiar Cold War threat in their own state, their alma maters, and sometimes their children's schools. The committee proved much more skilled at finding homosexuals and threatening to expose them than it had at identifying Communists within the NAACP. Charley Johns would capitalize on this success, expanding the search for gay and lesbian teachers to all corners of the state. At the same time, civil rights activism in Florida, as in much of the rest of the South, would take a new and dramatic turn away from the NAACP's legal challenges directed at schools to youth-driven, nonviolent protests aimed at integrating public spaces. Segregationist politicians and their supporters witnessed the stirrings of a mass movement that at once proved their worst fears and forced them to adopt new strategies for resistance.

Figure 1. Group portrait of the Pork Chop Gang, Tallahassee, 1956. Courtesy of the State Archives of Florida.

Figure 2. Governor-elect LeRoy Collins (*left*) and acting governor Charley Johns (*right*), inauguration day, 1956. Courtesy of the State Archives of Florida.

Figure 3. Reverend C. K. Steele (*center left*) and Reverend Dan Speed (*center right*) during the Tallahassee bus boycott, December 24, 1956. Courtesy of the State Archives of Florida.

Figure 4. State senator Charley Johns, 1961. Courtesy of the State Archives of Florida.

Figure 5. Ernest Salley (*left*), an employee of the State Road Board, secretly recorded a speech made in Florida by Scott Nearing, a well-known socialist and pacifist. Salley played the tape for FLIC chief counsel Mark Hawes at a hearing held in Tallahassee on February 10, 1961. Courtesy of the State Archives of Florida.

Figure 6. Governor Farris Bryant signing Florida's obscene literature bill, May 1961. *Left to right*: Representative George L. Hollahan Jr., Charley Johns, Senator Sam Gibbons, and Board of Control member Gert H. W. Schmidt. Courtesy of the State Archives of Florida.

Figure 7. Governor Farris Bryant with Board of Control members J. Broward Culpepper (*left*), executive director, and Baya Harrison (*right*), chairman, January 17, 1963. Courtesy of the State Archives of Florida.

Figure 8. Charley Johns with B. R. Tilley (*left*), president of St. Johns Junior College, and A. E. Mikell (*right*), superintendent of the Levy County schools, who appeared as witnesses before the Johns Committee on April 17, 1963. The committee held hearings to determine what policies were in place to detect and remove homosexual teachers and professors. Courtesy of the State Archives of Florida.

Figure 9. Mark Hawes, chief counsel for the FLIC, addressing a joint session of the Florida legislature, April 18, 1963. *Seated, left to right*: Representative Richard Mitchell, Speaker of the House Mallory Horne, Senator Charley Johns, Senator Houston Roberts, Representative George Stallings, and Representative Ben Hill Griffin Jr. Courtesy of the State Archives of Florida.

Figure 10. *Left to right*: Jane Smith, parent of a University of South Florida student and critic of professors and reading material at the university; FLIC attorney Mark Hawes; FLIC member William G. O'Neill; and Charley Johns, May 7, 1963. Courtesy of the State Archives of Florida.

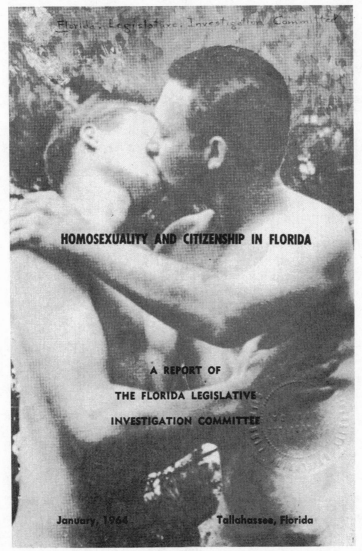

Figure 11. The title page of the FLIC's controversial 1964 report, *Homosexuality and Citizenship in Florida*. Courtesy of the Florida Heritage Collection and the George A. Smathers Libraries Special Collections, University of Florida.

Fetish appeal is shown in this photograph taken from a homosexual's collection. The use of the bindings is frequent in artwork of this nature, and an apparently strong stimulant to the deviate. In many photos offered by "Art Studios" primarily for the homosexual trade the black posing strap will be drawn in with a material easily removed after it has been mailed to the purchaser.

Figure 12. Photograph allegedly confiscated from a homosexual who collected pornographic pictures, used by the FLIC in the "purple pamphlet." Courtesy of the Florida Heritage Collection and the George A. Smathers Libraries Special Collections, University of Florida.

This photograph was taken by a Florida law enforcement agency of a homosexual act being performed in a public rest room. Such occurrences take place every day in virtually every city in every state. It is significant that the removal of the toilet stall doors to facilitate photography did not deter these and numerous other practicing homosexuals.

Figure 13. Photograph of a homosexual encounter in a public restroom, included in *Homosexuality and Citizenship in Florida* to illustrate the dangers of homosexuality. Courtesy of the Florida Heritage Collection and the George A. Smathers Libraries Special Collections, University of Florida.

Figure 14. The FLIC held one of its last public hearings in July 1964, this one covering the activities in Florida of the National States Rights Party. *Left to right*: Charley Johns, Representative C. W. "Bill" Young, Senator Robert Williams, Representative George B. Stallings, and committee director John Evans. Courtesy of the State Archives of Florida.

3

Surveillance and Exposure, 1959–1960

Every time I see one of these little sissy boys hanging around some college, the more I think every one of them ought to be made to play football. What we need today is more he-men and fewer sissies.

Georgia Board of Regents member Roy V. Harris, *Time*, 1953

The Johns Committee began 1959 as it had ended the previous year, with secret hotel room interrogations and men's room stakeouts on the University of Florida campus and around Gainesville. By the spring, the university had removed more than a dozen professors on the grounds of homosexuality. The purge was the beginning of what would become the committee's five-year campaign to expose and expel lesbian and gay public school teachers across the state, or, as committee attorney Mark Hawes put it, to stop "this thing" that seemed to have invaded Florida's schools and universities.[1] Florida lawmakers granted the committee another term in 1959. During those two years, while Strickland and assistant investigators fanned out across the state searching for gay and lesbian teachers, the region witnessed a shift in civil rights activism, as the staid legal approach of the NAACP gave way to student sit-ins and demonstrations throughout Florida and the South. The committee relied largely on monitoring meetings and publications, to little effect, while in the search for homosexuals, Johns and his men were wildly successful, gathering hundreds of names, questioning dozens of men and women, and pressuring many of them into surrendering their teaching jobs on the spot. Strickland's modus operandi was to inform each suspect that resistance would be rewarded by "a subpoena to appear before this Committee in a public hearing."[2] In its efforts to contain civil rights activism, the committee proved largely impotent, continuing to try to prove subversive influences while remaining mired in legal battles with the NAACP. At the same time, the civil rights struggle itself was becoming more diffuse, which made it more difficult for the committee to keep tabs on the growing numbers of activists in state and local groups.

*　　*　　*

When Charley Johns and his committee began targeting homosexual educators, they were at once covering familiar territory and blazing new trails. Teachers had long been feared as potential carriers of political subversion. After President Harry Truman issued an executive order in 1947 establishing a loyalty-security program intended to cleanse the federal government of Communists and fellow travelers, this "project," as historian Ellen Schrecker has written, soon filtered down into a wide range of professions and institutions. Among those most acutely affected were colleges and universities. Although professors had drawn fire and even lost their jobs as a result of their political views, actions, or affiliations, and although twenty-one states had passed laws requiring teachers to sign loyalty oaths as early as the mid-1930s, the Cold War elicited unprecedented scrutiny of the faculty and curricula of the nation's universities.[3] It also brought a new sexualized component to the regulation of teachers' behavior outside of the classroom.

The Johns Committee's campaign against homosexual professors and teachers resembled the State Department and federal government purges from the late 1940s and 1950s. Much of the shrillest hysteria associated with McCarthyism had waned, but political subversion, gender and sex nonconformity, and the interconnectedness of the two continued to resonate in America's political culture at the end of the decade and the beginning of the 1960s. What was new in the committee's model was its attention to schools as a locus for battling these forces, which stemmed both from popular preoccupation with teacher loyalty, "brainwashing," and teenagers' vulnerability and from the fact that the South's schools were currently the most volatile sites of radical change that the region had witnessed in a century.

In late 1958 and early 1959, witnesses in the University of Florida homosexual investigation proved exceedingly cooperative in naming names and confessing misdeeds. Several faculty members' names came up repeatedly. One was Lawrence Wathen, a humanities professor identified by a handful of students and instructors as an initiator of homosexual activity. John Park, a twenty-eight-year-old instructor in the Music Department and director of the men's glee club, told Johns, Hawes, Strickland, and Tileston, all of whom had gathered in room 10 of the Hotel Thomas in early January 1959, that when he had first started teaching at the university, Wathen invited him over to his house to listen to records; they ended up fellating each other. A middle-aged husband and father, also part of the music faculty, admitted to "mild" homosexuality in the second floor men's room at the library: "I just had a feeling of wanting to feel the other organ, is all."

"In other words, you would masturbate another man?" asked Charley Johns.

"No, just feel it," he answered.

Park also shared with the committee his low opinion of Professor Wathen, whom he described as "quite an obnoxious person." He talked about seeing him "in certain fraternity houses where I happened to be and where he was going to speak, and I've noticed him just always calling all the boys 'Sport' and always putting his arms around them."[4]

Johns and Hawes posed questions that reflected their own era's understanding of homosexuality. Johns asked, "Do you think that a man with sufficient will power can unlearn that, like any bad habit?" The professor, sensing a possible escape route, replied, "Most definitely." Next Hawes suggested that the "lack of a strong administrative stand and policy against this kind of conduct actually, by implication, has encouraged the increase of this sort of conduct out there, hasn't it?"[5] Again, the witness agreed wholeheartedly. Johns and his committee were operating on the popular midcentury belief, articulated chiefly by psychiatrists, that homosexuality represented a flight from adulthood, and adult masculinity, rather than being biologically or genetically determined. Others blamed the influence of overbearing, overprotective, feminizing mothers on what was deemed to be the rising numbers of homosexual men, and still other explanations included the ascendance of an impersonal, alienating mass society as well as the spread of secular humanism and general moral decay.[6]

On January 5, 1959, the same day John Parks was questioned, Lawrence Wathen appeared at the Hotel Thomas but never admitted to being a homosexual. At 8:00 that evening, Professor James Congleton appeared and threw himself on the mercy of the committee. Numerous witnesses in the investigation had named Congleton, and his homosexuality was something of an open secret around campus. At fifty-seven, in his twenty-second year of teaching in the University of Florida's English Department, Congleton was desperate to salvage his career. Like so many other suspects, he viewed, or at least claimed to view, his behavior as a bad habit, an uncontrollable compulsion that struck sporadically. "I don't think anybody at that University has worked as hard as I have," he told Mark Hawes. "I have never taken a drag off of a cigarette, never once. . . . I promise you and Mr. Strickland and Mr. Tileston and Senator Johns and everybody else that I'm going to break it."[7]

On the second day of motel room testimony, the committee faced its first challenge. The chief pharmacist in the Department of Student Health, thirty-one years old, married, and the father of two, asked if he could consult an attorney before answering any questions about homosexual activity. Mark Hawes assured him, "This is no criminal investigation. Homosexuality is a felony under the statutes of Florida, as he can advise you. It is a crime, and the penalty for it is a term of years in state prison. It is not presently our purpose to prosecute you." Hawes went on: "It is our purpose to find out the extent of this condition around that university out there, and to determine what measures should be taken civilly to correct the situation. If need be, for those people who do not co-operate with us, and who we have sworn testimony on, in order to get to the root of this thing and the extent of it, we may have to turn this information over to the State Attorney for criminal action; but for those people who co-operate with us and tell us the truth, we do not intend to take any criminal action at all."[8] The pharmacist returned that afternoon with two attorneys. He pleaded the Fifth Amendment and his lawyer told Hawes, "We challenge the authority and the jurisdiction of this committee to pursue that line of questioning." Unfazed, Hawes replied, "We have been challenged on that ground many times. Thank you, gentlemen."[9]

The overwhelming tendency of witnesses to play to committee assumptions about homosexuals reinforced, over and over again, the belief that the condition could be acquired through association. Most of the witnesses questioned in Gainesville told investigators just what they expected to hear. A twenty-six-year-old graduate student and math instructor, a husband and father of two children, claimed never to have engaged in a homosexual act but said he had gone to the courthouse merely to experiment. He had seen and heard similar acts in the men's room at the

University of Florida library and in the bushes behind the auditorium on campus:

> Q. What you saw in those rest rooms and outside of the library and what you saw down here in this rest room at the courthouse began to prey on your mind, didn't it?
>
> A. Yes.
>
> Q. And you began to have a desire to try it out?
>
> A. I don't know whether it was a desire or not, but I can honestly say it did begin to prey on my mind.
>
> Q. Desire or curiosity?
>
> A. I guess it was more curiosity than anything. I wouldn't call it a desire, but curiosity. I realize it may be rather hard to separate the two, but in my mind they are separated.[10]

The student painted it as an unbearably tempting curiosity ruthlessly "preying" on him. As Strickland asked him, "Don't you think the condition is such that it tends to draw young men that come up to this University into that sort of conduct?"

"I think so, yes. I know it has done it to me."[11]

Another suspect confirmed not only that homosexuality was picked up through association, but that it could progress from passive involvement to active. At twenty-three, he was a freshman attending the University of Florida on the GI Bill. He was also married but had been caught in the courthouse bathroom:

> Q. In your homosexual experience have you been both the active and the passive partner?
>
> A. Yes. It started out with me being passive, but lately it has been both.
>
> Q. This thing has sort of grown on you as you have practiced it, has it?
>
> A. Yes.
>
> Q. When you were first picked up had you ever had any desire to handle or fondle or take another man's penis into your mouth at all?
>
> A. No.
>
> Q. And it gradually grew on you after you submitted to other men passively?
>
> A. Yes.[12]

On January 8 the committee relocated to the Manor Motel in Gaines-ville to resume questioning, which continued for the rest of the month. The thinly veiled threats of exposure convinced most suspects to confess and to name names. Professors gave the names of students they had had sex with or knew to be gay; students similarly showed little compunction in doing the same for faculty and college mates. In mid-February, the Johns Committee met with the Board of Control in Jacksonville to sub-mit a nineteen-hundred-page investigative report. Johns issued a public statement announcing that his committee had "gathered this information in the interest of Florida educational institutions and to determine what if any legislative action is required and not for the purpose of damaging any institution or individual."[13] Johns assured UF president J. Wayne Reitz that he was not trying to impugn his university, but Reitz could not be mollified. He resented the intrusion and believed that the "irregularities" uncovered at the University of Florida could be found at many schools.[14] When the story of the report broke in the papers, the Alachua County sheriff denied that the county courthouse men's room was a homosexual meeting place, explaining that long ago he had had all the doors to the stalls removed. He neglected to mention that this was a common tactic for deterring bathroom sex, and just as commonly known not to work.[15]

Homosexuality did not creep up on Americans as a social problem in the late 1950s. Many knew individual homosexuals, and many more knew of their existence. Millions had read—or at least purchased—Alfred Kinsey's 1948 surprise bestseller, *Sexual Behavior in the Human Male*, in which homosexuality was a significant undercurrent. Americans con-sumed Hollywood magazines and scandal sheets that offered tantalizing hints in gossipy prose about which movie star was not quite the leading man he appeared to be. They were aware of the military code designed to keep homosexuals out of the service or had a spinster aunt or a bachelor uncle. When U.S. Army head counsel Joseph Welch made a sly reference to fairies during the U.S. Army–McCarthy hearings, the gay innuendo was not lost on the national television audience glued to their sets. What was new in the 1950s, however, was the notion that homosexuality was encroaching on the American family, like communism and juvenile delin-quency, that the number of homosexuals was increasing at a frightening pace.[16]

Thanks in no small part to Kinsey, the avuncular biologist from Indiana University, the pages of *Time*, *Newsweek*, *Good Housekeeping*, and *Reader's*

Digest, as well as newsrooms, universities, and kitchens, resounded with talk of sex. A great deal of this reflected Americans' surprise about what people claimed to be doing in their bedrooms. Kinsey reported that 10 percent of adult males considered themselves exclusively homosexual, and that more than one-third had engaged in homosexual acts.[17] The perception of a rising tide of homosexuality was bolstered by the media coverage of Kinsey's research, the military and federal government purges of gays and lesbians in the late 1940s and early 1950s, and local police raids on gay bars. With all this talk, this "endless stream of negative headlines and news articles," the homosexual menace seemed to loom ever larger during the 1950s.[18] Florida's investigating committee operated on the assumption that sexual perversion was seeping into and undermining the cornerstones of American democracy: government, the nuclear family, and now schools.

In April 1959, as the Board of Control pondered policy changes, the University of Florida fired fourteen faculty members, including Wathen, Congleton, and Park, along with librarians, a math instructor, and professors in geography, business, and nuclear engineering. Although the men who were actually involved in the investigation very likely discussed their situation with friends, and the details must have been buzzing across gay social networks, most students had only a murky understanding of the mass firing. In a letter to the editor of the student newspaper, the *Florida Alligator*, two students questioned why the purge had been carried out in secret. Because they had no idea of the extent to which the committee had extracted names and acts, they speculated angrily that the victims were not homosexuals at all but were targeted for taking a "pro-integrationist stand." Even a year later, the student newspaper was reporting ongoing investigations and expulsions of students and faculty, this time at the instigation of the campus police, but acknowledged by the vice president as part of the "legitimate self-policing" of homosexual activity promised to the Johns Committee in the spring of 1959.[19]

*   *   *

The University of Florida investigation was an epiphany for Charley Johns. While serving as acting governor in 1954, he had dealt with homosexuality as a political issue. That summer, a seven-year-old girl was kidnapped from her grandparents' house, raped, and strangled to death. In the headline-fueled rush to find the suspect, several local gay bars were raided and their patrons brought in for questioning. A crackdown on these and other establishments known for hosting drag shows soon followed. Police officers began showing up at local restaurants, hotels, and public spaces with a reputation as meeting places for homosexuals, including Bayfront Park, the Greyhound Bus Station, and the public beach on 22nd Street. According to the writer James Sears, in September 1954, "a dozen or so bars, ranging from Leon & Eddies to the Club Echo, were raided nightly."[20] In response to public officials' fears that known perverts would escape Miami and move elsewhere in the state, acting governor Johns appointed an attorney to oversee efforts to track homosexuals arrested in Miami. He also charged the Crime Commission of Greater Miami with investigating gambling, corruption, and sexual deviance. Daniel Sullivan, who a year earlier had called Miami "a gathering place for sex degenerates" and implied a link between gay bars and pedophilia, headed the commission.[21] Two years later, the campaign for Dade County Sheriff was marked by gay baiting from one of the candidates. ONE magazine described the atmosphere as a "new type witch hunt" and noted, "That some few (like many heterosexuals) offend with minors, is no valid ground for general attacks on homosexuals. This is as foolish as the Southern canard that every Negro is a rapist. It's time the two lies were laid together."[22]

Gay men and, to a lesser extent, lesbians endured a popular presumption that they were sexually drawn to children and adolescents. Estelle Freedman and other historians have traced the origins of the cultural mythology of the homosexual as child molester in the United States to the 1930s, when the figure of the unattached male became a symbol of economic and social dislocation and corrosion. In addition, psychiatric explanations of sexual deviance and sensational stories of child murder and sex crimes stirred public fears of the "sexual psychopath," often coded as homosexual.[23] As the scholar Philip Jenkins has shown, fear of sexual predators reached deep into the national psyche during the sex crime panic of the 1930s, and terms such as "sex fiends" and "sex psychopaths" were used interchangeably by doctors and in the press to refer to a range of behaviors, from rape and murder to consensual homosexuality, voyeurism, and indecent exposure. Criminologists often did the same, and thereby justified the disproportionate targeting of male homosexuals as sex offenders, sex perverts, and sex criminals.[24]

The enormous body of writing about homosexuality in the postwar period defies broad generalizations. Still, some themes, ways of defining problems, and uses of language from the mainstream literature recur in the interrogations and reports of the Johns Committee. The most commonly reiterated were the theory of homosexuality as a personality disorder, the comparison and linkage between same-sex desire and addiction, and warnings about outwardly normal homosexuals' powers of deception. Two prolific authorities on homosexuality, psychoanalysts Albert Ellis and Irving Bieber, argued that in most cases homosexuality stemmed from one's environment. In his 1962 work *Homosexuality: A Psychoanalytic Study*, Bieber compiled the responses of seventy-seven psychoanalysts who treated gay men and lesbians and concluded that a majority of these patients had dysfunctional parents, most commonly a domineering mother and a detached, distant father. The anxiety that resulted from this unhealthy upbringing, Bieber concluded, caused sons' and daughters' "flight into homosexuality."[25] Ellis, too, devoted much attention to the role of "parental conditioning," but he also theorized about the importance of early positive experiences with the same sex and, conversely, negative ones with the opposite sex, in directing sexual desire toward what he deemed normal and abnormal outlets. He noted the withdrawal of lesbians and gay men from the "heterosexual rat race," which resulted from their inability to cope with the "real difficulties" of being a "full-fledged member of one's own sex." For men, this meant facing the expense, hassle, and sexual frustrations that came with courting and marrying women. For women, it meant facing the terrors of vaginal penetration, pregnancy, and childbirth.[26] Borrowing a page from Freud, postwar psychiatrists presupposed that homosexuals displayed an immature or regressive sexuality, an inability to grow up into healthy heterosexual adulthood.

Though neither Ellis nor Bieber drew explicit connections between sexual immaturity and desire for young people, others did. One doctor, Clifford Allen, argued in his 1949 textbook on sexual perversions that pubescent boys and girls were unusually vulnerable because they were passing through a homosexual phase and would be more open to an advance by a member of the same sex. Seduction at the hands of an older person, he warned, "is particularly dangerous since it is likely to make them remain so the rest of their lives."[27] Many attributed a combination of factors leading to the homosexual's preference for youth: easy access to sexually awakening and curious youth, a need to "reproduce," if not biologically, and an immature personality driving him or her to seek out people on the same emotional level. As a former chief deputy district attorney for

Los Angeles County explained in 1950, the homosexual "presents a social problem because he is not content with being degenerate himself; he must have degenerate companions, and is ever seeking for younger victims."[28]

Press coverage of homosexual arrests and raids reinforced these explanations of sexual deviance. In the fall of 1953 in Atlanta, twenty men were arrested in a sting operation inside the men's bathroom at the Atlanta Public Library. In addition to exhaustive coverage, on six different occasions both of the city's major newspapers published the names and addresses of defendants. Editors pondered the danger posed by these men, none of whom was accused of having sex with minors: "Experts here say that evidence indicates that otherwise normal children sometimes come under the influence of molesters and are actually converted to a life of sex perversion. In his more innocuous form, the pervert too often is regarded as merely a 'queer' person who hurts no one but himself." The editorial went on to pilfer from the introduction of *The Sexual Criminal*, which had been published three years earlier: "The public loses sight of the fact that these sex degenerates are inveterate seducers of the young of both sexes."[29]

Two years later, in Boise, Idaho, a group of teenage boys accused several older men of molesting them. City leaders and the *Idaho Daily Statesman* sided with the teens. One editorial exclaimed, "Homosexuals must be sought out before they do more damage to youth, either by investigation of their past records or by appeal to their unbalanced minds. Psychiatric treatment should start wherever it will be accepted in order to work against further acts by homosexuals. Immediate plans must be made for the proper assistance to boys who have been victimized in order that they do not grow into manhood to become homosexuals."[30] In 1957, a sweep in Greensboro, North Carolina, led to the arrest and conviction of thirty-two men on charges of crimes against nature. The chief of police explained to the local press that it was the department's obligation to "remove these individuals from society who would prey upon our youth," although none of the men had been sexually involved with a minor. Twenty-four received prison sentences, and some served on chain gangs.[31]

The most common trope used in public discussions of homosexuality during the postwar period was disease and contagion, and it appeared regularly in FLIC investigators' interrogations. It was a popular metaphor for communism as well, and this was not by coincidence. The Cold War ideas of containment, guilt by association, and the infiltration of weakened minds influenced the ways homosexuality was discussed at midcentury.

Disparaging allusions to sickness abounded: Homosexuals "are often as annoying and pestilent as flies," and homosexuality "is spreading like a contagious disease," wrote one psychologist. According to another, the "homosexual must have a sexual partner, therefore, he can't keep his perversion to himself, and if he can't do this, then he *is* contaminating someone else."[32] One criminologist claimed that the "plea for compassionate understanding and tolerance" of gay men and lesbians "on the ground that one's own brother, daughter, sister, or son may become a homosexual loses force when one realizes that, as in crime and tuberculosis, the statistical chances that one's own brother or son may become a homosexual increases with the number of homosexuals in the community."[33]

After committee investigators uncovered the underground homosexual culture in Gainesville, Charley Johns grasped the political potency of the issue of gay teachers. What his men found led Johns to believe that he had stumbled on either a vital national and state security issue, or at least a battle that he could win—and win public support for. Hidden homosexuals on the faculty of the state's most prominent university, a university that had produced governors and senators, civic and business leaders, and public school teachers, had gone undetected for years. Here, thought Johns, was a worthy substitute for the kinds of subversives the committee had searched for in the NAACP. Before the committee launched its investigation of the University of Florida, one member, Senator John Rawls, serving on the Interim Legislative Committee on Education (ILCE) as well as the FLIC, participated in discussions about "standards of ethical and moral conduct for teachers of Florida." In June 1958, the ILCE discussed strategies for identifying and removing teachers who engaged in immoral conduct, including homosexuality. The committee also recommended fingerprinting all state employees, to facilitate the tracking of teachers' behavior outside the classroom. The Johns Committee made a similar recommendation in its 1959 report to the legislature.[34]

Homosexual scandals were not uncommon in the 1950s in the United States. The State Department purges in the nation's capital made headlines for months in the spring of 1950. Gay rumors and innuendo peppered Whitaker Chambers's confessions as well as McCarthy's reckless insinuations. Fear of secret homosexuals underlay Eisenhower's strengthening of the loyalty-security program, as it did the ongoing removal of gays and lesbians from the military and the civil service, as well as the discursive obsession in both political parties with "softness."

During World War II, homosexuality had been defined as incompatible with military service—and eventually as an outright threat to national security. The U.S. armed forces enlisted psychiatrists to screen out mentally unfit volunteers, draftees, and enlisted men and women. These experts framed homosexuality as a form of mental illness that could destroy morale through homosexuals' assumed gender nonconformity and sexual insatiability. They also lumped it together with various social problems, including alcoholism, delinquency, drug addiction, and even unemployment.[35] The demonization of homosexuals during and after the war accompanied the rising prestige of the psychiatric profession itself. Whether intentionally or not, psychiatrists benefited enormously from their wartime role in setting the boundaries of mental and sexual health for America's men and women in arms. By the end of the war, approximately twenty-four hundred army doctors and seven hundred navy doctors, most with no prior psychiatric training, were serving as military psychiatrists, and many would continue practicing as civilians after 1945. The same men who had developed the homosexual screening program taught these doctors, and their ideas about sexual perversion and personality disorders were passed down from one generation to the next.[36] One of the fundamental assumptions that emerged in postwar psychiatry was the Freudian notion of homosexuality as immature or arrested development, a condition that a man or a woman could overcome. As another historian explained it, this definition comprised three categories: the well-adjusted, sexually mature heterosexual; the deviant, sexually immature homosexual; and the regressive heterosexual who "reverted" to homosexuality because of "unusual circumstances or the influence of others."[37] It was this third category that fed the homosexual panic of the 1950s and 1960s, because this susceptibility was believed to make adolescents an easy target for adult homosexuals.

In 1950, a homosexual scare swept the nation's capital, precipitated by the dismissal of ninety-one State Department employees. During an appropriations committee meeting, conservative Democratic senator Pat McCarran pressed Under-Secretary of State John Peurifoy to admit that "most" of the ninety-one had been fired because they were homosexual. A month later, Washington, D.C., vice squad lieutenant Roy Blick testified before a congressional committee that 5,000 homosexuals lived in the nation's capital, some 3,750 of them employed in the federal government. The numbers generated considerable publicity. Republicans seized upon the issue of homosexuals as security risks and used it as one of many weapons in their attack against the Truman administration, as yet another example of how the president and the Democrats were soft on communism and had failed to keep perverts out of the government. The State Department's security division had actually begun conducting internal investigations of suspected homosexuals in 1947. By 1952 it featured two full-time employees devoted solely to that mission. They performed background checks, questioning former employers and scouring bank accounts, credit records, and the like. Historian David K. Johnson, in his definitive study of the lavender scare, explains, "Invoking the characteristic 'guilt by association technique,' the investigators checked whether any of the employee's friends or associates were homosexual. . . . If suspicions were high but evidence lacking, those suspected might be placed under surveillance to determine whether they frequented 'known homosexual places or associated with other known homosexuals.'" By Johnson's count, the number of gay men and lesbians removed from the State Department between 1947 and the end of the 1960s, though impossible to calculate precisely, approached five thousand.[38]

Eisenhower's administration accelerated the purges. His 1953 executive order specified sexual perversion as a criterion for excluding individuals from federal employment. Moreover, the loyalty-security frenzy seeped into virtually every sector of the government. A 1958 study cited by Johnson showed that one in five "employed adults in America had been given some form of loyalty or security screening.[39] Coupled with the loyalty oaths required of teachers and professors in most states, the reach of the national security state was breathtakingly long. In Florida, the efforts of the Johns Committee served to further expand the purview of government interest in the personal lives of educators.

*   *   *

When the Florida legislature convened in the spring of 1959, the FLIC submitted a report justifying another two-year extension to continue the search for homosexuals in Florida's schools and universities. The report consisted of Mark Hawes's summary of committee activities in Gainesville, the FLIC's interpretation of homosexuality as a social problem in Florida, an overview of the "medical aspect" of the problem, and suggestions of new laws to remove gay and lesbian teachers and to keep them from being rehired in the state. It described what investigators found, what committee members believed, and how they planned to confront the homosexual menace in Florida's schools. The ideas ranged from the dispassionate—that gay teachers and students could be found at every level within the university and public school systems and that Florida was not alone in this problem—to the alarmist: "Some of the State's instructional personnel at the higher educational level have been and are recruiting young people into homosexual practices and these young people have been and are becoming teachers in the public school system of Florida, and some of them are recruiting teen-age students into homosexual practices," a quote that appeared in many Florida newspapers, including the liberal *St. Petersburg Times*.[40]

Hawes painted a dire picture of this gay network, citing the 1957 Hillsborough County investigation that identified twenty-seven gay teachers, who in turn provided the names of thirty more alleged homosexuals in the county school system. For reasons unexplained, the Hillsborough County investigation was never completed, and committee members argued that they ought to be the ones to pick up where the local sheriffs' deputies had left off. Even more pressing, the report claimed, was the lack of centralized record keeping, which allowed disgraced teachers to pick up and move to another county and resume teaching. Finally, in a moment of deserved self-promotion, Hawes noted, "It is not difficult for a qualified investigator who knows what to look for to develop concrete proof concerning a homosexual's conduct in the vast majority of cases." The attorney reported that the committee's conclusions were drawn entirely from "the most highly qualified men" available and from the testimony of "admitted homosexuals." Based on these authorities, the FLIC found that there were "several classes" of homosexuals who could be separated according to age, the "degree and extent" of homosexual activity, the amount of time spent engaging in homosexual behavior, and "his individual desire to correct his sexual deviation." Finally, Hawes declared, "there is no useful means of treatment for this problem save and except psychotherapy."[41]

Also during the 1959 legislative session, Representative George Stallings and Senator Randolph Hodges, both porkchoppers and members of the Johns Committee, authored bills that would ban from public schools and universities any books written by Communists, any individual who had invoked the Fifth Amendment when questioned by an antisubversive committee, or anyone whose name had appeared on the U.S. attorney general's subversives list. The proposed legislation, which some critics were calling "book-banning" and "book-burning" bills, followed closely on the heels of a bill sponsored by state senators and FLIC members Dewey Johnson and Charley Johns that would mandate the firing of any teacher or administrative employee of a public school, junior college, or university who advocated racial integration. This flurry of restrictive bills in 1959 angered some students at the University of Florida who resented the presence of the Johns Committee on their campus. They organized protest rallies and collected two thousand signatures on a petition criticizing the legislation. The following week, Stallings met with a group of UF students to discuss the role of the state legislature in shaping educational curricula. The conservative from Jacksonville assured them he did not support censorship but merely wanted to provide "the helpless parent who is forced to see his child studying a slanted, subversive textbook, some recourse to do something about it."[42] The Committee on Public Education eventually defeated the bill by an overwhelming vote of sixteen to one, but it argued that keeping a watchful eye on reading material in the state's schools was still a good idea because the committee governing state textbooks had indeed been careless in allowing books with insidious ideas about America to creep into Florida's classrooms.[43]

On May 6, 1959, less than three weeks after the University of Florida purge, another incident rocked the campus and exacerbated parents' fears about what was going on at the state's flagship university. At 8:00 that evening, the day after nine hundred students had staged a peaceful rally protesting the censorship bills, the electricity went out in three of the men's dormitories. Students spilled outside and began milling around. Soon cries for an impromptu panty raid rang across the quad. "We want panties!" the young men shouted on their way to Broward Hall, a women's dorm. When the dean of men arrived and tried to calm them down by singing the school fight song, he was greeted with jeers and chants of "We want Johns!" The crowd moved to another dorm and then on to sorority row. By eleven o'clock, hundreds of students had joined the fray, throwing rocks at campus police and setting fire to Dumpsters. The police eventually quelled the panty raid–turned–riot, but not before several students were hospitalized and two were arrested and later expelled.[44]

Many students were appalled by the events of that night, but they were equally concerned about the larger issues that had been raised by the Johns Committee's investigations and by the proposed censorship bills.

One student wrote to the *Alligator* condemning his peers for sitting idly by while "the State is trying everything within its power to take away your liberty, while a lopsided legislature is attempting to remove what little freedom you have left after McCarthy." Instead of getting angry about these looming problems, he complained, UF students got excited about power outages and panties and ended up displaying the very sort of delinquent behavior that adults found so disconcerting. Not only would the rest of the country conclude that "Florida students must not be intelligent" but, closer to home, legislators would be able to point to the riot and dismiss any serious student organizing or protests by saying, "Don't pay any attention to those kids; they don't know anything."[45] An outside observer from Ft. Lauderdale wrote to university president J. Wayne Reitz, "It's a pretty sad state of affairs when you force men out of college because of a little *normal* undergraduate fun, but you close your eyes to extensive homosexuality, not only among the undergraduates, but in your own faculty." Apparently unaware or forgetful of the recent homosexual investigation, he argued that professors should be "thoroughly screened" because "they are the ones who fashion the minds and characters of our future strength." Reitz responded brusquely, "You might be interested in knowing that of the 14 staff members dismissed, 12 of them had been on the staff prior to my assuming the presidency." He added, "I believe you would be interested to know that in only two cases involving the staff did we find that there was any relation with students."[46]

Reporting on its NAACP activities, the FLIC repeated charges of the Communist Party's designs on Negroes since 1928, its success in infiltrating the NAACP, and claims that 60 percent of the "national officers" of the NAACP have "records of affiliation with Communist organizations." Closer to home, the committee had "gathered in its files a list of approximately 150 present and past members of the Communist Party in Florida. It is a proven fact that each of these people were under direct orders to infiltrate into and to influence, if possible, the NAACP." The report described Miami witnesses' failure to cooperate at FLIC hearings and blamed them for its inability to catch any Communists. It also documented the tangled litigation that had resulted from the contempt charges against Theodore Gibson, Ruth Perry, and other NAACP activists, claiming it was "useless for the Committee to undertake its other planned hearings seeking to determine the nature and extent of Communist penetration and influence . . . in the field of race relations." The report concluded with a reminder that the case was currently pending in the U.S. Supreme Court, which had issued a stay order against the FLIC. "The Committee feels," wrote Johns, "that the State cannot afford to abandon this litigation and allow an adverse decision to go by default, and for this reason and because of the necessity of completing the investigations, which the pending litigation has up to now obstructed, that this Committee should be re-enacted by this Session of the Legislature."[47] And so it was, in May 1959. The state house and the senate passed the renewal bill, which became law in June—once again, without the signature of Governor LeRoy Collins.[48]

That month, the FLIC secured the revocation of teaching certificates of four Florida men declared "unfit for service in the public schools." Three of the four never responded to the notification by mail from the state Department of Education, and two were returned to sender, indicating that they had already moved. Only one, a teacher in Alachua County, alerted the department that he would not contest the decision. Another, charged with "assault on a male child under fourteen years of age in a lewd, lascivious and indecent manner," was sent to the state psychiatric hospital in Chattahoochee and then to the St. Johns County jail.[49]

* * *

On June 24, 1959, the Johns Committee, featuring several new faces, held its first meeting of the new biennium at the state capitol. Cliff Herrell, the moderate representative from Miami, was elected chair, and Senator W. Randolph Hodges, porkchopper from Cedar Key, vice chair. Other members from the house included William G. O'Neill (Marion County), Ben Hill Griffin Jr. (Polk County), and John Mathews (Duval County); Charley Johns and H. H. Hair joined Hodges from the senate. Before going into executive session at Johns's request "to discuss certain matters of a confidential nature," the men went over the previous biennium's committee expenditures. Of an appropriation of seventy-five thousand dollars, the FLIC had spent roughly sixty-seven thousand dollars, more than half of it on staff salaries, twelve thousand dollars on travel, and another forty-six hundred dollars on informant fees.[50]

Just as the expulsion of homosexuals from the State Department had a ripple effect across other federal agencies, the University of Florida purge inspired some state agencies to enlist the Johns Committee in their own homosexual investigations and to assist the committee by handing over names of suspicious employees. A member of the Florida Industrial

Commission, for example, alerted Charley Johns in August 1959 to a handful of employees in the St. Petersburg office who were likely homosexuals. Although the individual admitted that the evidence was "strictly hearsay," he was certain that the "information will be of some benefit to you and your Committee. I am sure you will be doing a great service to the Agency if you should conduct an investigation."[51] This pattern was repeated in subsequent years, as local citizens and grass-roots organizations in Florida reached out to the Johns Committee to address grievances, most of which related to social issues in their cities, towns, and schools.

In the summer and fall of 1959, R. J. Strickland traversed the state, gaining new informants and compiling confessions and names. He spent the first two weeks of July in Tampa–St. Petersburg and, just to the south, the Bradenton-Sarasota area, where he picked up the leads left over from the Hillsborough County tuberculosis hospital investigation and public school inquiry in 1957. The trail led to several gay public school teachers, including one man recently charged with having sex with more than thirty high school students.[52] Strickland's time in the Tampa Bay area also led him to a number of women confined to the Lowell State Prison for Women. In August, he traveled to the maximum-security prison, located between Ocala and Gainesville, which had just opened in April 1956. There he interrogated several women, including a bartender from the popular Tampa lesbian bar Jimmy White's, a stripper, a waitress, a factory worker, a prostitute, and others. Many of them had children who were being raised by relatives or who had been taken away by the state, and most had not graduated from high school.

Strickland focused his interviews on acquiring female teachers' names. The prisoners offered a wealth of details about the gay underground in Tampa, but little in the way of identifying lesbian teachers. The bartender, a woman named Gertrude, described a Tampa judge who frequented Fungi's, a lesbian bar that had since closed, and enlisted lesbians to strip and "put on parties" for him as well as for police and FBI agents, allegedly in exchange for keeping them out of trouble. She discussed a bartender named Monica at another gay bar, the Pelican, who was a regular at these strip parties. Monica lived in the Airport Trailer Park in Tampa. During the investigations of 1957, Gertrude recalled that "things started getting hot for homosexuals in Tampa" and a particular police officer "kept asking [me] for dates. His sister was a homosexual and I've seen her come over to the house crying with black eyes where he had beat her up." She also claimed to have seen Tampa mayor Nick Nuccio at a policemen's party that featured a lesbian strip show. When asked if she knew any homosexual teachers or public officials, Gertrude told Strickland that she was only acquainted with "regular people that have ordinary jobs."[53]

Other inmates provided some information about lesbian teachers. One woman caught Strickland's attention after her name came up several times—a teacher at the Florida Industrial School for Girls, a facility for delinquents under the age of seventeen. Gertrude's partner, Hazel, also incarcerated at Lowell, told the chief investigator that Monica, the "big blond headed" stripper, had regularly palled around with the teacher at Fungi's. Hazel also identified a Tampa physical education teacher and her partner, who was a secretary. Strickland frequently used these interrogations to collect other kinds of data:

> Q. Do you feel like that you've acquired this through association and environment, the places that you were staying around, and the people with whom you were associating?
> A. I didn't know anything about it when I first started going to Fungi's and when I first started going to Fungi's I went with my husband, and I saw the girls and everything and I had been married twice and I knew that I didn't care anything about men and I was just looking.

Strickland also heard a lurid story from her about the Tampa municipal judge who propositioned Hazel and her girlfriend Gertrude. As he posed the question, "He wanted you to give him what is commonly known as a 'Blow Job'?" Hazel replied, "Yes, sir," adding that he also wanted to "go down on" her.

"In other words, he wanted to commit an oral act and a physical contact on you himself personally?" asked Strickland.

"Yes, sir."[54]

Others confirmed the homosexuality of the teacher from the Ocala reform school. One, a twenty year old serving five years for robbery, had been sent to the Industrial School for Girls for truancy and running away from home. She remembered the rumors about the teacher being gay, but denied any sexual contact with the woman. The next day, a twenty-one year old told Strickland that as a seventh grader, her music appreciation teacher at Oak Grove Junior High in Tampa would "fondle and caress" her. She also served time in the Ocala reform school at the age of sixteen, and she confessed to having sex with the teacher in question, named Vonceil Benson, in her cottage on campus:

> Q. How many times approximately, realizing you didn't keep a tabulation on it, did you go there?
> A. I don't know. I went there several times, but it did not occur every time. There were a couple of times it didn't occur. I just went down there and talked and smoked, which we weren't supposed to do.
> Q. She allowed you to smoke?
> A. Yes, sir.[55]

Two other witnesses testified to Benson's lesbianism and recalled widespread homosexual activity among the girls there. Over the coming months, which stretched into years, Strickland would doggedly follow these leads around the state.

* * *

While the issue of homosexual teachers came to occupy the Johns Committee in 1959, Florida NAACP members were in the early stages of a long legal odyssey revolving around the limits of state power and the constitutionality of the FLIC's methods of operation in the arena of civil rights. In December 1958 the Florida Supreme Court had complicated matters by ruling that the committee had not abridged witnesses' rights by asking questions about fellow and past members of the NAACP, but also declaring that the committee could not compel them to turn over membership lists. The NAACP appealed the decision, and the case eventually went to the U.S. Supreme Court.

That summer, the Miami branch of the Congress of Racial Equality (CORE) conducted a series of downtown lunch-counter sit-ins. Within months, the first African American students entered a previously all-white public school, Orchard Villa. In the midst of these public demonstrations and the first cracks in Florida's segregated school system, Strickland scrambled to organize a regional organization of southern investigators. In June he contacted his friend H. A. Poole of the Georgia Bureau of Investigation, figuring that they could bring together like-minded segregationist law enforcement agents from Florida, Georgia, Alabama, Mississippi, Louisiana, Tennessee, and South Carolina. "I think that by uniting ourselves in this manner it would strengthen our efforts in each state immediately," he wrote. "At least, it would give us a point of contact and referral as these people move from one area to another."[56] It is not clear if the chief investigator was referring to civil rights activists or gay teachers, but either way he knew he had an ally in Poole.

Strickland was also keeping tabs on Florida members of the Southern Conference Educational Fund, which he called "one of the most cited radical Communist infiltrated organizations in the South."[57] The SCEF was created in 1946 within the Southern Conference for Human Welfare to combat white supremacy in the South. It became a separate agency the following year. As far as critics were concerned, SCHW was bad enough for attempting to socialize the South, but to have native white southerners working for racial equality was too much. Led by James Dombrowski and Aubrey Williams, two white southerners steeped in the values of the social gospel and the New Deal, the SCEF, through research and polling, meetings and conferences, and reporting in the pages of its monthly publication, the *Southern Patriot*, sought to change attitudes about race and economic justice.[58] In 1954, the Senate Subcommittee on Internal Security questioned SCEF members about the group's subversive aims and influences, subjecting them to the scripted theater of Red scare smear politics. Commenting later on her confrontation with committee chair James Eastland at the hearing, SCHW founding member and SCEF stalwart Virginia Foster Durr recalled his obsession with the idea "that the Supreme Court was a Communist-dominated outfit if it handed down this ruling that 'niggers' and white folks had to go to school together. Oh, you know how he goes on, all about mass rape, and black men and white women." In her blunt estimation, he "was a vicious little fat toad of a man."[59]

By R. J. Strickland's count, there were 125 Floridians who paid their dues and subscribed to the *Southern Patriot*. "I feel that for this organization to get a foothold into the public school systems of our state through the student body, as they are apparently attempting, would be very detrimental to our American way of life," he informed new FLIC chair Cliff Herrell. By the end of 1959, he had enlisted the services of a female student at Central Florida Junior College in Ocala as an undercover agent to attend meetings and participate in SCEF activities in the central part of the state.[60]

The Johns Committee held hearings in Tallahassee on November 4 and 5, 1959. Many of the witnesses were whites from Miami, most of them Jewish, suspected of having once belonged to the Communist Party in

Florida. NAACP leaders Theodore Gibson and Edward Graham also appeared. A year earlier, the Florida Supreme Court had ruled that witnesses did not have to physically hand over membership rolls to the investigating committee, but they were required to bring such lists with them as they testified so they could refer to them in answering specific questions without actually showing them to committee members. Yet when Gibson took the stand, he stated up front that he had not brought any documents. R. J. Strickland testified that he had uncovered evidence of fourteen former Communist Party members attending NAACP meetings in Miami. He read the names and showed Gibson their photographs; Gibson claimed not to know them or to have seen them at any NAACP function. He was cited for contempt in the Dade County circuit court and later fined twelve hundred dollars and sentenced to six months in prison. Gibson appealed, and the case would not be resolved until 1963. In the interim, the committee's campaign against the NAACP languished.[61]

In December, committee members and other Florida segregationists were disheartened to learn that the Fifth Circuit Court of Appeals had found Florida's pupil assignment law "inadequate" in carrying out the Supreme Court's mandate in *Brown*.[62] The tiny fissures in the edifice of segregation were proliferating. Within a matter of months, they would begin to crack wide open.

*   *   *

Rather than utilizing public hearings, which were so effective in airing accusations and innuendo against civil rights activists, the Johns Committee relied on closed, private interrogations to extract information, confessions, and names from suspected homosexuals. Whether conducted by R. J. Strickland or local police officers, junior investigators, committee members, or Mark Hawes, the questioning of accused gay men and lesbians largely followed the same script. First, witnesses were asked their name, age, educational background, and employment history. Next came a twist on the Cold War query about membership in the Communist Party: "Are you now or have you ever been involved in any type of homosexual activity?" The follow-up question addressed the suspect's being "approached" by a homosexual. It was crucial to determine if he or she had been the aggressor or the victim. Then followed questions about how long the suspect had been involved in homosexuality. Once interrogators had laid the foundation, they could venture off down several different avenues, but they asked almost every witness to analyze him or herself and to ponder how they had entered into the world of homosexuality, and it usually took some form of "Do you feel like you've acquired this through association and environment, the places that you were staying around, and the people with whom you were associating?"[63]

Strickland conducted homosexual investigations around the Tampa Bay area in early 1960. In addition to hearing names of teachers, he found it easy to enlist fearful suspects to act as informants. One man, a twenty-eight year old arrested for indecent conduct in November 1959, offered the names of teachers, waiters, male nurses, and hairdressers and then professed his aversion to a local St. Petersburg gay bar called Tim Murphy's. "To me," he said, "it's all very disgusting, walking into a place, seeing men dancing together, seeing men dressed up like a woman, playing the piano, bartenders drunk and carrying on something terrible."

"Did you see or did you observe what you thought were juveniles in there?" asked the chief investigator.

"Oh, definitely." He then quickly agreed to assist Strickland in identifying gay teachers and passing their names on to a St. Petersburg police detective. "Uh-huh. Would be very happy to," he obliged.[64]

In March 1960, a month after a wave of student-led lunch counter sit-ins had spread across Florida cities and the rest of the South, the Johns Committee made the news when a suspected homosexual went to the *St. Petersburg Times* to report anonymously that Strickland had asked him to provide names of gay teachers and students in Sarasota and Manatee counties. For his part, Strickland played it cool. "Due to the recent Negro sit-downs, everyone around the state is tense," he explained to the *Times*. "I can't tell you my purpose here, but the committee wants to know about many things. Among them are racial problems, homosexuality and other matters."[65]

In the Cold War climate of 1960, the committee stumbled upon some unusual characters eager to play the part of informant, spy, or secret agent, especially if their employment or their good name depended on it. Strickland met just such an individual in May 1960, when an eighteen-year-old freshman at Florida State University contacted the Johns Committee for an urgent meeting. Kathryn, the student in question, drove from Tallahassee to Ocala to meet with the chief investigator and committee member William O'Neill. Also present were an assistant state's attorney, a state's attorney, a local sheriff, and an FBI agent. If her story or her motives surprised those gathered, they did not register it for the record. As she told it, she had been horrified by her friend's confession that she might be a lesbian. Kathryn immediately reported the information to unnamed "authorities" at Florida State, and her friend was put on probation, which she immediately violated by traveling to West Virginia with a woman unaffiliated with the university. She was expelled. But Kathryn was not finished. She began investigating other lesbians at the school, and reporting her findings to a staff member there. As she told the group assembled in Ocala, "I made out this list" of approximately twenty names, "including faculty members, students, and also the Dean of Women's name came up several times." The list also included an education major from Palatka, a member of a sorority, and an employee of the Florida Fish and Game Commission. Strickland asked the obvious question about her motives. Kathryn answered, "Frankly, I had seen what it had done to Kathy out at the University, and I could not sit down and just watch it going on without doing something about it."

"In other words," Strickland asked, "by your close friend becoming involved—you saw how destructive it was as far as she was concerned, then you decided to make an effort to try to do something about it, is that correct?" Kathryn answered yes.[66]

She also reported to the group her recent discovery that a lesbian in her dorm had "converted two more people" and that the "entire" softball team sponsored by Tallahassee Savings and Loan were "all homosexuals." Strickland wondered how she managed to gain the trust of so many lesbians. Kathryn explained that she simply made it seem as though she were "sitting on the fence, so to speak." Or as Strickland rephrased it, she made them "think that you were very interested in becoming converted."[67] Strickland pressed Kathryn in a subsequent interview: "When you say 'go right along with them,' you mean make them think or believe that you also were a homosexual?"

"That's right, sir."

"But not to actually participate in the fulfillment of the acts with them?"

"Absolutely not."[68]

There is no indication that Strickland followed these specific leads or enlisted the student's help as an informant. But it is important because it reveals the extent to which the Johns Committee's presence and mission impinged upon some students' identities as citizens and as potential allies—or targets—of the committee's. In this instance, Kathryn may have been sincere and eager to assist in the FLIC's battle against sexual deviance, or perhaps she wanted to divert attention away from herself and toward other girls. It could also have merely been a matter of settling a personal score. Whatever the case, it is clear that Floridians were beginning to view the committee as an agency to address personal or local complaints.

Strickland had a special talent for making witnesses squirm by quoting detailed testimony from other suspected homosexuals-turned-informers. One man, who had taught in Florida's public school system for thirty-two years and had a wife and four children, listened as the investigator read back another man's claims of sexual encounters with him at St. Petersburg's Bayfront Park. Others had sworn that they had encountered him at gay bars like the Surf and Sand and Tim Murphy's. Strickland asked, "Have you ever made the statement to a student that you can recall whereas you stated that there was no lunch like the cream of the crotch?" But the witness refused to budge. "That I have no knowledge of."[69] At a school in Hawthorne, located near Gainesville, several male students complained of sexual advances made by their principal. When confronted with the accusations, he denied everything, including the testimony of a student who recalled telling him, "No sir, I'm not coming over there, I know what you are, you're a dick-sucking daddy."[70]

In the fall of 1960 in St. Petersburg, the Johns Committee encountered its first serious resistance in the gay investigations. Strickland, along with police officers and an assistant superintendent of education, questioned three teachers: one African American, William Neal, and two white women, Ina Riggs and Mary Bradshaw. Neal, a music teacher at Gibbs Junior College in St. Petersburg, admitted only to receiving oral sex from a man in New York City, never in Florida, and never playing the active role. Riggs, who graduated from the University of Florida and now taught physical education, confessed to a series of relationships with women but downplayed their sexual component. And Bradshaw, a math and science teacher in a Pinellas County junior high school, simply refused to answer any sex-related questions, arguing that "since the same questions will be asked at the hearing, I feel that it is not necessary for me to go through this procedure twice."[71] Threatened by the chief investigator with a humiliating public hearing, Bradshaw called his bluff. The committee decided to include Neal and Riggs, along with two other suspected gay teachers, Anne Louise Poston and Dottie St. John, on the list of witnesses to appear at the hearing. The Pinellas County Board of Public Instruction suspended them. By early December, having still not even received a date for the hearing, the teachers hired lawyers and petitioned the National Education Association to investigate their case because, as Superintendent of Public Instruction Floyd T. Christian put it, "they feel their rights have been denied." In a December 6, 1960, letter to J. T. Kelley, the director of the Department of Education's Division of Teacher Education, Certification and Accreditation, Christian admitted, "Frankly, I am of the opinion that far too much time has been lost from the date of the suspensions, October 20, until the time of their hearings, which makes it very difficult to keep down the rumors and also affects the peace of mind of other teachers who are fearful of this Legislative Investigation Committee."[72] The hearings would be held in 1961 before the Florida Board of Education (BOE), as required by law, and, as with the NAACP contempt cases, the teachers' battle for their livelihoods was one that would be settled by the U.S. Supreme Court.

* * *

As the Johns Committee continued scouring central Florida in the fall of 1960, gathering teachers' resignations and certificate revocations, Miami police were investigating the production and sale of homosexual pornography. Detective J. Duane Barker, the lead investigator, contacted Strickland in early 1961 and shared some of his evidence, including a deposition taken from a young man who kept a diary filled with meticulous details of his pornography business: how many pictures he sold, to whom, and the dates of purchase. Perhaps as added enticement, Barker also told Strickland that the city police had long lists of local teachers "who have been involved in numerous aggressive homosexual acts with juveniles in Dade County."[73] It worked. Strickland joined Barker, and together they devoted the early part of 1961 to infiltrating the underground culture of male hustling, teenage prostitution, and pornography. This marked an important shift for the Johns Committee, which now added a new subversive threat to the list of the dangers facing young Floridians: obscenity, indecent literature, and pornography.

Florida was not alone in the purge of gay professors, the eradication of pornography, and the tendency to treat the two as interrelated social ills. In the fall of 1960, local police and a federal postal inspector raided Smith College English professor Newton Arvin's Northampton, Massachusetts, apartment and confiscated his collection of male erotic photographs. They also seized Arvin's journals, in which he had detailed sexual encounters with men, many of them much younger. In custody, Arvin almost immediately gave up the names of fifteen other men who collected and traded similar photographs; he pleaded guilty to possession of "obscene pictures" and "lewdness" and agreed to spend a month in a psychiatric hospital. The professor, like many liberals, had supported leftist causes in the 1930s, and in 1954 he became one of five Smith faculty members named by a committee, headed by the sister of William F. Buckley, as subversives who merited investigation. But it was his sexuality and his fondness for male erotica— including the popular bodybuilding magazines of the day—that got Arvin in trouble with the law. His arrest was part of a statewide crackdown on obscene literature carried out by a committee of the Massachusetts legislature. His story appeared in the pages of *Newsweek* and other national magazines.[74]

Many experts either compared homosexuality to addiction or delineated how an individual's addictions to drugs or alcohol could lead to gay sex. Albert Ellis, for example, included addiction in his litany of possible causes of homosexuality, along with low self-esteem, rebelliousness, and emotional disturbance: "Alcoholism, drug addiction, and similar kinds of sick behavior are occasionally etiological factors in homosexuality." With substance abuse and intoxication came lowered inhibitions, and heterosexuals became more likely to "experimentally engage in homosexual behavior which later becomes habitual."[75] Another expert charged that gays and lesbians "seduce normals who are in mental conflict, or alcoholics, drug addicts, and others who have an outright fear of sexual intercourse." Even more unnerving, the homosexual could actually be in cahoots with "drug peddlers" and "pushers," who help him or her "seduce newcomers to the realm of abnormal sexual behavior" in which "the 'kicks' are repeated night after night, until, finally, the victims are 'hooked' both ways—drug addiction and homosexuality."[76]

Another significant theme in the postwar construction of homosexuality was its assumed furtiveness and deceptiveness. Men and women who either refused to hide their sexuality or whose mannerisms and outward appearance implied homosexuality were not unheard of—and, in fact, gender nonconformity was still seen as a particular type of personality disorder by mainstream psychiatry, and police still regularly rounded up women and men in gay bars who chose to dress, speak, and act in ways that violated gender norms. They tended to be working class, and they generally bore the brunt of police harassment because of their reliance on public spaces for socializing.[77] As homosexuality came to be imagined during the Cold War, however, scrutiny shifted to the homosexual who could pass for straight—who, in the role of teacher, minister, Boy Scout troop leader, or camp counselor, would never raise suspicions among the parents of his or her youthful targets.

*   *   *

Black youth evoked an entirely different sort of discomfort among conservatives. In February 1960, a new era of African American activism began. Although the Woolworth's lunch counter sit-ins in Greensboro, North Carolina, have become iconic in civil rights history, they were not the first. Similar demonstrations had occurred sporadically since the 1940s. In Miami, the local chapter of CORE, which had just been organized there in early 1959, led a series of what it called "sit-downs" that fall. The actions were the result of CORE's Action Institute, which brought 600 participants from across the country to Miami to learn nonviolent direct action techniques and to practice them in Miami restaurants, lunch counters, and movie theaters. Based on Gandhian principles of nonviolence, the goal of the demonstrations was to publicize in dramatic terms the immorality of segregation and, conversely, the moral justness of using peaceful means to protest it. The sit-ins did not succeed in Miami, but they did inspire workshop participants to take this new approach, along with a new sense of empowerment, to their own communities.[78]

The Greensboro demonstrations marked a sea change in the civil rights struggle. Unlike previous episodes, most notably the Montgomery bus boycott, which grabbed national attention and elicited a regional backlash, the sit-ins inspired a massive, spontaneous wave of copycat demonstrations in dozens of southern cities. More than that, however, it led to a new ethos of student participation and leadership as well as nonviolent direct action, and a new major organization, the Student Nonviolent Coordinating Committee (SNCC). It energized the movement at a time when the NAACP's legal efforts seemed to be producing agonizingly slow results, made worse by the unrelenting white attacks against it, when the whiff of communism still clung to the organization and to any liberal group that supported it, and when infighting, lack of resources, and uncertainty threatened the stability of the Southern Christian Leadership Conference (SCLC).

CORE field director James McCain, who had helped lead the non-violence workshops in Miami, was in Tallahassee organizing a fledgling chapter when the Greensboro sit-ins began. He encouraged the new group to launch its own sit-ins in the state capital. On February 13, eight Florida A&M students, along with two African American high school students, obliged at the downtown Woolworth's lunch counter. No violence occurred, but the students were not served; eventually, the manager closed the counter. A week later, the group returned, but this time the police and the mayor showed up, and a handful of demonstrators were arrested. After a series of CORE meetings that attracted hundreds, on March 12 an interracial group of local college students staged simultaneous sit-ins at the McCrory's lunch counter as well as Woolworth's. Dozens were arrested at both sites, and a large group of angry whites, including a local Citizens' Council leader, loomed menacingly with sticks and bats but did not attack. The police, however, launched tear gas into a crowd of students watching from near the entrance to Florida A&M, and bedlam ensued. On March 17, city judge John Rudd sentenced eight African Americans, six of them FAMU students, to sixty days in jail when they did not pay their three-hundred-dollar fines for breach of peace and unlawful assembly. Before he handed down the sentences, Rudd impugned the defendants as "young Fidel Castros," blaming the demonstrations on the sinister influence of "professors who read so many books they have completely left the earth."[79]

On March 12, the most volatile day of the Tallahassee sit-ins, the Johns Committee sent several spies into a meeting at the Unitarian Church in Orlando of representatives from CORE, SCEF, and the Florida Council on Human Relations. SCEF field director Carl Braden led the proceedings. Also present were members of the American Jewish Congress, the Southern Regional Council, and the NAACP. In part a response to the wave of sit-ins, the meeting was designed to improve communication and coordination among disparate civil rights groups throughout Florida. One of the infiltrators was the newest FLIC secretary, Mary Mueller, who had begun working for the committee in October 1959. Her résumé included U.S. Army intelligence at Fort Sam Houston, Texas, U.S. Air Force safety officer in Wichita, and the Motor Vehicle Department at Fort Sill, Oklahoma. Now she was posing as a liberal supporter of civil rights, receiving a free copy of the *Southern Patriot* from Carl Braden himself. She told Strickland that a CORE member who was also a teacher at Gibbs Junior College in St. Petersburg boasted at the meeting, "CORE moved right in—those were his words, 'CORE moved right in'—with any kind of assistance that these students needed, and they specifically moved in to tell the students when to sit-down, how to do it, and just what to do in case of arrest." She went on: "He made the remark that it was absolutely necessary that white people be used—white students or other white people—be 'used' in these sit-downs." Offering further evidence of the group's deviousness, Mueller recounted the speech made by the wife of Jack Gordon, a liberal Miami businessman who would soon be elected to the Miami Dade School Board and who served as a state senator in the 1970s and 1980s. Perhaps most damning in her estimation, he was a business associate of former U.S. senator Claude Pepper. According to Mueller, Mrs. Gordon "got up and said that no one in Florida would support them if they put the issue to them of integration or segregation, that the issue must be stated another way so that people would go for it. . . . That would get them, she said."[80]

When Strickland asked her to describe the attendees, Mueller called the whites "mis-fits socially," with a "battered, rag-tag appearance . . . pretty scroungy looking, mangy hair, bad teeth, dirty fingernails—and they were just badly and very cheaply dressed." These kinds of disparaging comments about the dirty, disheveled, and nonconformist appearance of white supporters of civil rights were not uncommon. In Mississippi, for example, Sovereignty Commission members frequently noted white Freedom Summer participants' unorthodox clothing and suspect grooming as prima facie evidence of their subversiveness, describing men who had not "had a haircut for months" and let their "whiskers grow out, with dirty, filthy, nasty clothes on."[81] Historian John Howard has suggested that invocations of the "dirty beatnik" could also have sexual connotations, from questioning the masculinity of white Freedom Riders—"pallid fellows with pallid voices and the watery passiveness of the conscientious objector"—to the willingness of "barefoot," "dirty," and "unshaven" Students for a Democratic Society members to live in the homes of Negroes during Freedom Summer.[82] Mueller characterized the interactions between the races in nightmarish terms: "I got the feeling that the negroes there thoroughly and completely hated the whites who were there, but the whites were just panting, trying to do everything for the negroes, trying to be kind to them, but the negroes, it seemed to me, were actually looking down their noses at them."[83] In the Johns Committee's report to the legislature the following year, SCEF was singled out for its growing membership in Florida and its cooperation with the NAACP, which in turn was used to remind legislators that the Southern Conference Educational Fund was a "Communist-front organization." The report noted that SCEF "openly proclaimed" its intention to organize "the efforts of individuals and organizations in the State of Florida in the field of race relations," almost as if committee members were surprised by the sudden brazenness of civil rights activists.[84]

Governor LeRoy Collins used the March 12 sit-ins, and the entire sit-in movement across the region, to weigh in on the larger moral implications of the struggle and to take his strongest stand yet in favor of equal rights. In a March 15 speech in Lakeland, he remarked that "if the leaders in the Kremlin had worked up a plan to weaken us throughout the world, I can think of none which would be more effective than the script we are now following"—of racial discord, mutual suspicion, fear, and injustice. "I think if the men in the Kremlin were writing a prescription for destroying American influence they would include discrediting American freedom and democracy by presenting us to the world as a nation torn by internal dissensions—incapable of dealing justly with one another in a spirit of mutual respect and brotherhood."[85]

At the end of the month, as Florida State University and Florida A&M officials attempted to crack down on student involvement in demonstrations, and as segregationist legislators, including Johns Committee member Randolph Hodges, called for a special session devoted to stopping the sit-ins, Collins gave the speech of his life. In typical fashion he sought to restore calm to a situation that threatened to spiral out of control. But this time he brought something new as well, a sense of righteous indignation, of moral certitude, and a warning to intractable segregationists. From the television studios of WFGA in Jacksonville and broadcast on TV and radio stations across Florida, Collins began by telling his audience, "I have no ambition to seek any other public office and as long as I am in this office I will say what I think is right whether it is popular or not." A business owner may have the legal right to allow Negroes in one part of their establishment but not another, he said, "but I still don't think that he can square that right with moral, simple justice." Referring to people who believed order could be restored by blacks simply staying in their place, the governor claimed, "Now friends, that's not a Christian point of view. That's not a democratic point of view. That's not a realistic point of view. We can never stop Americans from struggling to be free."[86] He also announced that he was creating a new statewide biracial committee and he urged individual cities to follow suit, as a way to solve local problems and avert further public demonstrations and possible violence.

Tepid support greeted what could only have seemed an earthshaking speech from a southern governor, even a moderate one. Porkchoppers groused, and few legislators took his call seriously, though several Florida cities did create biracial committees. As for the public's response, Collins received many more supportive letters than critical ones, though the latter are especially revealing in their vitriol and anxiety about interracial sex. One woman quoted a marriage counselor from the University of Pennsylvania about integration leading to interracial marriage and then asked, "Is this what you want for your daughters or granddaughters? I don't believe you do. I know I don't." Another woman questioned, "Have you ever seen white and black teenagers dancing together, spooning? I have, and it is the saddest sight to behold." A Gainesville man speculated that Collins considered "amalgamation of the races as not undesirable and as moral." One of the most convoluted theories came from a man in Zolfo Springs: "I read that the Queen of England is being advised to marry her children into negro families and if she falls for that trick England also will become mongrelized. Russia will then be the one and only white top nation to rule the world." Sumter Lowry struck a similar note in asking the governor, "Will it be 'morally wrong' to reject social contact and dancing between the races in our public schools? . . . to refuse marriage between whites and negroes?"[87]

* * *

As whites in Florida and the rest of the South tried to come to grips with the sit-in movement, the Johns Committee continued trading blows with its original foe, the NAACP. Theodore Gibson and Edward T. Graham of the Miami NAACP were required to appear before the committee on July 27, 1960, and to bring the membership lists. The two showed up yet again without them, and again faced contempt and jail time. Gibson made still another statement about his decision not to turn over the membership rolls, explaining the national and local policies against allowing Communists or any subversives into the organization. He reiterated his testimony from the November 1959 hearings, in which he denied that specific individuals named by the committee as Communists had been members of the Miami branch, and he claimed, "If I bring the NAACP membership

lists before this Committee . . . the fears, concern and worry about exposure and reprisals based upon NAACP association will be more firmly
embedded in the public's mind in Florida than it was before." Moreover,
Gibson declared, "in our judgment this is as gross an interference with
freedom of association and freedom of speech," and "while the activities
of the Association in fighting for freedom from racial discrimination and
for equality for Negroes may seem revolutionary to the present power
structure in Florida, and in respect to the mores of the South, it is true
to and in accord with the most fundamental tenets of the American social order."[88] And with that, the NAACP's counterattack against the Johns
Committee continued. At the end of August the two appeared in state
court and were charged with contempt sentenced to six months in prison.
They appealed to the Florida Supreme Court in September.[89] Meanwhile,
the injunction prohibiting any new investigation of the organization by
the FLIC remained in place.

Over the summer of 1960, sit-ins continued across Florida, and the
Johns Committee simply observed, though Strickland encouraged Hawes
to subpoena those who had attended the March 12 Orlando meeting.
In Miami and Tampa, a handful of lunch counters and other facilities
were integrated. In most places, including the seat of state government,
it would take several more years.[90] In Jacksonville, tensions surrounding
sit-ins erupted into violence at the end of August. That month, the local
NAACP Youth Council had initiated downtown lunch counter sit-ins. After a few days, department store owners ordered their restaurants closed
for business. Protesters switched to picketing, and the Ku Klux Klan
planned its own demonstration for Saturday, August 27. That morning, a
white mob assembled and began beating Negroes with fists, baseball bats,
and ax handles. (One downtown department store allegedly had noted a
sharp jump in sales of these items the week before.) The mayhem lasted
for hours, and African Americans soon formed their own large groups
in a part of town known as Little Harlem. Among the participants were
members of street gangs, who were concentrated in Jacksonville's housing
projects. Despite the presence of two hundred police officers to stop the
rioting, violence continued on both sides throughout the day and night.
The Youth Council temporarily suspended all downtown demonstrations,
and an uneasy cease-fire ensued.[91]

*   *   *

The Johns Committee established its reputation as a homosexual-hunting body during the 1959–60 biennium. The University of Florida investigation led to a statewide scouring of schools that would continue through 1963. At the same time, Strickland's presence in Miami offered the committee another avenue for battling subversion, this time in the form of pornography and male prostitution. While committee members gathered names and confessions of gay and lesbian teachers, they remained impotent against the NAACP. Across the South and the state, the sudden transformation of civil rights agitation away from legal cases and schools into a more diffuse, student-led movement that relied heavily on public demonstrations and impassioned demands for equal access to public facilities struck a new fear into the hearts of segregationists. The Johns Committee, in constitutional limbo as far as the NAACP was concerned, had no strategy in place for this new wave of activism and so continued to employ the longstanding anti-Communist tactic of surveillance and infiltration.

In 1960, Americans elected a new president who promised a New Frontier. Floridians elected a new governor, Farris Bryant, a segregationist who promised to turn back the clock on the perceived racial liberalism of LeRoy Collins. Both were Democrats, yet they represented the divergence that would soon transform the party. The divergence stemmed almost entirely from ideas about race. In Florida, the crowded field of Democratic gubernatorial hopefuls included the segregationist mayor of Jacksonville; the brother of former governor Dan McCarty, who played the race card enthusiastically; a business moderate in the mold of Collins; and the conservative speaker of the state house. In the end, it was Doyle Carlton Jr., the moderate, and Farris Bryant, the segregationist, who battled it out for the Democratic nomination. Bryant's promises to put a stop to Negro demonstrations, to restore order to Florida's cities, and to maintain segregation won the day.[92] For the first time, the Johns Committee would have a friend in the governor's mansion.

4

Subversion and Indecency, 1961–1962

The Communist Party is attempting to exploit the rise of materialism, ir-religion, and lack of faith in our society. In an era when moral standards have been lowered, when family life has been disrupted, when crime and juvenile delinquency rates are high, communists have tried to set forth a goal—dressed in attractive phrases—that would captivate the longings and hopes of men and women.

J. Edgar Hoover, *Masters of Deceit*, 1958

C. Farris Bryant was inaugurated as Florida's governor on January 3, 1961. A conservative Democrat from Ocala, Bryant had served as a member and as speaker of the state house of representatives and failed in his 1956 bid for governor. Soon after taking office, he created two advisory committees to address the problems of homosexuality and obscene literature. Under Bryant's watch, the Johns Committee's public school investigations continued, and the committee gained a measure of authority through cosponsoring with the Florida Children's Commission (FCC) a series of educational conferences about the need to eradicate indecency from public life and to expose and remove homosexuals from state agencies, particularly schools. This momentary triumph, however, led the FLIC to overreach in a controversial investigation of the curriculum, speaker policies, and hiring practices of the University of South Florida, where every problem bemoaned by segregationists and conservatives appeared to have taken root among the faculty: communism, interracialism, indecency, anti-Christian bias, liberalism, and homosexuality.

This attention to social issues came at a time when the black struggle for equality, in Florida and elsewhere, was moving to the streets and department store lunch counters, interstate highways and Greyhound Bus waiting rooms, parks, beaches, golf courses, and college campuses. At the same time, Cold War tensions escalated in the first two years of the Kennedy administration, and Florida felt them acutely, given the ninety-mile proximity of the Soviet Union's newest ally, Cuban leader Fidel Castro. Moreover, committees for decency in literature at the local, state, and national levels, many established during the 1950s, proliferated in the early 1960s. In Florida, ordinary citizens as well as politicians turned to Charley Johns and his committee as the appropriate body to address the problems that, in their view, loomed in dangerous concert with these national and international developments. In their original mission of resisting blacks' entrance into Florida's public schools, committee members remained devoted to exposing Communists and subversives within the civil rights movement, at the same time extending their role as defenders of traditional values into new arenas.

*   *   *

The FLIC joined an investigation into male prostitution and pornography in the Miami area in early 1961 at the request of Thomas J. Kelley, director of the Dade County Department of Public Safety. In the previous two months a team of detectives headed by J. Duane Barker had uncovered two men who produced and sold pornographic pictures of boys and men of varying ages. Barker notified R. J. Strickland that he had information about "numerous teachers at Dade County Schools that are homosexuals" as well as a gay physician suspected of taking nude pictures of boys. Barker drew up a report on the investigation in which he identified the main target as "producers who are all aggressive homosexuals, and who are inducing young juveniles to pose and then to commit, or allow the subjects to commit unnatural sex acts upon them."[1] He likely included gay teachers in an effort to entice Strickland and the Johns Committee to join him, and it worked. The investigator was in Miami by the first of the year.

Miami represented a unique project for the committee. Rather than seeking to expose homosexual teachers, now the FLIC was helping police track down men engaged in exploitative, criminal activities involving the abuse of underage boys. Barker and his fellow detectives rounded up more than a dozen teenagers who had been hustling on the streets of Miami.

They cooperated with the police, providing names of customers and men who had taken nude or sexual photographs of them, and some of the witnesses drove around the city with detectives pointing out private residences, clubs and bars, hotels and motels where they had engaged in these activities. One informant, aged nineteen, told Barker he had been hustling for six years. It started when an older man had picked him up after school and given him "money to mess with me." He also "gave me beer and let me drive his car." When asked how far he had gone with men, the witness reported that had drawn the line at anal sex until recently, when a man paid for a trip to Orlando and a pair of shoes "if I would let him brown me, so I let him."[2]

Several boys told similar stories about trading sex for cash, liquor, and other coveted items. They also described gay parties. Coupled with what detectives were hearing and seeing—they claimed to have confiscated thousands of photographs—these tales reinforced the most damning stereotypes of homosexuals. Another nineteen year old, for example, recalled how he was paid to be "cornholed" or "browned" by other young men in front of a group of spectators at the Apache Motel in Miami.[3] One teenager who worked as a high-dive performer at Sam Howard's Aqua Show described a "real weird-like" party filled with "queer people." He received money in exchange for serving drinks and performing "some handstands, some free exercises in the middle of the room" while nude.[4] Still another informant discussed a local doctor's Halloween party, in which nearly half the guests were dressed as women. "They were drinking and kissing and petting and playing with each other . . . masturbating each other and a lot of smooching going on . . . and they were laying all over the floor and everything—just having a regular orgy going on down on each other—screwing each other and everything." Of his own activities that night, he remembered going into a bedroom with a man, where "we got on the floor and he started going down on me and then another guy came in—he has something to do with naval reserves, and then he was having a party with me—went down on me a couple of times." The sailor was reportedly wearing "a dress—a red sweater with falsies and a skirt."[5]

Strickland joined Barker in his follow-up questioning of many of the men named by the teens, and he filed his final report to committee chairman, Representative William G. O'Neill, in which he described the arrests on pornography charges, raids of houses that netted extensive pornography collections, and a list of people charged with crimes against nature and providing alcohol to minors. The FLIC apprised Governor Farris Bryant of these findings, and he in turn invited representatives from the Sheriffs Bureau, Florida State Hospital, Division of Corrections, Parole Commission, and the juvenile court system to attend a meeting to discuss ways of ridding the state of homosexuality and pornography. "Recent crime investigations in our state clearly indicate that homosexual activity is widespread," Bryant wrote. "The true impact of this menace to our society is not fully felt until we realize that our youngsters, the youth of our state, are prime targets for homosexuals who continually seek to proselyte [*sic*]."[6]

Bryant also appointed twenty-four men and women to the Advisory Committee on Decent Literature. In March, the committee made its first report, which consisted of a series of exhibits and legislative proposals to combat "the traffic in obscene, indecent and noxious literature." The exhibits included a statement by J. Edgar Hoover and letters of support from the Florida Prosecuting Attorneys Association, the Florida Police Chiefs Association, the Obscene Literature Control Commission in Massachusetts, and Citizens for Decent Literature.[7] One advisory committee member, a state assistant attorney general, drafted an anti-obscenity bill and sent it to Charley Johns and a state representative, who introduced it in their respective chambers. In April 1961, it passed easily and Bryant signed it into law the following month. The new law made it illegal to possess, sell, or distribute "obscene, lewd, lascivious, filthy, indecent, immoral, sadistic and masochistic materials, matters, articles and things" and called for "vigorous enforcements by sheriffs, constables and prosecuting attorneys" as well as "prescribing the test of obscenity." Though it may have served a symbolic role in demonstrating conservatives' tough stance against smut, it would be impractical in enforcement and in the even thornier question of defining obscenity, something the U.S. Supreme Court still grappled with in the early 1960s.[8]

At midcentury, Americans fretted that new forms of mass culture, especially comic books, pulp fiction, and girlie magazines, with their graphic depictions of sex and violence, had caused a "breakdown of generational communication and control." A new teen culture forged in high schools and hyped by advertising agencies and other media now "stood between parent and child."[9] After World War II, economic prosperity, the growth of suburbs, and unbridled consumerism translated into rising teenage purchasing power. More teenagers took after-school and summer jobs or received an allowance and had their own money to spend on clothes, records, magazines, and any number of amusements. As they developed distinctive fashions, musical tastes, and slang, parents and experts decried the rise of juvenile delinquency. Popular movies like *Rebel without a Cause* and *The Wild One* celebrated the brooding, sexually ambiguous teenage antihero. In their living rooms, Elvis Presley, Little Richard, and Jerry Lee Lewis scandalized parents with overtly sexual performances, androgyny, and the blurring of racial lines.

Purity and decency crusades had arisen and receded regularly since the nineteenth century, but in the 1930s the Legion of Decency and the National Organization for Decent Literature had become a national force in the regulation of visual culture. These groups, which were affiliated with one another and with the Catholic Church, screened movies and reading material, respectively, for dangerous and objectionable content. They encouraged the creation of local decency committees, comprising like-minded citizens whose membership often overlapped with the PTA, the American Legion, civic and church groups, and women's clubs.[10] The anti-obscenity movement in the 1950s and 1960s increasingly came under the purview of social scientists, sexologists, and politicians, as well as the secular Citizens for Decent Literature (CDL), linking obscenity to a wide array of ills, including susceptibility to communism, juvenile delinquency and crime, and sexual perversion. The best-known proponent of the idea that sexualized, violent crime and horror comics could turn healthy American children into twisted and sadistic criminals was the psychiatrist Fredric Wertham, whose *Seduction of the Innocent* appeared in 1954 and figured prominently in Senator Estes Kefauver's Subcommittee to Investigate Juvenile Delinquency in the United States during the mid-1950s. According to the subcommittee's interim report of 1954, these comics "offer short courses in murder, mayhem, robbery, rape, cannibalism, carnage, necrophilia, sex, sadism, masochism, and virtually every other form of crime, degeneracy, bestiality, and horror." Kefauver concluded, "This country cannot afford the calculated risk involved in feeding its children, through comic books, a concentrated diet of crime, horror, and violence."[11]

Efforts to eradicate obscene literature ran the gamut from local communities to states to national organizations in the 1950s. From New York to California, from Georgia to Minnesota, lawmakers, school boards, and local committees banned library books, screened motion pictures, blacklisted Pulitzer Prize–winning novels, and fought against the distribution of certain magazines through the mail and in newsstands.[12] A 1958 *New York University Law Review* article found that "in most cases the group conducting a drive against literature it deems objectionable is one informally organized by local citizens who are supported by no outside organization," citing the American Legion, Boy Scouts, PTA, Veterans of Foreign Wars, and Women's Christian Temperance Union. The authors also determined that "over 2,500 separate instances" of local groups attempting to persuade stores to remove reading material "have been reported to a single official of the American Book Publishers' Council during the past five years. He estimates that the actual number of communities affected has been far in excess of that figure."[13]

Like the crackdowns on gay and lesbian bars and public spaces, and anxieties about sexual psychopaths and juvenile delinquents, the movement to eradicate obscenity resonated nationally and in some instances became intertwined with Cold War ideas about citizenship and national security. The postmaster general, Arthur Summerfield, barred the November 1955 issue of *Confidential* from the mail and waged an ultimately unsuccessful battle against the homophile publication *ONE* magazine. Summerfield appealed to the American public to help his crusade against "filth merchants" by turning over any obscene materials they received in the mail to their local postmaster and pursuing legal action. That year he also banned *Lady Chatterley's Lover*. Although that and his *Confidential* suppression were subsequently overturned in court, the postal service received Congress's approval in 1960 to screen and seize people's mail if they were suspected of distributing or receiving obscene materials. (Smith Professor Newton Arvin was one victim of this law.)[14]

One of the first state-level agencies to articulate these concerns was the Georgia Literature Commission, created by the state's general assembly in 1953. Governor Herman Talmadge appointed Atlanta minister James P. Wesberry to chair the agency, which was authorized to declare a publication obscene, notify its distributor, and request its withdrawal from public availability under threat of prosecution. The first books deemed obscene by the commission were the lesbian novels *Spring Fire* and *Women's Barracks*, as well as Erskine Caldwell's *Place Called Estherville* and *Element of Shame* by pulp novelist Cicely Schiller.[15] In 1961, members of Farris Bryant's advisory committee on decent literature contacted the Georgia commission for advice about drafting anti-obscenity laws and coping with the "vital problem of indecent literature and offensive material."[16] The commission lasted until 1973 but was most active through the mid-1960s, reviewing dozens of books and requesting, with varying degrees of success, their removal from Georgia shelves. In the group's first report to the legislature, in 1954, Wesberry summoned familiar justifications for alarm over indecency. The most obvious and common was the trope of uncleanness: "A veritable cesspool of indecent literature infests our nation" and "Tragic beyond words is the fact that many of our school children are being contaminated by this iniquitous flow of sexually suggestive literature."[17] Another was the refrain that sex deviants were a driving force behind the creation of pornography, and that they used it to pervert normal children, sometimes resulting in violence and murder. The report quoted a principal from "a leading boys' high school in Atlanta" who had confiscated "extremely salacious material" from his students. According to him, the "boys learn about various forms of perversion, such as sodomy, from this literature," and he added: "I could not have given a good definition of sodomy. I had never heard of it, but now I have seen it and I have seen lots of it and I have heard lots about it and I know a lot about it. The first case I had was a little boy who was killed in the Ansley Hotel."[18]

In 1955, attorney Charles Keating founded Citizens for Decent Literature, which began as an informal network of concerned businessmen and civic leaders in Cincinnati, Ohio. Over the next decade, similar state and local organizations proliferated, including the Dade County Decent Literature Council, created in 1957. They were dedicated to the premise that obscene literature in the hands of young people—in the mail, through advertising, or in drugstores and newsstands—would lead to both personal and national decay.[19]

Legal and cultural standards were indeed changing. Between 1957 and 1964, a series of U.S. Supreme Court decisions narrowed the definition of obscenity. In 1957, *Roth v. United States* changed the criteria by which material could be defined as obscene. Labeling would now depend on "whether to the average person, applying contemporary community standards, the dominant theme of the material appeals to prurient interest." This marked a departure from an eighty-year-old precedent based on the "Hicklin rule," which defined obscenity as anything that tended to "deprave and corrupt those whose minds are open to such immoral influences." Later Supreme Court decisions declared that obscenity had to be defined as material that was patently offensive and lacking in socially redeeming value, and that the "community standards" originally referred to in *Roth* had to be national, not local.[20] These rulings opened the door to more explicit sexual content in books and magazines. Many politicians and parents feared the effects of change on children and teens who thumbed through the magazines at the local newsstand, perused the paperback books, or merely glanced at their ever more stimulating covers.

Playboy, founded in 1953, spawned an entire industry of men's magazines that became popular in the 1950s and 1960s, and sales of beefcake magazines such as *Physique Pictorial*, *Trim*, *Manual*, and the *Grecian Guild Pictorial* soared. The popularity of racy gossip magazines such as *Eyeful*, *Titter*, *Wink*, and *Whisper* in the 1940s prefigured the success during the following decade of *Confidential* and *Hush Hush*, which regularly featured stories about celebrities' adulterous affairs, closeted homosexuality, and interracial romances. At the same time, paperback and pulp novels poured into corner drugstores and newsstands across the country. The mass-market paperback, introduced by Pocket Books, debuted in 1939. In addition to reprinting literary classics cheaply, paperback publishers began putting out a wider variety of material during and after World War II, expanding into mystery, crime, and romance novels. Heated competition with magazines and comic books, and among book publishers themselves, led the paperback industry to take a "lowest-common-denominator approach," which resulted in even higher sales. In 1948, 147 million paperbacks were sold in the United States. The following year 184 million were sold, and by 1950 sales reached 200 million.[21] The growth of decent literature organizations around the country, and the early 1960s campaign against homosexuals and pornography in Florida, was part of a larger impulse to resist very real changes in sexual behavior and attitudes. But they also stemmed from ongoing Cold War anxieties about vulnerable young minds and bodies and the moral health of the nation.

The movement in the 1950s to stamp out smut was by no means a unified one. Decent literature councils, local obscenity laws, and grass-roots organizations varied widely from state to state. In broad terms, however, the loose confederation wanted to contain and keep out of teenagers' hands any depictions of sex outside of heterosexual marriage. Many believed that prolonged exposure to salacious sexual material would lead the consumer of obscenity down the path to deviance. As one observer of the "high price of pornography" put it, it mattered little whether the sexual content was heterosexual or homosexual; removing sex from the proper bounds of marriage and using it to titillate readers were themselves considered deviant acts that would encourage abnormal sexual behavior. The availability of obscene reading material to adolescents threatened the integrity of the family and the nation. Richard Kyle-Keith, one anti-obscenity activist, argued that "the future of the nation may be at stake if young people are permitted to grow up with morals that can only be considered destructive of civilized society."[22]

There was no consensus about the damage caused by the consumption of obscene materials, but many psychiatrists were enlisted in the crusade against it. Kyle-Keith's 1961 study cited two doctors, Benjamin Karpman, chief psychotherapist at St. Elizabeth's Hospital in Washington, D.C., and Nicholas Frignito, chief neuropsychiatrist and medical director of the Philadelphia Municipal Court, as evidence that the "overwhelming opinion of psychiatrists and social workers supports the view that smut is substantially responsible for the increase in sexual deviations and sex offenses by young people." Frignito argued that teenage boys who were overstimulated by pornography often became "sexually aggressive and generally incorrigible. The more vicious delinquent or psychopathic type," he cautioned, "may become an exhibitionist, a rapist, a sadist, a fetishist."[23] In Miami in early 1961, investigators Strickland and Barker were gathering just such evidence, of connections between homosexuality, male prostitution, and pornography, which they would later use to make the case to Floridians that homosexuals must be ferreted out of the public school system.

*   *   *

While R. J. Strickland continued to pursue homosexual suspects and concluded his investigations in Miami in the spring of 1961, FLIC chair William G. O'Neill, a conservative representative from Marion County in central Florida, called a public hearing about the Southern Conference Educational Fund's role in the civil rights meeting in Orlando the previous year. Carl Braden was subpoenaed but did not answer questions, so the committee questioned some of its own spies who had attended the meeting. No new evidence emerged, but O'Neill nevertheless ended the day with the familiar boast that the committee had "clearly" demonstrated the "Communist Party, the Communist Fellow Travelers, and those persons who would destroy our country have infiltrated the organizations of this country."[24]

Two months later, President Kennedy ordered military action against Cuba. Since 1959, south Florida had been awash in Cuban exiles plotting and training to take back power from Fidel Castro. The CIA and other federal and military agents set up militia camps and a massive apparatus for an invasion of the island nation—all in the Johns Committee's back yard. In its report to the legislature in May, the FLIC claimed to have proven that Communists had infiltrated and inspired "racial agitation moves that are being promoted and carried on in the Sit-ins, Kneel-ins, Wade-ins, lunch counters, Freedom Riders, etc." Strickland distinguished between "do-gooders and joiners who are actually and basically good American citizens" blind to Communist influences within organizations such as CORE and the Southern Regional Council and "leaders" who "are not stupid people who are willing to be set up in the position of a dupe but who are fully aware of what they are doing."[25]

In other parts of the South, segregationists disparaged the morals of civil rights activists, implying that their racial views were tainted by moral perversion. To take just two examples, Bob Zellner, a white activist from Alabama who had worked at the Highlander Folk School and served as a field secretary for SNCC, was arrested in Baton Rouge in 1961 during a jailhouse visit to a friend and fellow activist. Zellner had brought with him cigarettes and reading material, including a copy of the *Nation*. Zellner was charged with "criminal anarchy" and accused of smuggling obscene material on race mixing and attempting to overthrow the government of Louisiana.[26] And in Atlanta, during the summer of 1961, a group of southern politicians met to "establish better communications between the various states and to familiarize those present with past and current activities of Communistic, Socialistic, Subversive and Agitative individuals and groups." Among those singled out was Jane Stembridge, a white woman identified as "a sex pervert, and an associate of Negro men of this group." In fact, Stembridge was both—a lesbian and a founding member of the Student Nonviolent Coordinating Committee.[27]

The Johns Committee's 1961 report to the legislature also included a list of teachers in Florida whose certificates had been revoked by the Department of Education on the grounds of homosexuality and chided school administrators for failing to prevent gay teachers from being rehired in another Florida school district. State school superintendent Thomas Bailey bristled at the accusation, vowing to continue putting homosexuals "out of business."[28] Committee members identified this as a problem they would address in the next biennium. The legislature renewed the committee for another two-year period, and Strickland mailed six copies of the report to the chief investigator for the Mississippi Sovereignty Commission. In addition to recounting the lingering problem of Communist influence within civil rights groups, the 1961 enabling act also articulated the aim of investigating "the extent of infiltration into agencies supported by state funds by practicing homosexuals."[29] The search for homosexual teachers was now codified.

The boundaries of the committee's role vis-à-vis the Board of Education, however, were not. In a 1959 meeting, Strickland, Senator Cliff Herrell, and Thomas Bailey had determined that the FLIC would act as "the investigative arm of the state," presenting evidence to the BOE in morals cases. But it was an informal agreement, forged not by law but with a handshake. According to Bailey, during this two-year partnership, the board revoked teachers' certificates in all forty-five cases brought by the Johns Committee.[30] In 1961, state representative Tom Whitaker of Hillsborough County sponsored a bill designed to protect the due-process rights of teachers accused of morals violations. Although his intention was to prevent witch hunts, the new procedures addressed the concerns of the three teachers accused of homosexuality who had filed a lawsuit against the state the previous year. The law cleared up any doubt about the Johns Committee's sanctioned role in the process. Its investigatory powers were taken away, and the only capacity in which it could now act was to initiate charges against teachers. It was left to the BOE to determine probable cause for revoking teaching certificates, a hearing officer to investigate, and a state's attorney to present evidence against the teacher.[31]

The legislature also passed a law in the 1961 session that mandated the teaching of thirty hours of course work per year in "Americanism versus Communism" in Florida's public high schools, to begin in the fall of 1962. Johns Committee member George Stallings sponsored the bill in the senate, where it passed overwhelmingly, as it did in the house.[32] Many states, from Louisiana and Texas to Oregon and New Hampshire, joined Florida in the rush to insert the study of communism into high school curricula.[33] Not only had the American Bar Association recommended that the highest caliber of teaching be devoted to the subject in American public schools in order to "instill a greater appreciation of democracy and freedom under law and the will to preserve that freedom," but anti-Communist segregationists also supported it as a vital tool against subversives.[34] Mississippi judge Tom Brady, for example, urged such instruction to "counteract the Marxian Christians who will soon be openly teaching and preaching the propriety of the amalgamation of the white and Negro races. Unless the true facts in these issues are placed before the youth of our country, we are doomed."[35]

*   *   *

In the fall of 1961, members of the Florida Children's Commission announced that at the request of Governor Bryant they would conduct a statewide campaign to educate Floridians about the dangers of obscenity and pornography and to advise the governor on further steps to suppress it. The campaign would also instruct parents, teachers, and law enforcement about the rising numbers of homosexuals in the state. The inaugural gathering of the agencies that would run the program—the FCC, the governor's advisory committees on homosexuality and decent literature, and the Johns Committee—took place in Tampa on November 4, 1961. One attendee, a local juvenile court counselor, declared that "some publications and other materials" have actually "caused an increase in homosexuality."[36] The keynote speaker, Gert H. W. Schmidt, Jacksonville businessman, chair of the decent literature committee, and later a member of the Board of Control, held up what he called a "Russian textbook used to train their agents on how to take over the world." He read aloud from what was actually a pamphlet published in 1955 under the imprint of Kenneth Goff, an ex-Communist turned fundamentalist Christian: "By making readily available drugs of various kinds, by giving the teen-ager alcohol, by praising his wildness, by stimulating him with sex literature and advertising to him or her practices as taught at the Sexpol, the psychopolitical operator can create the necessary attitude of chaos, idleness and worthlessness into which can then be cast the solution which will give the teen-ager complete freedom everywhere—Communism."[37] Schmidt's audience may not have been quite sure what a psychopolitical operator or the Sexpol was, but they well understood the message: Pornography, alcohol, and drugs were not merely social ills. They were threats to American democracy.

Newspaper coverage of the meeting reflected the lingering conflation of predatory sex criminals with homosexuals at midcentury. The *Tallahassee Democrat*, for example, explained the governor's mission as addressing the problem of "sex offenders," and that the educational program had grown out of the Johns Committee's recent investigation of homosexuals in Tallahassee, Panama City, and Tampa. In the next paragraph, Roy W. Russell, chairman of the Florida Parole Commission, stated that certain unspecified types of sex offenders who "prey" on children need to be confined and rehabilitated. The entire focus of the article then shifted to Russell's report on sex offenders, invoking the familiar metaphor of contagion: "Many young people can avoid contamination, if stricter methods of investigation and selection were instituted by our public agencies." Discreetly dismissing gay employees but then allowing them to move, undetected, to another city in Florida would only result in "spreading the disease."[38]

Another meeting took place in Florida that month. The newly formed Southern Association of Intelligence Agents gathered in Miami Beach to set an agenda for sharing information and intelligence about subversive groups in the region. There is no indication from the committee's records about who first proposed the idea of the association or who organized it. It is possible, however, that the Johns Committee's chief investigator may have been instrumental in putting the group together, given that the planning meeting took place in Florida and was run by Strickland. The inaugural meeting included presentations by H. A. Poole from the Georgia Bureau of Investigation, Billy Joe Booth of the Louisiana Department of Safety, and T. B. Birdsong, commissioner of public safety in Mississippi, among others. They discussed Martin Luther King and the SCLC, the left-wing Highlander Folk School in Tennessee, and the role of the Communist Party in the Freedom Rides. Strickland presented an overview of the FLIC's efforts in removing homosexual teachers from Florida schools and argued for the importance of monitoring SNCC. Tom Scarbrough, investigator for the Mississippi Sovereignty Commission, lauded the meeting as "very informative" and singled out Alabama, Florida, and Georgia for their "progress in combating groups which Mississippi is now struggling with. . . . The South's first line of defense opposing these left-wing groups are the Southern States Investigators, and God knows we need all the help and cooperation we can get from our sister southern states." Members of the FLIC and the Sovereignty Commission had been sharing information in some capacity since 1956, though the record is incomplete in terms of how often they communicated and the extent to which they conferred on investigative strategies. Months later the *New York Times* noted, however, that civil rights advocates were reacting to the new agency with understandable concern.[39]

One instance of this information sharing came in June 1961, when Strickland sent to the Mississippi Sovereignty Commission the names of more than two hundred people who had recently traveled to Cuba under the auspices of the Fair Play for Cuba Committee. Of those, two were arrested in the Freedom Rides in Jackson. Both came from outside of the South—Madison, Wisconsin, and Chicago. These facts confirmed widespread charges among southern segregationists that this new tactic of the civil rights movement was being orchestrated by outside agitators and, as James Eastland, Bull Connor, and others repeated, Communist-inspired subversives.[40]

While Sovereignty Commission investigators gathered intelligence about the backgrounds of Freedom Riders jailed in Mississippi, the Johns Committee did not, despite the fact that two rides took place in Florida in the summer of 1961. One group was arrested in Tallahassee after being refused service at the airport restaurant. Judge John Rudd, who by this time was well known for his rigid sentencing of bus boycotters, carpoolers, and sit-in demonstrators, used his courtroom to lecture the riders against "forcing your views on the community" and dismissed the notion that they had come to Tallahassee "on a noble, Christian purpose and acted accordingly."[41]

* * *

The FCC's educational conferences marked the first joint action between Governor Bryant's advisory committees on homosexuality and decent literature. Bringing together experts from various fields, including education, law enforcement, mental health, and politics, the meetings were ostensibly designed to alert parents, teachers, and the public about the threat posed to young people by gay men and lesbians. What they accomplished, however, was to bring a new level of publicity and approval to the FLIC, by spotlighting committee members and investigators as legitimate authorities. They sanctioned and repeated the ideas that homosexuals preyed upon and recruited children and that gay teachers had to be exposed and removed. Perhaps most of all, they stirred up fear among parents and the public that they were not safe—that, in addition to agitating Negroes and treacherous Communists ninety miles to the south, now Floridians had to fear pornography-wielding deviates.

During the summer, before the conferences began, the committee scoured two of the state's juvenile detention centers and schools in search of child predators. On July 15, 1961, Strickland questioned a former student from the Ocala School for Girls, fifteen-year-old Yvonne Ross, at her family's home in Gainesville. Ross had left the school in 1960. She told her father about what she had seen there, and he was so disturbed he turned to Charley Johns, the man who by 1961 had cultivated a reputation for investigating homosexuals. In his appeal, the girl's father included a seven-page letter by Yvonne describing aggressive lesbian students, rumored lesbian teachers, and indifferent administrators. She documented a long list of girls' first names, courtship rituals, types of sex acts, and an elaborate system of code words and numbers used by students to express their affection for one another.

According to Yvonne, the girls "start out with sweetying. This is courtship. They have making-out parties, where a group of partners are together. They kiss and fondle each other. The more making-out parties they have, the more they want each other. They finally get to the stage where nothing else matters but sex." But there was more: "When the girls get worse off, they go through an act that we call eating. They put lips to vagina and they tongue each other; they kiss and fondle each other in any way and anywhere that will give them a better feeling. This becomes more serious until it's done every chance possible." The girl confirmed several of the committee's assumptions about how homosexuality worked: The real or authentic lesbian, insatiable and obsessed with sex, finds new victims and marches them through an escalating array of acts, finally becoming actual lesbians when they have committed the ultimate lesbian sex act. As the victims progress along this scale of perdition, Yvonne noted, they become "worse off." Just as the committee feared, and even more horrifying, these lesbian predators flaunted their sick talents. "They just show off, I mean they are skilled at doing it, they know how to do things like that, they just lead it on, do it slow until you finally agree with them."[42]

Although women made up almost 50 percent of Florida's roughly twelve thousand secondary school teachers in 1960, they did not constitute half of the suspects questioned by the committee.[43] Committee members themselves never explained this discrepancy. We are left to speculate about the postwar pop psychology of writers such as Philip Wylie and the urgent need for stay-at-home mothers to raise well-adjusted, sufficiently masculine, and properly heterosexual sons. Cultural concerns about mothers and their influence on the development of young men, especially in the midst of rising numbers of wives and mothers entering the labor force during and after World War II, may have outweighed fears of lesbians.

This is not to say that Americans, or Floridians, were not worried about female homosexuals. Historian Donna Penn has argued that the Cold War anxiety about lesbians "had less to do with women choosing other women as sexual objects than with the degree to which lesbians, particularly butch women . . . challenged what it was to be a woman."[44] The example of the FLIC, however, with its focus on sexual object choice and on the physical acts performed between people of the same sex, women and men alike, cautions against such a generalization. Occasional references to masculine mannerisms or appearance are scattered throughout the interrogations of lesbians, but the committee rarely, if ever, used that as evidence of a woman's guilt. Indeed, investigators were much more likely to note gender nonconformity in gay men. But just as with gay men, they scrutinized every aspect of accused lesbians' sex lives, compelling confessions of specific sexual acts and the role played in each one, most commonly articulated by interrogators as "passive" or "aggressive," to measure their potential for seducing the innocent.

Given the close association in the public's mind between pedophilia and male homosexuality, it may seem surprising that the Johns Committee went after women teachers at all. Lesbians' sexuality rendered them deviant and threatening, but in a somehow more benign way than gay men, and it set them apart from "normal" heterosexual women. They inhabited a no-man's-land in more ways than one. There was some cultural precedent for the fear of lesbians, particularly in the pulp novels of the 1950s, and in the psychiatric literature of the day. Here lesbians were often represented as masculine, maladjusted hunters of straight women and girls.[45] In one typical passage from a freelance investigator and would-be psychologist, lesbianism is breathlessly described in doomsday terms: "The female who is held captive by a lesbian soon becomes a mental and physical wreck, who suffers from the pangs of hell and remorse, but like a drug addict she is unable to ward off the repeated advances made towards her by the octopus-like creature who continually saps her strength."[46]

As part of its search for homosexual teachers, the FLIC also targeted a juvenile detention center, the Florida School for Boys, near the Panhandle town of Marianna. Supervisors were alleged to have used excessive force and made sexual advances to the teenage residents, and it is possible that someone from the local police, the state legislature, or a social service agency had informed Charley Johns. Founded in 1897, the school offered rehabilitation to the state's "socially handicapped boys" and reflected national currents of thought about the causes and treatment of juvenile delinquency. Students took classes and did chores and engaged in a "wholesome use of leisure time" with plenty of sports, games, camping, music, and reading. They could also "discuss their spiritual problems in private with conferences" with the chaplain and attend Bible study and church services.[47] Above all, the school sought to provide mentors for troubled young men, who "may have become delinquents partly because of their poor relationship with adults such as parents, teachers, and neighbors."[48]

In this purpose the institution evidently failed by the early 1960s. Robert L. Currie, head of the guidance department, faced the most serious charges of physical abuse and sexual impropriety. Before coming to Marianna in 1956, Currie had worked in a state prison in southern Michigan, which he left because of a "question as to whether or not I was homosexual at that time." He explained that he had been "given an alternative of a public hearing, which I was advised would be attended by newspaper people."[49] In an appeal to the state legislature in 1963, the Johns Committee used examples like this to argue for the need to fingerprint all state employees, including teachers, thoroughly check the backgrounds of prospective teachers, and keep track of the comings and goings of those who had been discharged or resigned from Florida's schools. To this end, Johns proposed at one point a statewide database for holding just such information.[50]

Currie, having gone through a similar experience in Michigan, faced off with Strickland. The chief investigator told him that the committee had "testimony to the extent that some of the employees have seen you actually kissing these boys, is that true or false?"

"That would be false."

When asked if he had been in the habit of "going around in the dining room and pinching these boys on the butt," Currie again denied the charge.[51] Other accusations included watching and touching boys while they showered, visiting their rooms late at night, and taking them off campus for several hours at a time. Currie denied it all, including the charge that he and other administrators used physical force to punish boys who claimed to have been sexually abused in the first place. At this point in the questioning, Strickland demanded, "Isn't it a fact, Mr. Currie, that these boys are so afraid" of sadistic teachers and house fathers "and the spanking that they might get, that they just don't say anything" about homosexual activity?

The counselor replied, "From what has been said about me, today it certainly looks like I'm about the worst thing that could live. I don't know—I don't know why these particular individuals say these things. . . . It does destroy what I have tried very hard to do. I'm ruined professionally, I'm ruined every which way."[52]

Using the testimony gathered in 1961 from a wide range of sources, from teachers to hustlers, Strickland created much of the informational basis upon which the educational conferences on homosexuality and indecent literature were based. For several months beginning in December 1961, the Florida Children's Commission carried out sixteen conferences across Florida. At each, the morning session featured lectures on sexual perversion, "with special emphasis on problems associated with current homosexual trends." This included a variety of topics, such as understanding sexual terminology; identifying sex offenders and forms of "overt homosexuality," including sadism and masochism, child molestation, "fetishism, voyeurism and sexual fantasies"; and suppressing "various forms of indecent literature, photographs and drawings." In the afternoon, the program shifted to panel and group discussions about how to treat "sex deviates" after they had been apprehended. Nearly two thousand people attended the conferences. The largest numbers came from law enforcement (672) and the public school system (116).[53]

On March 21, 1962, the Florida Cabinet allotted two thousand dollars to the FCC and promised another fourteen thousand dollars to "carry the fight" against homosexuality and obscenity through the next fiscal year. Farris Bryant had nothing but praise for the "fine job" the commission was doing. "I am so proud of them," he beamed. Part of the money would go toward the purchase of two film projectors on which to show to audiences around the state "examples of trashy literature" used to "lure children into homosexual practices."[54] Two representatives from the FCC explained to the press that their organization intended to use the facts gathered by the Johns Committee on "the ways homosexuals make contacts" and to "pinpoint characteristics of the abnormal subculture." They told the *Tampa Tribune* that educating Floridians about these problems was the first and most important step toward solving them, even if a "'shock' treatment approach" had to be taken.[55]

Both the *Florida Times-Union* and the FCC newsletter paraphrased the assistant director of the Children's Commission, George Young, who warned about advertisements in girlie magazines encouraging "young people to send for literature and pictures which stimulated homosexual practices." Not another word of explanation followed, however, leaving readers to wonder, and fear, just which magazines and which advertisements he was referring to. The FCC's published version of Young's speech focused on his theory that homosexuals used "objectionable obscene materials, such as movies and photographs" as, in Young's words, "warmups" in seducing youngsters into homosexual acts. The article then described Young showing slides of "these and other materials" to "give the group an idea of the extent of the problem."[56]

The reflections of a seventeen-year-old member of Future Farmers of America who attended one of the conferences appeared in the pages of *Florida's Children*. Recalling how he had been "shocked into realizing that homo-sexual practice has become a very serious threat," he went on to explain his epiphany that "these 'freaks' are not freaks of heredity or nature, but environment." This was a repackaging of the same message that the governor's advisory committee, the FLIC, and the Children's Commission were spreading through the educational conferences, through the first-hand account of an all-American boy who could have been victimized by a homosexual were he not informed by state agencies and committees.[57]

When the conferences ended in the spring of 1962, the Florida Sheriffs Bureau called them a stunning success, noting that they had "created a strong desire" to "do something about sex deviates, particularly where youths are involved."[58] Hillsborough County sheriff Ed Blackburn joked that homosexuality was "like sin and taxes. It's always with you."[59] Florida's law enforcement professionals also responded enthusiastically to the educational conferences. E. Wilson Purdy, chief of police in St. Petersburg, wrote an upbeat letter to Governor Bryant informing him of a "crime prevention program for the youth of our community" that has been so "effective and successful . . . it has gained considerable national and international recognition." He went on to explain the slideshow and lecture delivered by Policewoman Pat and her puppet sidekick Yabby about the "Too Friendly Stranger," which taught children how to identify and avoid potential molesters. Purdy urged the governor to use it in his own anti-homosexual and anti-obscenity work: "Due to recent interest shown by the Governor, in the State's homosexual and child molesting problems, we humbly submit this idea as one of the most successful methods of prevention."[60]

Summaries of conference participants' addresses reflect a similar mishmash of stereotypes, medical and pseudo-medical theories, and hysteria. One psychiatrist involved in the conferences claimed, "You get a clear picture of the wide variation that exists in homosexuality. Psychological factors are: shyness, withdrawal, fear, lack of self-expression, etc." Another explained that Florida had such a large "underworld organization" of homosexuals because "you get people who are dissatisfied and unhappy and the wonderful land of the future opens up for you" in the Sunshine State. One conference attendee recommended that the Florida Highway Patrol take an active role in battling homosexuality because "many of the patrolmen who travel around the highways [know] a great deal about the problem of indecent and pornographic literature and would undoubtly [sic] be of great value" in "putting the story of homosexuality over to the public." The leap from indecent literature to homosexuality went unnoticed. Another conference participant suggested that whatever measures the state adopted, it should be made clear that "there are many homosexuals who are not dangerous but there are also some homosexuals who are actually criminals in that they solicit children and sometimes even attack children."[61]

The state's newspapers helped further cement these ideas as truth. An editorial response in the *Lakeland Ledger* to gay arrests in Hillsborough and Polk Counties demanded that homosexuality not "be allowed to go on in open, rampant, fashion, most especially because so many adult sex deviates victimize teen-agers and younger boys and girls, thereby making them misfits in normal society."[62] The press also treated Farris Bryant and Charley Johns as authorities on homosexuality and indecent literature and simply repeated their warnings of impending social chaos. A January 1962 *Tampa Tribune* editorial, for instance, paraphrased Bryant's statement that until he "or other experts" could come up with the "best answer to curbing homosexual practices before they corrode innocent persons' characters, there will be no attempt by the administration to hamstring or slow down the work of the Johns Committee."[63] The *Tallahassee Democrat* covered a 1962 Florida Board of Health report indicating an increase in syphilis among teenagers and young adults. The article quoted at length the director of the Bureau of Preventable Diseases, who blamed "a class which seems to be increasing, the homosexual, man or woman, who is completely promiscuous and will have relations with either or both sexes of any race."[64] The director had quite neatly summed up the prevailing wisdom about hypersexual and diseased deviates, even adding an interracial twist that in his view offered further evidence of the subversive depravity of the homosexual and reflected widespread beliefs about the prevalence of venereal disease and promiscuity among African Americans.

During the final month of the educational campaign, the FLIC held hearings to determine what policies, if any, were in place in the public schools, junior colleges, and state agencies to keep homosexuals from being hired in a different county once they had been exposed. More than a dozen county superintendents testified, as did several junior college deans and representatives from the state nursing board, the Florida Development Commission, and the Florida Children's Commission. Most witnesses testified that they had been unaware of a problem before the Johns Committee began investigating homosexuals, that there was no communication among agencies, county school districts, or junior colleges about homosexual removal, and that there was no standard procedure for monitoring homosexuals. They also universally agreed that the Johns Committee was doing valuable work, because homosexuality made people inherently unsuited to be around children. The executive secretary from the Florida Educational Association, for example, declared, "We feel that of all the activities of the government the most sacred trust we have is what happens to these children and, therefore, anyone who has shown any of these tendencies . . . we think the youngsters ought to be protected from such influences."[65]

At the conclusion of the statewide conferences on homosexuality and pornography in May 1962, the FCC continued to publicize its message about the dangers posed by gay men and lesbians. The commission formed a research committee on sexual deviation, chaired by a psychiatrist for the state Bureau of Mental Health and made up of six physicians and one layperson. The research subcommittee held its planning meeting on May 21, 1962, and laid out the "fundamentals" upon which it would operate, noting "concern about the problem of sexual deviation and the character disorders in general," belief that "this problem threatens the family and sexual health of the children and youth of Florida," and expressing support for "the present activities of the Governor, the Johns Committee, and the law enforcement agencies."[66]

*   *   *

Soon after, the FLIC's activities came under fire at the University of South Florida, the state's newest public university. In 1954, the Board of Control had appointed the Council for the Study of Higher Education, a group of outside educators who issued a series of recommendations on the expansion of Florida's university system, which had to keep pace with the state's population boom. The council recommended that a new four-year institution be built near one of the fastest growing urban areas, the cities of Tampa and St. Petersburg. Construction began in 1957 on the northern outskirts of Tampa. The BOC selected John Allen, acting president and former vice president of the University of Florida, to be USF's first president. With nearly two thousand students enrolled, the inaugural semester began on September 26, 1960.[67] In its original plan, the state legislature did not allocate any funds for building dormitories, and USF was a commuter school drawing students from nearby Tampa and St. Petersburg, and smaller towns in neighboring counties.

Like previous Johns Committee investigations, the origins of the USF campaign are murky, and evidence points to several possibilities. One committee member had his eye on the university months before the investigation began. In November 1961 George B. Stallings, University of Florida graduate, attorney, and conservative state representative from Jacksonville, read an Associated Press article about a public forum on integration held at USF. The story cited one professor, Thomas Wenner, who irritated Stallings by "blowing off about how the University has accepted Negro students and should announce it to the nation." He vented to Johns, "It seems to me that if this guy wants to make such an announcement he should not be salaried in a tax supported institution of the State of Florida." Stallings concluded, "I hope that our committee will be able to do something about this bird and his big mouth."[68] Johns forwarded the letter to Strickland with a note: "The next time you are down that way, see what you can find out about this Professor."[69] The news item caught the eye of others as well. One Orange County resident and "taxpayer in several of our good counties" wrote to Governor Farris Bryant, "It seems clear that this is not a question of academic freedom, but rather a deliberate opposition to the pubic policy of the State and public sentiment."

Echoing Stallings, he declared, "I do not believe we should be paying faculty members" to promote integration.[70]

Two months later, Stallings snubbed Wenner by refusing to participate in another USF forum, this one addressing the mandatory Americanism versus communism course in Florida high schools. Wenner, in an abrupt turnabout or perhaps an effort to avoid the committee's wrath himself, began funneling hearsay about homosexuals and Communist sympathizers at USF to state representative Joe McClain, a conservative Democrat from rural Pasco County, just north of Tampa.[71] He claimed that USF president John Allen "has characteristics of a homo" and called the head librarian "effeminate" and "possibly a homosexual."[72] McClain was already riled by the recent announcement that USF had invited Jerome Davis to speak on campus. Davis, a graduate of Oberlin Seminary with a doctoral degree in sociology from Columbia, was a union organizer and a YMCA leader in Russia during World War I. He taught sociology at Dartmouth in the early 1920s and in 1924 became a professor in the Yale Divinity School. In 1935, Davis wrote *Capitalism and Its Culture*, in which he concluded that democracy and capitalism were ultimately incompatible. Critics called for his immediate dismissal. Instead, the following year, he was denied tenure and left Yale in 1937. Davis devoted the rest of his career to writing, speaking, and activism on behalf of labor unions and peace. After World War II, he made frequent trips to the Soviet Union and was deemed by the FBI a Communist sympathizer.[73] Although Davis was by now in his early seventies, Representative McClain was not happy to hear that a man with such a long and dubious record would be invited to speak at a public university where some of his constituents sent their kids. He complained to President Allen and then contacted Charley Johns as well as the Tampa office of the FBI.[74]

In early 1962, around the time of the Jerome Davis invitation, USF officials announced their plan to hire D. F. Fleming, a political scientist from Vanderbilt University who had published a two-volume work on the Cold War in which he held the United States primarily responsible for its origins and escalation. By July, Allen again capitulated to his critics and decided against hiring Fleming. He later defended his actions by claiming that proper procedures in interviewing Fleming and negotiating his salary had not been followed, that Fleming was no longer in good standing with Vanderbilt's chancellor, and that the professor had grown "sour over the years at what was happening in this country."[75]

As discontent simmered, a group of USF parents began meeting to discuss their misgivings about the new university. Jane Smith from Plant City, a small town twenty miles east of Tampa, headed the group. Her son, Stockton Smith Jr., known to his family and friends as Skipper, had transferred to USF from Washington and Lee University, where he had excelled in football and academics. Jane Smith took a special interest in Skipper's education now that he was living at home and commuting to school. As she put it, "He would say, 'Mother, what do you think of this? Mother, what do you think of that? Mother, I do feel that higher education should encourage morals, patriotism and faith, and what I have been required to read thus far would not only discourage those things, but might destroy them.'"[76]

Both Skipper and his mother took offense at some of the reading assignments. By the time her son had completed a summer session in 1961, Jane Smith claimed to have heard enough of his complaints about the "vile approach to sex, destruction of faith in God, and extolling of ideas that are of socialist and communist origin" in the classroom.[77] In the fall she and three others, Helen Funkhouser and Dr. and Mrs. James Hodge, met with the dean of academic affairs, Sidney French, and several professors. The parents said they were dismayed by the liberal bias among the faculty, especially in the English Department. French defensively called them a "pressure group" and promptly saw them to the door.[78] Later that fall another parent, Neil Smith (no relation to Jane and Skipper), spent two hours with John Allen discussing various readings he and his daughter found objectionable.[79]

In the spring of 1962, Jane Smith was growing impatient. On April 4 she and her husband, with help from Bert and Neil Smith and Helen and Morton Funkhouser, drafted a letter and mailed it to "50 couples in Tampa, chosen as responsible citizens, interested in the affairs of our community," inviting them to an April 9 meeting at the home of Mr. and Mrs. Smith. The topic of conversation was the "daily problem of extreme, liberal, atheistic teaching by those who feel they have a monopoly on the cry for 'academic freedom'" at the University of South Florida.[80] Twenty-five people attended, including Tampa mayor Julian Lane. Evolution, moral relativism, acceptance of interracial dating, and the fallibility of the Bible were dangerous notions to be putting in the heads of college kids, Smith argued. She and many of the other parents at the meeting also complained about the Jerome Davis incident. After a long evening, the group voted overwhelmingly to ask the Johns Committee to investigate the university.

Within ten days, the committee had circulated a confidential memo outlining the game plan for the USF investigation. In order to secure information and allies, it stressed that the "Tampa student and citizens element must be picked up with the greatest care for reliability, knowledgeability [sic], ability to be *good* witnesses, and courage." Allies included Charley Johns, Mark Hawes—designated the "quarterback"—Joe McClain, Edward Whittlesey, the former chief of public relations at the University of Florida under then–vice president John Allen (who Whittlesey called "that rascal"), Thomas Wenner, and Jane and Skipper Smith. This "Inner Group," as it was called, met with R. J. Strickland on April 28.[81]

Strickland began questioning students on May 10 in room 170 of Tampa's Hawaiian Village Motel. John H. Sullivan, an investigator from Panama City who had worked with Strickland on previous homosexual investigations, assisted him. They arrived with a list of faculty and staff names and the specific complaints against them, and their interrogations consisted largely of confirming stories they had already heard. Strickland asked a high school principal from Zephyrhills about grumbling from teachers who were taking classes at the university. According to them, the Human Behavior Department's reading list included "some pornographic literature," its professors' teaching about evolution violated the "personal feelings" of some students, and "there was a very definite movement at the University to soft-pedal any opposition to Communism."[82]

As to rumors of homosexuality, one former student reported that in December 1960 he and his girlfriend, along with some other students, had gone to the home of Human Behavior teaching assistant James Teske, who allegedly proffered alcohol and pornographic pictures, both heterosexual and homosexual, and initiated sexual contact with a male student. Strickland sent another investigator, J. Duane Barker from Miami, to interview this student in Orlando. He recalled having too much to drink at Teske's apartment, spending the night there, and awaking the next morning to find the instructor engaged in oral sex with him.[83] Barker wanted to know how USF administrators handled the incident. The student told him that he had immediately gone to his adviser, the drama instructor John Caldwell, with the story. Caldwell "advised me that he thought that I should just forget about it if I could, instead of getting involved and getting my name in court and the papers and everything. He said it wouldn't be worth it." Caldwell reportedly also counseled him that "in the theater group, sometimes you find an unusually high amount of homosexuals" and "if he ever found out about any that were in his drama class, that they would automatically be thrown right out."[84]

Another former student, working for Morrison's Food Service on USF's campus, discussed his "past life" as a homosexual and offered up his own mixture of personal experience and conjecture to Barker on May 10. The detective asked, "You have at one time considered yourself a gay person" and "you and your wife do know and entertain these people from time to time" so "your opinions would be a little bit stronger, or carry more weight?"[85] The young man repeated gossip about a dean who "stirred up a big stink last year with the idea of not wearing shorts on campus, and he was called a panty waist and several other names." This witness characterized the dean as "sort of on the feminine side." He remembered an English professor who was "a very bashful, shy person; he comes through the line quite often where I serve, and when he orders, he will sort of blush and shy away." He saved the most damaging testimony for drama teacher John Caldwell, with whom he had shared a motel room on a theater department trip to Tallahassee. The two chatted "after we were in bed, and his statement to me, as well as I can remember it, was that as far as homosexuals were concerned, he did not condone it, but if a homosexual did approach him, and he knew the homosexual, he would not turn the homosexual away if he thought the homosexual needed sex; that he would be the receiving partner of the sex act."[86]

Other witnesses described inappropriate sexual comments in class, liberal discussions of race, and profanity in the classroom and assigned readings. Cheryl Beckner, who had just completed her first year at USF, found some of the reading material unpalatable.

"Cheryl, a majority of these books that is required reading, do you think that they are educational?" Strickland inquired.

"Well, I can't say that I think they are educational."

"There is books that, as a whole, the University could do without?"

"I think so, yes."[87]

Throughout the questioning, women were considered especially vulnerable to the affronts of sex jokes and off-color language. One young woman relayed to Strickland a list of words spoken by a professor that had offended her. Unable to utter them aloud, she wrote them down, and the chief investigator repeated them for the record: "testicles," "penis," "bitches," and "whores."[88] Another female student, questioned in her pastor's office in Tampa, reported that some students actually enjoyed the "trashy" readings, especially the "bigger-mouthed boys," while "the girls usually just sit there and don't say anything, not unless it's a, well, a girl that I wouldn't know."[89]

Some students were just as insulted by liberal racial views. One woman got into a "heated discussion" with a professor after he told the class he supported integration. Another student complained about having to read John Dollard's "very irresponsible statements" in *Caste and Class in a Southern Town* regarding "the prejudice that he felt southern people had toward the Negroes." In the next breath she criticized a film she had to watch for another class because "it showed Negro men and white women together, holding hands, and I remember in one scene she, I believe, took a cigarette from his mouth and started smoking."[90]

*   *   *

On May 17, one week into Strickland's investigation, John Allen learned of the clandestine interrogations and publicly invited the Johns Committee to come to the campus for public hearings with a court reporter present during all questioning. To prepare the students and faculty for the arrival of the committee on campus, Allen addressed the university on Monday, May 21. He reassured the audience that, although they might be questioned, their livelihoods were not in jeopardy. He advised them to remain calm. And he reminded them that they were not obligated to answer unfair questions, or be interrogated anywhere other than the designated conference room, or be questioned at night or at other "odd hours."[91]

Two days later, at 9:30 in the morning, Johns, Hawes, Strickland, and four other committee members filed into the conference room. Herbert Stallworth, assistant director of the Board of Control, took a seat beside the other men to observe the proceedings. The committee first addressed the selection of reading material in a course called "The American Idea," housed in the College of Basic Studies and the College of Humanities and Natural and Social Sciences. As Dean Russell Cooper and administrator Margaret Fisher explained it later, "The American Idea took an instrumental approach to the study of public policy, using basic documents and critical works (in paperback) that analyzed the developmental process of organization and policymaking and identified and proposed alternative approaches to matters of policy and practice. The course was avowedly oriented toward shared values of democracy: freedom, equality, and justice, constitutional principles of the grant of governmental powers, reserved powers, and guarantees of civil rights."[92] Committee members also zeroed in on the All-University Book, chosen each term by a committee of faculty members and students for classroom and campus-wide discussions, which had come under fire by some parents and students. John Warner, who taught the American Idea course, was slated as the first witness. It quickly became apparent that committee members assumed his reading list reflected the declining cultural standards and morals of the day. After attacking choices like Somerset Maugham's *Razor's Edge* and J. D. Salinger's *Nine Stories*, Charley Johns flared, "Doctor, I want to ask you if the literary field has got to such a low ebb that you all couldn't find anything to put in your library but this trash?"

"I don't rate this trash myself, sir, and I think that, with more time and studying it and analyzing it with one of our good teachers, you wouldn't either," Warner replied.[93]

Later, after Mark Hawes read aloud from Salinger's short story collection, Johns demanded angrily, "Will you advise me what is literary and a genius about writing such crap as he just read?"[94]

Warner did not answer.

The committee's questions on the first day of hearings reflected conservative midcentury attitudes, as legislators invoked a mythical—and now imperiled—wholesome past. Late in the afternoon, Senator Richard Mitchell informed Warner that he, Hawes, and Stallworth had all been at the University of Florida in the late 1940s. He then implored, "Will you tell me how, from 1950 to 1962, this world has changed so much that it is necessary to have such kind of books as we are talking about as recommended reading, or suggested reading, or as a reading list delivered to the young people of this University? Tell me how in twelve years that has changed." Charley Johns may have made the most revealing comment that day when he asked rhetorically, "I am 57 years old, and when I read this stuff it stimulates me. What does it do to these teenage children?"[95]

The USF hearings lasted two weeks. Reading material and professors' in-class behavior dominated the first week. On Thursday, four days into the questioning, Mark Hawes put Human Behavior Department professor Henry Winthrop through the ringer for his alleged use of words like "hell," "damn," "Christ," and "God damn" in a lecture. Winthrop wearily observed, "It's fantastic that this kind of thing would come to the attention

of you gentlemen." He explained that he had used these words when quoting from *The Catcher in the Rye* "to illustrate the roughness and crudeness
and coarseness of lower class speech."[96] On Friday, another professor defended his use of *The Inhabited Universe*, a 1959 book by aerospace scientist and popular writer Kenneth W. Gatland, in his literature class. In his
testimony, the professor admitted that he agreed with the book's central
argument, that "orthodox religion as we generally understand that term,
is immature, and unthoughtful and not predicated on anything factual,
and constitutes a large amount of superstition."[97] By the end of the week,
the hearings had proven only that a vast cultural divide existed between
conservative politicians and liberal intellectuals. For professors like Warner and Winthrop, the university's mission was to encourage students to
question and to equip them with analytical thinking skills. If that meant
exposing them to progressive racial ideas about integration and equal
rights, or discussing faith versus reason or sexuality outside of marriage,
then so be it. For cultural conservatives, these ideas were abhorrent. But
they provided the committee and concerned parents with ammunition to
rally other like-minded people to their cause.

Johns also implied a link between liberal teaching and sexual perversion. As he asked one professor, disingenuously, given his dealings with
homosexuals in Miami in 1954, "Would you believe me when I tell you
that six years ago, when I was appointed on this Committee, and when we
got into this homosexual situation, that I was naïve and didn't know that
existed?" Johns continued, "Further, would you believe me when I tell you
God knows I would have been better off if I never found it out, as far as
being a citizen. I would have been happier."

"Yes, sir."

"Then you all teach this kind of stuff to our children, warping their
minds."[98]

The hearings resumed on Monday, May 28, and within two days the
questioning had shifted to homosexuality. Mark Hawes began by asking
Sidney French, dean of academic affairs, if he had ever received a complaint about a gay faculty or staff member. He had not. When asked about
the procedure if he were to hear such a complaint, French replied, "If it
involved a faculty member, then I would become concerned with it. If it
did not . . . then this is outside of my area."[99] Margaret Fisher, director
of student personnel, was asked about official procedures dealing with
homosexual students. She stated that if she encountered a gay or lesbian

student, she would refer him or her to a counselor and keep the student's name on file "because of the possible future difficulties which might arise in their professional and educational career."[100] She admitted that USF had no specific policy for dealing with gay faculty and staff.

Mark Hawes seized on her confession, reminding Fisher that when John Caldwell came to her to discuss James Teske, the instructor accused of inappropriate sexual advances to a student, she never reported the incident to a higher-up, despite her testimony to the contrary. Caught in a lie, she tried to shrug off the seriousness of the charges against Teske, calling them ambiguous. George Stallings asked, "The staff member involved helped put him to bed and then he woke up later with this man, with his penis in his mouth. Now, there couldn't be any question about misunderstanding whether this was actual outright homosexual conduct or not."

"Uh huh."[101]

As the hearings wound down, Charley Johns ended with some "fatherly advice," as he called it, to the university to "take a hard boiled attitude against" homosexuality, to "keep it out of here, and build an institution that this State can be proud of." He paused. "But you can't take the attitude you have got."[102]

*　　*　　*

After the hearings concluded, Strickland traveled to Hot Springs, Arkansas, for another meeting of the Southern Association of Intelligence Agents. He informed the assembly, "Homosexuality is playing a big part in our present racial problems and in the promotion of communism." Neither Strickland nor any other committee member had ever made such a claim in public, and their investigations had not led them to search for specific ties between racial agitators and homosexuals. But Strickland persisted, hoping to convince his colleagues to take note in their respective states of the sexual and political immorality that underlay civil rights agitation. As an investigator for the Mississippi Sovereignty Commission noted, "It was surprising to learn just how influential these homosexuals are and how they have used it in recruiting members for the various racial agitative groups."[103]

An episode involving a white civil rights activist in Mississippi who was also a homosexual did occur early the following year. William Higgs was an attorney from Jackson and a graduate of the University of Mississippi and Harvard Law. Historian John Howard called him "among the most hated white men in the state" for working in the early 1960s as a legal adviser to black political candidates, his role in cofounding a civil rights newspaper with an African American grocer, assisting the legal efforts of James Meredith to desegregate the University of Mississippi, and filing a federal lawsuit against the Sovereignty Commission, claiming that its disbursement of public funds to Citizens' Councils was unconstitutional.[104]

In early 1963, Higgs was arrested by the Jackson police on what one historian has called "a phony moral charge" of contributing to the delinquency of a minor. Upon closer inspection of the boy's testimony, coupled with Higgs's unwillingness ever to return to Mississippi after being convicted and sentenced to prison in absentia, it is plausible that the charge was neither phony nor, as Howard has suggested, a means of silencing an outspoken white integrationist.[105] The deposition of William Daywalt, the teen in question who at the time was in ninth grade but had been held back a year in school, bears striking similarities to accounts of young male hustlers gathered by R. J. Strickland and Duane Barker in Miami. It is filled with minute details about clothes, meals, and cigarettes purchased by Higgs for him, as well as descriptions of specific sexual activities between the two.

Higgs first met Daywalt in the lobby of the downtown Jackson YMCA. Daywalt had left his parents' home in Pennsylvania days before, riding with another man who was on his way to Texas. Higgs lived about six blocks from the YMCA, but there is no indication from Daywalt's testimony about why Higgs was there. In any event, Higgs brought Daywalt to his house. On the first night, Higgs allegedly asked the young man to sleep in his bed with him. In Daywalt's words, "When I got to bed, I just closed my eyes because I find I relax much better and get to sleep fast and Mr. Higgs must have thought I was asleep or something, and he started rubbing around my chest. . . . And my stomach, and his other hand started rubbing around my leg and all, started feeling around with his hand, and it got so . . . well . . ."

Q. Go ahead.
A. Well, he put his hand through the elastic of my shorts and started fooling around like that and stuff like that. He got it in his hand, and, well . . .
Q. What did he get in his hands?
A. (No answer. Witness is embarrassed.)
Q. I don't want to embarrass you at all. The point of the matter is,

I don't want to put words in your mouth. I just want you to tell us exactly what happened as you know it and as you would repeat it elsewhere.

A. Well, he got it in his hand, my . . . well . . .

Q. Go ahead. It's kind of like diving into cold water. It's all right. Go ahead.

A. And the words I use should just be my own?

Q. I like for you to use your own words.

A. Well, he got my peter in his hand and started messing around with it and stuff.

Q. All right?

A. And that's all as far as he went the first night.

Q. For what period of time; how long did he hold your peter in his hand?

A. Approximately about five minutes.

Q. Did it cause an erection?

A. No sir.[106]

Daywalt went on to describe how their sexual activity changed over subsequent days and nights, to include oral and anal sex, both performed by Higgs. This testimony was interspersed with vignettes related to their day-to-day lives together over a two-week period. The attorney doing the questioning also focused on Higgs bringing the teenager with him to African Americans' homes and churches and discussing voting rights, school integration, and other civil rights issues. According to Daywalt, Higgs encouraged him to socialize with Negro girls: "He expected me to hold a conversation with girls that—, you know,—are not even my color. I guess he wanted me to take one of them out and I—

Q. (Interposing) Did he suggest that to you?

A. Well, not in plain words, but he was getting around to it.

Q. What did he say?

A. He asked me if I ever took out a negro girl. 'No,' I said, 'I'd stick to girls of my race.'

Q. What did he say about that?

A. Oh, well, he was a little mad. I mean I could tell that he was mad.[107]

The veracity of Daywalt's statement, and the question of whether he was coached or otherwise influenced by Mississippi officials, remains unclear. What is evident, however, is the degree to which segregationists viewed Higgs as a threat to white youth and a symbol of the most abject moral degeneracy of a white man, and a pervert at that, who would betray his own race.

In Florida, the Johns Committee investigation of the University of South Florida raised a different set of questions about morality and spurred the Board of Control into reforming its hiring policies, procedures for handling parents' complaints, and guidelines for inviting speakers to Florida's college campuses. The board's response actually lent credibility to the FLIC. It became a question of which state agency would solve the problems identified by the committee, not whether the problems actually existed or whether their significance outweighed other questions such as professors' salaries, faculty retention rates, national rankings, and so on. In mid-July 1962, J. B. Culpepper, the BOC's executive director, contacted all state university presidents and assigned each one to tackle a specific issue, but his instructions were vague. He asked one to develop a hiring plan that would ensure professional competence and "loyalty and good morals" as well as a "reasonable spiritual outlook." In planning a statewide policy for choosing textbooks and library books, he told another president to emphasize selection based on "a most desirable and effective academic climate and learning situation which will be compatible with our concept of American democracy."[108] The directive doomed the Board of Control and the council of presidents to incite the ire of professors as well as the public. Whose standards would be used to measure a professor's "spiritual outlook"? And why would a public university use religion as a litmus test for hiring in the first place? These and other questions would remain muddled and contested.

Culpepper shared the Johns Committee's assessment of the homosexual menace in Florida's classrooms and campuses, and by including the issue in his directive, he again validated the legitimacy of the committee. One of the board's central concerns, he wrote, was to create "plans for protecting the Universities against homosexuality, moral turpitude, drunkenness, profanity in the classroom, personality instability, and other behavior deemed to be detrimental to the institutions."[109] Not only did this list lump same-sex sexuality together with things such as alcoholism and emotional instability, perhaps the two most predominant associations in the postwar model of homosexuality, but it also echoed earlier work by Governor Bryant and the Johns Committee to link homosexuality with obscenity.

The council of presidents proposed policy changes or clarifications that sent a clear message to the BOC and the state legislature: They must have a role in setting and enforcing policy and be shielded from reckless attacks by unqualified critics. If a student or parent lodged a complaint against anyone or anything at his university, that president would determine what inquiry, if any, was called for, oversee the investigation, and report the findings and the response to the Board of Control, which would decide on punitive action.

John Allen of the University of South Florida drafted the proposal on choosing speakers and guest lecturers. At the outset, he acknowledged that state law prohibited the employment of Communists or anyone who advocated the violent overthrow of the government. But he also argued that communism, along with "fascism, dictatorship, or other extreme ideologies and positions must be well understood by intelligent, democratic citizens if they are to be contained and combated successfully." Likening this approach to the practice of medicine, he argued, "We study cancer objectively in the laboratory in our efforts to contain, control, and eliminate it. We should study extreme ideologies in a similar manner." He recommended that controversial speakers be allowed on campus as long as sufficient question-and-answer time existed and a speaker with an opposing view had equal time.[110] This was the sort of compromise commonly employed by universities across the country since the 1940s. Although Allen and Johns may have agreed that communism was like a cancer and could be understood and treated as a disease, they disagreed on how dangerous ideologies should be taught, in what context, and by whom.

Kenneth R. Williams, president-elect of the newly announced Florida Atlantic University in Boca Raton, dealt with the question of homosexuality. It was the university's duty, he wrote, to arm future leaders with "a code of conduct which will stand the test of time." It must "take precaution against having as its leaders and spokesmen, individuals who are characterized by emotional instability, drunkenness, homosexuality, promiscuity, the use of obscene language, or other behavior patterns which are in severe conflict with those generally accepted." Williams parroted Culpepper's phrasing almost verbatim. He also insisted that any accusation of homosexuality, "either openly-made or even more maliciously circulated by innuendo and rumor," be taken seriously and investigated thoroughly. The entire university system needed a uniform policy to detect, remove, and facilitate psychiatric treatment for both students and faculty.[111]

In late summer 1962, the Board of Control also received a report from the special subcommittee that had studied the twelve volumes and twenty-five hundred pages of testimony from the USF investigation. The Johns Committee had released its report to the *Tampa Tribune*, which published it in its entirety on August 25, a move that outraged the board and the University of South Florida. Defensive in tone, the BOC subcommittee report argued that the board had "long had a standing policy designed to eliminate sex deviates." The evidence for this policy, however, was the "Policy on Morals and Influences," which had only been adopted by the BOC in December 1961. It also pointed out that the Johns Committee had not actually uncovered any Communists or fellow travelers in its investigation of USF, nor had it turned up any reading material that could be legally deemed obscene. The report concluded that most of the problems uncovered by the FLIC "were already under scrutiny" and reiterated that the board itself was "the proper body to receive, investigate, and take action upon any and all complaints" made against Florida's universities.[112]

*   *   *

The Board of Control quickly issued new guidelines for monitoring faculty. Each university president would maintain files on all professors. The information included "academic background, loyalty, attitudes toward communism, moral conduct, and general teaching ability." As of February 1, 1963, all university personnel were to be fingerprinted. Every student who applied to a state university would have a file, and if "the official detects any indication of antisocial or immoral behavior, such as communistic activities or sex deviation, he shall immediately report this to the President who shall see that a thorough investigation is made before the applicant is admitted." Presidents would be required to inform one another of these undesirables so that they could not gain entrance into another Florida university.[113]

Troubles continued to hound the University of South Florida. In October 1962, President Allen had suspended English professor Sheldon Grebstein for assigning a Norman Podhoretz article from the *Partisan Review* called "The Know-Nothing Bohemians." In the essay Podhoretz, later a neoconservative writer but at that time a stalwart New York social democrat, dismissed Jack Kerouac and the Beats as a "revolt of the spiritually underprivileged and the crippled of soul—young men who can't think straight and so hate anyone who can."[114] Grebstein used the essay to explain the shortcomings of contemporary fiction, but this critique got lost in the furor over the sexually explicit quotes that Podhoretz sprinkled throughout. One month after Allen suspended Grebstein, he reinstated the professor, who was so disgusted that he resigned from the university at the end of the fall semester.[115]

The Board of Control supported Allen's original decision to suspend Grebstein. As one member explained, Grebstein was all too representative of faculty who found such reading material not only acceptable but also "desirable." The board member apparently failed to grasp that he, Grebstein, and Podhoretz all agreed on some level about the degraded and inferior writing produced by Kerouac and other Beat writers. His bigger fear concerned the female students who might be exposed to this indecency. He urged "each men's civic, service, social, and fraternal organization" to read "The Know-Nothing Bohemians," especially any man "who has a daughter or a granddaughter, read this essay, and take note of the excerpts on sex." Then, he suggested, each man should "go home, take his mother's picture and study it thoughtfully; reread one particular excerpt; and then, take a hard, cold look at what he sees in the mirror."[116]

The Grebstein suspension outraged the American Association of University Professors and the American Association of University Women (AAUW). Both groups protested the action. The USF chapter of the AAUP blamed the Board of Control's recent policy changes. Grebstein's suspension showed what could happen when rules are "dangerously vague" and "arbitrarily and prejudicially applied." Now, thanks to the board, "faculties need be under constant surveillance for basest intentions and violations of morality and patriotism."[117] The Tampa AAUW blamed the Johns Committee for fostering an atmosphere that made the professor's removal thinkable in the first place. According to the group, above all else the FLIC had violated its own rules of operation, paying for information, editing testimony, and intimidating witnesses. Moreover, it had no legal right to investigate the ethical or professional standards of university faculty or to monitor the religious content of university courses, yet the committee had done both at USF without anyone batting an eye. The AAUW also noted that the Johns Committee was obligated by law to report directly to the state legislature, but Johns himself had sent the USF report to a local newspaper.[118]

In December 1962 the Board of Control weighed in by unveiling a new "Policy on Academic Freedom and Responsibility." The statement assured the rights of students and professors to "examine ideas in an atmosphere of freedom and confidence" but at the same time cautioned every college professor to "fulfill his responsibility to society and to his profession by manifesting academic competence, scholarly discretion, and good citizenship." Finally, in the "Morals and Influences" clause, the BOC enjoined administrators to "continue to guard against activities subversive to the American democratic process and against immoral behavior, such as sex deviation."[119]

Floridians, too, weighed in on the skirmishes of the past year. Conservatives and supporters of the Johns Committee embraced the new BOC statement as an important weapon in the fight against Communists and perverts. One woman from St. Petersburg asked, "Do we want our young people to be so 'free' that they can be indoctrinated with Communist theories and turned into Marxist monsters we do not recognize? Must we lose our country for the sake of 'academic freedom'?" A USF parent informed John Allen, "I don't care if my son even misses a college education." Placing him in the classroom with "bigoted onesided profs makes me feel that he would be better out in the big world where truths are not 'searched for' by ivory tower conceited and disloyal pink professors."[120]

Opponents thought the USF investigation proved that the committee had finally strayed too far from its original intent, and that it could mar Florida's reputation. One minister from the Tampa suburb of Temple Terrace asked Governor Bryant, "How shall we be able to secure able professors to join this new faculty if they read this scurillous [sic] attack? How shall we enlist students to enter classes here?" He warned, "We must not abet the already growing opinion that Florida is after all a state of 'crackers.'" But Bryant seemed untroubled by this possibility. "I have neither the authority nor the inclination to hamper their activity, because although in some instances it does injury the overall result of legislative investigations is good." Further, he wrote, "as a cracker myself I was not offended by that opinion, but I don't think anything will be done that will destroy the wonderful image that Florida has."[121]

Not everyone was so optimistic. A letter to the editor of the *Tampa Tribune* warned that if the Board of Control "does not quickly assert its authority over our university, the asinine, stone age pronouncements of Charley Johns and his barbarian pork choppers on such matters as philosophy, literature, and good taste, will make a laughing stock of higher education" in Florida.[122] The Florida State Chamber of Commerce passed a resolution in November 1962 demanding that the governor and the BOC "assume the responsibilities placed on them by law" to run Florida's universities in a "proper" manner, and blamed the Johns Committee for the "disruption" at USF.[123]

The terms of debate surrounding the Johns Committee's investigation of the University of South Florida were framed by a common set of Cold War assumptions, in this case the belief that softness on communism, religious relativism, sexual deviance, and obscenity had no place in higher education. Even most critics of the committee acknowledged this fact. They disagreed, however, about who should safeguard Florida's universities from these dangerous influences. The BOC, university presidents, the Johns Committee, and professors all wanted a say in the matter. And even though the public consensus pointed toward keeping the committee out of educational policy making, Johns scored a minor victory by pressuring the Board of Control to tighten regulations in light of what the FLIC claimed to have uncovered at the University of South Florida. The 1961–62 educational campaign of the Johns Committee, the Florida Children's Commission, and the governor's advisory committees had set the stage for the USF investigation. The fact that decency had become politicized allowed—and perhaps even inspired—parents to challenge professors' political views, religious beliefs, and use of profanity. At the same time, the cultural and political currency enjoyed by the FLIC led it to overreach at the University of South Florida, though it is worth remembering that although many people believed that universities should be monitored for "appropriate" teaching and hiring practices, they did not want a legislative investigating committee to be the arbiter of that propriety. The next biennium would bring still more trouble for the Johns Committee, as civil rights demonstrations gathered steam, student activism increased across Florida's campuses, court rulings limited its scope on many fronts, and committee members took egregious missteps.

5

Sex and Civil Rights, 1963–1965

We're not having any sex orgies or anything like that. This is a march for freedom.

Lester Maddox, Americans for States' Rights, Private Property Rights and Private Enterprise demonstration, Atlanta, 1965

The first half of the 1960s saw a dramatic climax of nonviolent civil rights protests in the South and the passage of sweeping federal legislation to protect African Americans' constitutional rights. By 1965, the movement had penetrated American politics and culture, awakening the nation's conscience in a way that individual episodes in the 1950s—from Emmett Till's lynching to the venomous white mobs in Little Rock—jarring though they were, had not. The stark contrast between the dignified resolve of peaceful demonstrators and the raging violence of segregationists came into ever sharper relief during the era of the Freedom Rides, Birmingham, the March on Washington, and Bloody Sunday and the subsequent march from Selma to Montgomery. A majority of Americans sympathized with the abstract principles of black voting rights and equal access to lunch counters. At the very moment when the greatest constitutional victories in a century had been won, however, the movement itself was already changing. Growing student activism across a widening spectrum, from the increasing radicalism of the Student Nonviolent Coordinating Committee to the emergence of the New Left, seemed to portend the fulfillment of postwar conservatives' and segregationists' most dire prophecies.

In Florida, the Johns Committee continued monitoring students active in civil rights and peace groups, defended an unpopular and soon notorious report on homosexuality and published a leering account of Martin Luther King's and SCLC's St. Augustine campaign. By 1964, with passage of the Civil Rights Act and the conservative triumph within the Republican Party, massive resistance had transformed from an overtly race-based articulation of white supremacy and fears of black contamination to an ostensibly color-blind defense of individual rights, in particular, the freedom of association. Politicians, legislative committees, and the FBI continued to discredit the civil rights movement as Communist-tainted. The seeds of this critique of liberalism had been sown in the immediate postwar years, but the commingling of conservative and segregationist attacks on the morals of blacks and whites on the left forged a crucial bond with nonsoutherners that would contribute to the reshaping of conservative politics in the decades that followed.

*   *   *

In December 1962, Mrs. Smith had stood before the Plant City Conservative Club and reminded members that the problems at USF remained unsolved, despite the Johns Committee's hearings and the Board of Control's new policies related to homosexuality, communism, and academic freedom. She framed her concerns around the question of rights. "Moral order is being attacked at our university," she warned, and "I have a right to act when they come into class and indoctrinate." At one point during the evening, she attempted to read from the Norman Podhoretz article that had been the source of Sheldon Grebstein's suspension, but her husband hastened to restrain her, cautioning that the content was inappropriately graphic for this particular setting. He allowed his wife, however, to read from John Dollard's chapter on interracial sex in his study of the Mississippi Delta, *Caste and Class in a Southern Town*. According to the *Tampa Times*, which chose not to quote her in this instance, "club members readily agreed that the book was unfit" for college students.[1]

Ill will lingered on all sides of the controversy after the Johns Committee left Tampa, but R. J. Strickland, unbothered, traveled around north Florida and the Panhandle in the early months of 1963, continuing his search for lesbian and gay teachers. In Ft. Walton Beach, Panama City, Tallahassee, Pensacola, and Jacksonville, Strickland located dozens of women and men and methodically interrogated them all. He found female softball leagues filled with lesbians, gay navy men in Jacksonville and Pensacola, and even an embittered victim of the Johns Committee

in Tallahassee who was allegedly plotting to kidnap the son of municipal judge John Rudd as payback for his antipathy toward homosexuals.[2]
Then, in February, the chief investigator made a grave mistake. He paid a
female informant to lure *Orlando Sentinel* reporter Robert Delaney to a
motel room in Tallahassee that he had booked in advance. Eavesdropping
from an adjoining room, Strickland arranged to have the local police burst
in when the woman gave the signal (according to Delaney, she "called
out something" and "shoved my head down") to catch him in an "unnatural act." The truth behind the setup did not emerge for a few months.
When the story finally appeared in the papers during the summer of 1963,
Strickland resigned from the committee, but not before the legislature
had renewed it for another two-year term.[3] For the time being, however,
with the homosexual investigations rolling along and the committee preparing its report for the upcoming legislative session, morale remained
high among committee members. Duane Barker was buoyant enough to
joke about having "converted" and joined the NAACP, the ACLU, and
UNESCO. "Also," he wrote to Strickland, "I war [sic] a wig and womens
[sic] clothes and go and spy on the local meeting of the Daughters of the
Confederacy."[4]

But trouble loomed. In late February, the Florida Supreme Court rejected the committee's appeal in *Neal v. Bryant*, the case involving three
Pinellas County teachers who had sued Governor Bryant as head of the
Department of Education for denying due process in revoking their teaching certificates. In late 1962 the court had decided in favor of the plaintiffs
and ordered their certificates restored, on the grounds that Strickland
had not been authorized by law to act as an investigator on behalf of the
Department of Education. Now in early 1963 this last-ditch effort to get
the court to reverse itself failed, and the Pinellas County Board of Public
Instruction was left to calculate how much the teachers were owed in
back pay. They had been ousted in the fall of 1960.[5] In the committee's
other major pending litigation, six exhausting years of skirmishes ended
in March 1963 with the U.S. Supreme Court ruling in *Gibson v. Florida
Legislative Investigation Committee*. In a 5–4 decision, the court reversed
Theodore Gibson's contempt conviction, arguing that the state had not
demonstrated a "meaningful relationship between the NAACP Miami
branch and subversives." In his opinion, Justice Arthur Goldberg, who
had only recently replaced the more conservative Felix Frankfurter who
stepped down after suffering a stroke in 1962, wrote that because of this

"utter failure" on the part of the Johns Committee, "groups which themselves are neither engaged in subversive or other illegal or improper activities nor demonstrated to have any substantial connections with such activities are to be protected in their rights of free and private association."[6]

The decisions debilitated the FLIC, now legally unable to pursue the NAACP or investigate homosexual teachers and provide the depositions to the Florida Department of Education. Moreover, many Floridians remained unhappy over the committee's activities at the University of South Florida. The *Florida Alligator* called the investigation and the Board of Control's adoption of the FLIC's agenda a "great leap backward." Tampa television station WTVT editorialized, "No responsible Florida official or citizen is trying to protect deviates, traitors or any other undesirables," but it agreed with "many other seriously concerned citizens who feel a committee of the Legislature has no business in the law enforcement field, or as book censors, or as a screening agency for university personnel." On the other hand, the Women's Republican Club of St. Petersburg offered a resounding endorsement of the Johns Committee, maintaining that "a person hired to form the minds of the young, if he be vulnerable to any questions whatever on immorality or subversion, ought not to bemoan 'methods' when the Committee asks him an embarrassing question which he has invited by his own questionable conduct."[7]

Charley Johns and Mark Hawes addressed the legislature on April 18, 1963, to summarize the committee's activities over the previous two years. Hawes started by explaining that the FLIC first came to Tampa to gather "information in the field of subversion and homosexual conduct." But the committee began "receiving complaints . . . in regard to the anti-Christian teachings and materials on that campus, and the alleged materials containing the vulgar and profane language out there." After recounting the ill-fated Jerome Davis lecture and the retracted job offer to D. F. Fleming, Hawes quoted J. Edgar Hoover's warning from *A Study on Communism* about the Communist Party's establishing "a speaker's bureau for the purpose of making themselves available to go around and become members of the faculty of the universities of this country and to make one-shot and two and three-shot speeches." He then commenced with the familiar list of student and parent complaints about the problems of USF professors: insulting and belittling Christian beliefs and those who hold them, "ethical relativity—the notion that there is no absolute standard of morality or immorality," the use of "coarse and vulgar, profane and vile" language in reading assignments and classroom discussions, and homosexuality and inappropriate behavior with students. Worst of all, thundered Hawes, administrators and faculty were closing ranks and crowing about the sanctity of academic freedom, which as construed by USF administrators meant nothing more than "the right to bring communist sympathizers and communists themselves to teach and indoctrinate, [and] the right to take this ordinary, everyday filth which I call intellectual garbage off the newsstands and put it in the classrooms as required texts, and it includes the right for these people to do these things without any restraint or policy at all on behalf of the people or the elected officials."[8]

Next, Charley Johns implored his fellow legislators to remember the children. He revealed the alleged plot to kidnap Tallahassee judge John Rudd's eleven-year-old son: "God knows what would have happened to him" if Strickland "hadn't nipped it in the bud." Johns noted that more than seventy teachers' certificates had been revoked, reminding legislators, "They are the teachers teaching your children." In a final plea for renewal, Johns emphasized that the "work of this committee has got to go on. It's larger than any of us." He then divulged that Strickland was so good at his job he had even helped an unnamed federal agency remove "thirty-nine homosexuals and two of 'em was in high, exalted positions of trust."[9] With that, Charley Johns took his seat.

Six days later, USF president John Allen stood before the legislature. He methodically identified all of the distortions and misstatements in the Johns Committee's report. What he also ended up doing, however, was to affirm that former Communists or fellow travelers such as divinity professor Jerome Davis indeed should not be allowed to give a lecture to college students, and that faculty and students ought to be screened for "homosexual tendencies," receive psychiatric treatment, and be removed from universities. He reassured legislators that the Podhoretz beatnik article was no longer part of the USF curriculum while in the same breath pointing out that it was reprinted in a "college casebook used by more than 75 colleges and universities across the nation."[10] In spite of Allen's defense of his university, replete with statistics about faculty PhD rates and impressive student achievements, and his warnings that the FLIC would do irreparable damage to the state's academic reputation and economic potential, it was clear that he had been backed into a corner by conservatives, implicitly conceding to the forces who urged government monitoring of the moral standards and practices of publicly funded universities.

Similar controversies had arisen at colleges and universities for decades, especially during the Red scares following World War II. Across the country, schools compelled teachers and professors to take loyalty oaths because conservative anti-Communists feared corrosive liberal influence in classrooms and campus organizations. FBI director J. Edgar Hoover never seemed to tire of warning about the Communist menace within schools and colleges. But many universities policed themselves, and had policies dating back to the 1930s that denied members of the Communist Party from employment and speaking appearances.[11] Just to be sure, virtually every state passed or attempted to pass laws during the late 1940s and 1950s banning the hiring of Communists and requiring loyalty oaths. Because politicians believed Communist teachers' primary allegiance was to the Soviet Union, rather than intellectual integrity or autonomy, they were viewed as unfit. Secrecy surrounding party membership was another strike against members. HUAC's first inquiry into subversive professors in 1953 ushered in a new era of scrutiny and created a consensus in the academy "that it had to respond to the congressional hearings. Once HUAC, SISS, or Senator McCarthy questioned a teacher and raised the issue of communism, the academic community rushed to investigate," wrote historian Ellen Schrecker.[12] Unpopular beliefs or untoward classroom behavior also inspired conservative attacks. William F. Buckley, a towering figure in the postwar critique of liberalism, published *God and Man at Yale* in 1951, a screed against the anti-Christian bias he detected at his alma mater, one of the nation's elite universities. Ten years later, E. Merrill Root, editor of the John Birch Society's *American Opinion*, wrote *Collectivism on the Campus: The Battle for the Mind in American Colleges*, a similarly scathing critique of the liberal professors, presidents, students, and textbooks that, he argued, had come to dominate academia.

In the post-*Brown* South, where schools and universities functioned as a different battleground—for the forces defending segregation against Negroes, outsiders, and the federal government—university self-policing as well as political investigations and other intrusions had become commonplace. In Mississippi, a minister's speaking invitation at Ole Miss was rescinded when his NAACP membership was revealed.[13] And in North Carolina, in the summer of 1963, the legislature passed "An Act to Regulate Visiting Speakers at State Supported Colleges and Universities." The speaker ban law prohibited appearances by anyone who had been a member of the Communist Party, who had advocated the overthrow of the state or federal constitution, or who had pleaded the Fifth Amendment in any legislative hearing on subversion or communism. Though it technically applied to all state-funded universities, the law was directed at the University of North Carolina at Chapel Hill, which had a long tradition of liberalism and had recently made headlines statewide as a source of student protests and civil rights demonstrations.[14] By 1963, three years of activism and increasingly violent white retaliation had led to a new awareness about students' transgressive political power. White students, participating in the demonstrations and joining civil rights groups in greater numbers than they had a few years earlier, caught the eye of the Johns Committee. These students were considered traitors to their race and to the South.

In the early 1960s, a young Jesse Helms railed against UNC rabble-rousers in his nightly editorials for Raleigh television station WRAL. The conservative editor of the school's newspaper, the *Daily Tar Heel*, Armistead Maupin (who later gained fame as a gay novelist), did the same. The object of their scorn was a group called the Student Peace Union, a local chapter of a national organization devoted to nuclear disarmament and civil rights founded in 1959. In March 1963 the group devoted its sole focus in the Raleigh–Durham–Chapel Hill area to civil rights, and students began a series of highly publicized demonstrations at segregated restaurants, hotels, and theaters. North Carolina legislators were furious. As one historian argues, they responded to this flouting of southern custom by concocting the speaker ban to "exercise direct political control over the university, some of whose students and faculty had been openly opposing the status quo."[15] The linking of racial subversion with communism had been hammered into the southern white consciousness, and now with Jesse Helms editorializing about it regularly on television across the state, the legislature seized on fears of universities as breeding grounds for liberal-inspired interracialism and moral corruption.

*   *   *

Demonstrations were gaining momentum in other southern cities as well, including St. Augustine, Florida, in 1963. Here the local NAACP Youth Council, headed by a young dentist named Robert Hayling, led the picketing, marches, and sit-ins against segregated restaurants and city facilities. Hayling was new to the area, having moved to St. Augustine three years earlier from Nashville. From the moment he joined the local NAACP, he was more impatient with the city's entrenched white leadership and its refusal to desegregate than were his native colleagues. His militancy may have given him greater appeal to the Youth Council, comprising mostly high school students and a handful of undergraduates. In early 1963, Hayling and other NAACP members wrote Vice President Lyndon Johnson urging him to cancel his upcoming visit to St. Augustine, and soon after contacted President Kennedy to demand that he quash a federal grant to help pay for the city's quadricentennial, to take place in 1965, because of discrimination in the city's schools, stores, and recreation facilities. Both requests were ignored, but the gathering storm attracted the attention of the FBI, which dispatched agents to St. Augustine to monitor growing racial unrest.[16]

The all-white city council proved equally uncooperative, refusing NAACP demands to desegregate public facilities, hire more African Americans in city government jobs, and establish a biracial committee. Meanwhile, fed up with the numerous death threats he had been receiving, Hayling further alienated St. Augustine whites when he angrily told reporters that he would not think twice about using violence if necessary for his own self-defense. Referring to the recent shooting in Jackson, Mississippi, he stated flatly, "We are not going to die like Medgar Evers."[17] Ten days later, sit-ins began. Mayor Joseph Shelley publicly condemned the protests as Communist-inspired, unknown assailants fired shots at Hayling's house, and white employers began firing or threatening to fire black workers who participated in any demonstrations. Undaunted, the Youth Council, the NAACP, and local black citizens continued picketing and sitting-in. From late summer into the fall, the demonstrations grew in size and the recriminations increased accordingly, not only from police, who displayed unnerving ease in manhandling black protesters, but also from various Ku Klux Klan groups and the John Birch Society, which had an active chapter in the city. By late October the Klan rallies and cross burnings had given way to gun violence on both sides. By the end of 1963, it was obvious that compromise would be impossible.[18]

In past years, the FLIC very likely would have sent R. J. Strickland to investigate racial agitators like Robert Hayling. But in the summer of 1963 the committee was in the middle of a dramatic shakeup, necessitated in part by the chief investigator's departure after his embarrassing botched hotel room sting operation, by the negative publicity surrounding USF, and by the judicial rebukes suffered earlier in the year. On June 24, Strickland submitted a letter of resignation in which he spoke of the honor of serving such "dignified, fair minded and impartial people."[19] That month Mark Hawes also resigned quietly. Neither was replaced until November, when Tallahassee attorney Leo Foster became chief counsel and Lawrence Rice, a former FBI agent, was hired as chief investigator. In addition, former Farris Bryant aide John Evans took over in a newly created position, staff director. Evans had also headed the Center for Cold War Education, a think tank devoted to teaching the evils of communism and the benefits of American democracy. Tallahassee representative Richard O. Mitchell, FLIC chairman during the 1963 to 1965 biennium, announced the new additions less than a week after President Kennedy's assassination. He used the national heartbreak to trumpet the committee's work, speaking as if it were responsible for protecting Floridians from dangerous characters like Lee Harvey Oswald: "We must find sound ways to combat those forces that produce warped minds and hatreds, and, unchecked, can lead to violence and tragedy. It is to that end we labor." Mitchell then indicated that his committee would be focusing on issues of "internal security" in the coming two years.[20]

*　　*　　*

During the Johns Committee's overhaul, its members sitting idly on the sideline, white college students—the very people the committee had long claimed to protect—were joining liberal groups and participating in public protests on behalf of racial equality. At Florida State, small numbers of white students formed chapters of the Young People's Socialist League and Students Act for Peace. They also joined in the picketing and sit-ins during the summer and fall of 1963 aimed at integrating the capital city's movie theaters, restaurants, swimming pools, and recreation facilities. The Congress of Racial Equality, which white students were also joining in larger numbers, organized the demonstrations, and hundreds of Florida A&M students, along with a small contingency from Florida State, participated. Police arrested and jailed them by the score. Many came face to face with the segregationist judge John Rudd. Also arrested and suspended from school were University of Florida students who, as members of the Student Group for Equal Rights, had come to Tallahassee to participate in the nonviolent direct action.[21] The Johns Committee did not investigate the demonstrations. At the very moment CORE picketed Tallahassee's movie theaters, two of R. J. Strickland's associates, investigators

Duane Barker and John Sullivan, were exposing homosexuals on Florida's east coast. Sullivan uncovered a former Marine and current teacher in Jacksonville who had been discharged from the military for making a pass at an officer, and Barker was compiling accusations against a number of instructors at Palm Beach Junior College.[22]

The upsurge in interracial civil rights activism during 1963 reflected both local circumstances and a national shift in priorities. In communities across the South, sit-ins and demonstrations had been taking place for nearly three years with little actual integration. Black patience wore thin, especially as white resistance stiffened. President John F. Kennedy had finally been convinced to push aggressively for civil rights legislation that would address, among other things, public accommodations. He had watched in horror along with the rest of the country as Martin Luther King and the SCLC led a youth march on May 2, in which Birmingham's black elementary and high school students were subjected to abuse by Bull Connor's police force, attacked by dogs, hurled against buildings, trees, and sidewalks by fire hoses, arrested, and jailed, all for demanding equal access to city facilities. Images from the melee, broadcast to national and international audiences, thrust Kennedy yet again into the awkward position of opposing Marxism in third world independence movements while deflecting criticism of the blight of segregation on his own nation's democracy. A week later, after the bombing of King's brother's house and the black-owned Gaston Motel in Birmingham, local blacks responded by attacking white police and firemen. The following month, Alabama governor George Wallace made his infamous and symbolic stand in the schoolhouse door to prevent two black students from entering the University of Alabama. Wallace's actions made for great political theater, but they infuriated Kennedy and persuaded the president to endorse a comprehensive civil rights bill.[23] In many Florida cities and towns, including Tallahassee, St. Petersburg, Tampa, Gainesville, Daytona Beach, and Jacksonville, the NAACP, newly unburdened from Johns Committee harassment and energized by college and high school students, launched a new series of demonstrations against segregated movie theaters, restaurants, beaches, and other public spaces.[24]

*   *   *

Early in 1964, the white South was on the brink of losing its grip on legalized segregation. Although some segregationists may have hoped at first that southerner Lyndon Johnson would stand with them, even Richard B. Russell, longtime Georgia senator and mentor to Johnson, knew that the Texan's sympathies and political sensibilities meant that Kennedy's civil rights bill would pass. More ominously for segregationists, blacks were shifting their attention to voter registration and legal challenges to disfranchisement across the region even as they stepped up sit-ins, picketing, and public school lawsuits. In Florida, the Johns Committee had reorganized, discontinuing its investigations of homosexual teachers and subversives within the NAACP. With John Evans, the staff director whose responsibilities tended almost entirely toward public relations, and Chairman Richard O. Mitchell as the committee's public face replacing Johns and Strickland, the FLIC began 1964 promising to investigate the matter of internal security. In light of the proliferation of student activist groups and escalating tensions in St. Augustine, the new committee believed this message would resonate with Floridians.

It is surprising, then, that the FLIC issued in March 1964 what most people viewed as a bizarre report on the threat of homosexuality. Releasing the report may have been one of the committee's few options. It could not legally interfere with the NAACP's announced voter registration drive that began in January, seeking to add 50,000 new names to the nearly 220,000 registered black voters in the state. The committee had begun recruiting informants at the University of Florida and Florida State University to infiltrate the Young People's Socialist League, the Liberal Forum, and Students Act for Peace, but it would take time to gather enough "detailed information on some of the key links in these organizations" to propose any legislative action. And Evans coordinated FLIC meetings with members of various antisubversive groups that spring, including HUAC, the Alabama Legislative Commission to Keep the Peace, and California's Senate Investigating Committee on Education.[25]

In addition, after the Florida Supreme Court ruling prohibited the Florida Department of Education from using evidence gathered by the FLIC, the committee simply stopped gathering the evidence about gay and lesbian teachers. But as John Evans told state superintendent of education Thomas Bailey in February, the committee was eager to share "information in our files" about "upwards of a hundred employees" of the state's public schools. He also impressed upon Bailey the need for the department to establish its own investigatory arm to "provide the nearly full-time attention to this problem that its gravity demands." Bailey responded by pointing out that the legislature had passed the Professional Practices Act in 1963, which among other things established the Professional Practices Commission within the Florida Education Association to investigate any charges against Florida teachers and recommend action to the Department of Education. He urged Evans to be patient and to give the new commission time to get on its feet.[26] Like the Board of Control's adoption of a morals policy that reflected the Johns Committee's mission while handing over investigatory and regulatory control to another government body, the Department of Education was now turning to the state's professional educators' organization to self-police their ranks to keep homosexuals out of Florida's schools.

The FLIC's plans for a report on the dangers of homosexuality had been in the works since the statewide educational conferences on pornography and homosexuality in 1961–62. At one Florida Children's Commission advisory committee meeting in January 1962, a participant had recommended educating the public by disseminating an informational pamphlet on the problem.[27] Two months later, the FCC announced in a press release that it had received suggestions from an undisclosed "committee on community education" that "all known information on the subject be compiled."[28] In June 1962, the Research Committee in Sexual Deviance, a subcommittee of Governor Bryant's Advisory Committee on Homosexuality, concluded that a "public education effort employing the so-called 'shock technique' may be needed immediately [if] the public is to be stimulated to want to do something about" homosexuality and pornography.[29]

Soon after his hiring as the FLIC staff director, John Evans began defending past campaigns and emphasizing the focus on creating new legislation. He also promised at the beginning of his tenure that the Johns Committee would produce "a definitive report, factual in nature and complete in its descriptions, of the relationship of homosexuality to sound citizenship in our state." And in direct contradiction to the ruling of the Florida Supreme Court in the Pinellas County teachers' case, he reassured Floridians that "investigative leads in the Committee's files and which came to its attention were promptly and properly followed up by appropriate agencies." In public appearances, press releases, and personal correspondence, Evans tried to convince audiences that this new and improved committee was no longer focused on rounding up gays and lesbians, but was still dedicated to investigating "organizations and individuals which can be broadly termed 'subversive.'"[30]

In January 1964 the committee completed its report, which was, according to one anonymous legislator, penned by Duane Barker. Members met at the end of the month to discuss how best to present their findings. State senator Robert Williams from Graceville, a small town near the Alabama line, proposed that distribution of the forty-four-page booklet be limited to "members of the Legislature, law enforcement officials, educators, members of the press, and to such groups as parent-teacher associations, city police departments, and others properly concerned." Johns seconded the motion.[31]

Homosexuality and Citizenship in Florida, published in March 1964, was supposed to be the Johns Committee's crowning glory, the culmination of years of painstaking interrogations, surveillance, and collecting informants' secrets. But the FLIC drastically overestimated the public's tolerance for being scared straight. Upon opening the swirling lavender cover, the reader was greeted by a black and white photograph of two men, naked to the waist, embracing and kissing on the mouth. On the next page appeared a preface explaining the importance of the report to "every parent and every individual concerned with the moral climate of the state," who "should be aware of the rise in homosexual activity noted here." The main text began on page 3, positioned next to a full-page photograph—"taken from a homosexual's collection"—of a teenage boy, clad only in a g-string, bound with ropes to a latticework door. As the caption explained, "The use of bindings is frequent in artwork of this nature" and "an apparently strong stimulant to the deviate."[32] Two other pictures were included in the report. One, on the opposite page from the "Glossary of Homosexual Terms and Deviate Acts," showed a man in a public restroom receiving oral sex from another man in the adjoining stall. The doors to both stalls had been removed, to no effect. His hips pressed against the partition, his face turned toward the camera but obscured by a black rectangle to conceal his identity, he wore a plaid shirt with the short sleeves rolled up. The man performing oral sex was seated on the toilet. The last image, placed next to the "Bibliography on Sexual Deviations," showed a series of images of a preadolescent boy in various poses—most of them resembling the popular muscle magazines of the day—and stages of undress. There was no frontal nudity, but in six of the twenty photographs the youth had his back to the camera, bare-bottomed. In the rest he wore a towel or a bathing suit. In all of them, he smiled.[33]

These illustrations demonstrated what committee members had been telling Floridians for years: Homosexuals coveted children, they took and traded dirty pictures, and they had anonymous sex in public places. This exposé of homosexuality was bolstered not only by the report's frequent references to "experts" and "authorities" or the hefty bibliography but also by the most inflammatory photographic evidence, intended to instill fear. Indeed, without these pictures it is difficult to imagine the report causing as much of a stir. To be sure, it discussed sex frankly and contained a glossary of gay terminology that would certainly have thrown 1964 audiences for a loop. Who knew, or perhaps needed to know, that "pygmalionism" (the "sexual desire for a statue or statues") was a problem at all, much less one related to homosexuality? Or that a "dinge queen" was a Negro homosexual, "sea food" referred to homosexuals in the navy, and "chicken" was slang for an extremely young homosexual?

A blurb printed on the back of the pamphlet offered individual copies for sale at twenty-five cents apiece. But there was considerable confusion about who constituted "properly concerned" or "properly qualified" persons invited to order their own copies of the booklet. The uncertainty was only heightened by a piece in the New Republic that claimed, "Two thousand books were printed at a cost of $720. The first thousand were sent off to legislators, newspapers, and other 'key' people, but anyone who sends the committee 25 cents can get one."[34] Despite committee members' claims that they had intended all along for the report to make it only into the hands of those with a vested interest in youth and education, the ambiguous statement on the back of the pamphlet, coupled with national publicity about the shocking report, led untold numbers of people from Florida and around the country to mail their quarters and their requests. The Dade County State Attorney threatened legal action to prevent the sale of the report and called it obscene.[35]

In the opening pages committee members established their credentials as authorities by emphasizing their impartiality and reliance upon "officials of Florida's mental health program, law enforcement agencies and courts," and their "extensive study of the many and divergent publications, both scientific and popular, in the field" to formulate "recommendations for effective recognition by the state of its present and potential bearing on the quality of citizenship in Florida." First, the report maintained that homosexuals constitute "a well organized society," including everything from separate customs to special meeting places and "national organizations through which articulate homosexuals seek recognition of their condition as a proper part of our culture and morals."[36] The report represented homosexuals as a secretive, organized underground community whose political agenda aimed at making their abnormality normal in the eyes of American culture.

The idea that so-called perverts sought acceptance of their way of life as "normal" was central to postwar opposition to pornography and obscenity. The Cincinnati-based Citizens for Decent Literature focused on the issue in its 1964 film *Perversion for Profit*, which was similar in tone and content to *Homosexuality and Citizenship in Florida*. Charles Keating founded CDL in the mid-1950s with the goal of restricting or eliminating altogether obscene paperback books, magazines, and tabloids. The organization grew rapidly in the early 1960s, claiming three hundred chapters across the country by 1965. Local chapters would send members out into the community—"PTAs, fraternal orders, women's clubs"—to enlighten them about the harm caused by this material. "After we had described the problem," explained one CDL member, "we'd pass around to the audience a typical group of pornographic publications. Invariably, everybody would be shocked."[37] And that shock would turn to action, as newly informed citizens wrote angry letters, joined the organization, or took other steps to try to clean up their communities' newsstands. In *Perversion for Profit*, narrator George Putnam, a popular news anchor in Los Angeles and later a conservative talk radio host, warned that obscene reading material enticed youth to "enter the world of homosexuals, lesbians, sadists, masochists and other sex deviates." Putnam held a placard with a picture of a gigantic octopus, tentacles outstretched, reaching into every corner of a map of the United States. As the camera zoomed in on the sinister image, the narrator intoned, "Here is the most vicious, the most insidious feature of these publications: they constantly portray abnormal sexual behavior as being normal; they glorify unnatural sex acts; they tell youngsters that it's smart, it's thrilling, it provides kicks to be a homosexual, a sadist, and every other kind of deviate." And, like Communists, they were insidious and sneaky, tricking young people into perversion gradually, while making this deviance appear perfectly normal, harmless, and downright fun. Girlie magazines that emphasized women's buttocks "appeal to the sodomist." Too many images of breasts turned healthy male appreciation into "a fetish." A normal heterosexual man who enjoys men's muscle magazines, Putnam announced, would eventually become perverted.[38]

Homosexuality and Citizenship in Florida, much like the regulations excluding gays and lesbians from government employment and military service, defined homosexuals as sexually insatiable and morally bankrupt. The danger of allowing gays to serve as teachers, according to the report, was their corrupting influence on children. They spent their time "cruising," defined as "driving or walking through areas where they believe they might find 'trade,' individuals, not necessarily homosexual, who will serve as passive partners in the performance of homosexual acts." Many of them "take their sex where they find it, be it in a rest room of a park or other public place; a car, be it moving or parked; a residence or a hotel room." Homosexual desire for youth runs through the entire report. In some places the author was careful to distinguish between the child molester—who "attacks, but seldom kills or physically cripples his victim"—and the homosexual, who "prefers to reach out for the child at the time of normal sexual awakening and to conduct a psychological preliminary to the physical contact. The homosexual's goal and part of his satisfaction is to 'bring over' the young person, to hook him for homosexuality." In perhaps the most concise summary of the post–World War II mainstream articulation of homosexuality, the report noted that it is "unique among the sexual assaults" because "the person affected by the practicing homosexual is first a victim, then an accomplice, and finally by himself a perpetrator of homosexual acts."[39]

The outcry was immediate. Some, like the *New Republic,* dismissed it out of hand as silly and alarmist and questioned the logic behind hunting Communists and homosexuals together: "Possibly the two deviations have become confused in the committee's collective mind."[40] Bill Baggs, editor of the *Miami News,* racial moderate, and close friend to the *Atlanta Constitution's* Ralph McGill and *Arkansas Gazette* editor Harry Ashmore, mocked the Johns Committee's gross miscalculation, writing to Ashmore, "The author of the tract did such a splendid job in No. 1, Vol. 1, Florida Homo, that we shall never see No. 2." He concluded sarcastically, "This is but another testimonial to the fact that Florida is not afraid to think new thoughts and explore new ranges. In short, we are at least not stuffy."[41] A feature article on "Homosexuality in America" in *Life* magazine included the FLIC and its "irresponsible" report, albeit in the context of national debates and attitudes about homosexuality.[42]

Critics included a handful of self-identified homosexuals. Hal Call, a leader in the San Francisco–based homophile group the Mattachine Society, in an open letter noted the report's many flaws—starting with its failure to achieve its primary goal, which was to document the extent of homosexual infiltration of state agencies. Call pointed out that the committee quoted no authorities, despite the substantial bibliography, and offered no proof that homosexuals recruited the young, spread venereal disease, or were "a factor in other forms of sexual deviations, in major crime occurrences, and in security matters." He concluded by observing, "Only about one-third of the material in the section on Florida laws has anything whatsoever to do with homosexuality" and "the remaining two-thirds was included in order to associate homosexuality with everything else that is considered abnormal or arouses emotional responses."[43] Some critics proved more diplomatic. One wrote, "As one of these 'degenerates,' I cannot but be somewhat concerned as to the fate of these now-existing 60,000 [homosexuals in Florida], once public sentiment is aroused . . . for I am not the 'queer' the general public has in mind, and I cannot help feeling that there must be thousands (yes, in addition to that 60,000 figure) who would suffer perhaps unreasonably in a great purge for the common weal."[44] One man from Ft. Lauderdale composed a scathing letter to Chairman Richard Mitchell, telling him, "I personally hope that you and every member of your infamous legislative investigating committee, and your staff henchman, John Evans, get just what you deserve—to rot in hell." He then asked, "How does it feel to be on the other side of the fence . . . to be getting a royal fucking instead of giving one?" The postscript was no less biting: "Your present ill-fame only serves to prove that you and your crowd have the dirtiest minds in the whole state."[45] Finally, another man scolded the Johns Committee for casting aspersions against all homosexuals: "Let me assure you there are thousands upon thousands of us right here in Florida who live sane and sensible lives. None of my friends would hardly know what one of your 'glory holes' is much less would we indulge in such degradation."[46]

Most people who commented publicly condemned the report for its style—the lurid photographs and bizarre glossary—but not the message. As a *Tallahassee Democrat* editorial put it, although the report was "obscene" and "shocking," and the "subject it treats is offensive," it is "a real subject that we have discussed too long behind the backs of our hands without recognizing the scope and implications of the pernicious problem it presents. This booklet contains information . . . that has only recently begun to dawn on the opened minds of some editors and reporters who like to think they are world-wise." Even on the question of the photographs, the editors remarked that they "have seen some of the pictures the committee has had before it during its investigation, and we'd say the ones it published were among the least objectionable." Finally, the editorial warned readers not to dismiss the pamphlet or the committee out of hand, or at the expense of gleaning a valuable lesson from the report, because there "might be something in it that will help you understand a public problem, or head off a family tragedy."[47]

A law professor at the University of Michigan, Hobart Coffey, had a similar reaction. Having requested and received a copy of *Homosexuality and Citizenship in Florida*, Coffey shared his reactions with Evans. Like others, he found the pictures distasteful and the glossary odd. The former, he wrote, did not "add much to the report and they do furnish ammunition to political enemies, smart-aleck journalists and the usual carping critics who pop up on all occasions." As for the list of slang terms, Coffey likened them to "thieves' cant, prisoners' jargon, or teen-agers' language." He concluded that the FLIC should be "praised rather than condemned for undertaking a study of this problem. We get nowhere by sweeping our problems under the rug."[48] *Confidential* published an alarmist article about the report, "Perverts Under the Palms," warning, "Don't shrug off this story! What is happening in Florida can happen in your state—and to your kids!" The article's introduction set the tone: "Florida has a sun-tanned sex problem. A perverted one. It seems all the fruit the Sunshine State raises is not confined to the grove."[49]

Some Floridians, everyday citizens who never actually saw the report, shared the view that, despite its flaws, its message was important and should be heard amid the cries of obscenity. Governor Farris Bryant told reporters, "I impute good motives in disseminating information on such bad practices that have grown up in Florida."[50] Most people formed their opinions on the basis of what the media said about the report, and they claimed to believe that homosexuality was indeed on the rise and parents needed to learn the facts to protect their children. A father from Hollywood, Florida, whose son was entering college, wrote that "the information as imparted in the booklet will be invaluable, in my guidance and counseling of my son, in his new environment, in this crucial period of his life." A Key West resident praised the committee for "enlightening both the public and officials on this subject which has been too hush-hush for many years, and which is now internationally recognized and dealt with in a much more sane fashion than in days past." A woman from Miami exclaimed, "It is about time some of our Legislators were shocked about the growing homosexuals in our community. I admire you very much for publishing this booklet and I do hope it will shock our State Legislate [*sic*] into making some new and stiff laws to control these sex deviates." A mother of five and grandmother of ten wrote to John Evans urging him to "do something about it before many of our young people are ruined and little children are killed as a result of these perverts being loose in our society."[51]

Evans spoke before the Florida Federation of Women's Clubs defending the report, gave numerous interviews, and responded to scores of letters from both opponents and supporters. He assured a Miami judge, in a rote recitation of the party line, that *Homosexuality and Citizenship in Florida* was "a definitive report, factual in nature and complete in its descriptions, of the relationship of homosexuality to sound citizenship in our state." He explained that the committee had formulated a strict policy about limiting distribution to specific groups—an explanation that never accounted for the note on the back cover stating the individual copies were available for twenty-five cents each—claiming, "The booklet has received wide use among the organizations for which it was intended, and if the reports that come back to us are any indication, it has made a significant contribution to better understanding and handling of the problem of homosexuality around the state."[52]

* * *

Two weeks before the report was released, the Southern Christian Leadership Conference held its annual meeting in Orlando. Black leaders from St. Augustine traveled there to ask King's advisers for his help in resuscitating their city's flagging integration movement. After C. T. Vivian visited the city and saw firsthand the influence of the Klan, the John Birch Society, and other segregationists within city government and law enforcement, as well as the palpable racial disquiet that brooded in the muggy St. Augustine air, he recommended that the SCLC launch a campaign there. Recognizing the potential for attracting national attention to the upcoming quadricentennial just as the civil rights bill was being debated in Congress, King agreed. He and the SCLC also decided to invite white New

England college students and clergy to come to St. Augustine during the Easter weekend and spring break and participate in the planned marches, sit-ins, and other demonstrations. On Easter Sunday, St. Augustine police arrested Mary Peabody, mother of Massachusetts governor Endicott Peabody. She spent twenty-four hours in jail after sitting down to a meal at the Ponce de Leon Motor Lodge restaurant with an integrated group. It was exactly the lightning rod the movement had sought. Upon her release from jail, Peabody appeared on NBC's *Today* show and described the city's stubborn segregation in unflattering terms. City officials fumed, and Governor Bryant received letters from around the country, many of them sympathetic to the city and state that had been "invaded" by outside agitators. One Salt Lake City man wrote sarcastically to Peabody and Bryant, "There should be something which a lady of your stature could do to keep from contributing to an already very serious situation in the South. There must be some bridge games with which you could occupy yourself up in Massachusetts, if you are unable to find anything constructive to do."[53]

The SCLC's first venture into St. Augustine lasted two weeks, and soon after activists departed, the local movement floundered. The organization announced that it would return to see the campaign through to the end this time, and on May 26 the second round of demonstrations began. This time it turned violent. Whites threw bricks, rocks, and whatever was handy at the black marchers who walked through downtown St. Augustine nightly. On a few occasions they beat up cameramen and demonstrators and shot at and set afire King's rental beachfront cottage—whose address the *St. Augustine Record* had published. Unshakeable city leaders, represented by Mayor Joseph Shelley, would not consider activists' demands that the city add a handful of black police officers, firefighters, and clerical workers. An even greater sticking point was the creation of a biracial committee, which Shelley refused to appoint. The mayor had the support of most St. Augustine whites, whose numbers were increased by Klan groups from around the state as well as Georgia and Alabama.[54]

Farris Bryant was unable to stop the nighttime marches, which had become a magnet for violence during the summer of 1964, as had the wade-ins at local beaches and a demonstration at a motel swimming pool. When a handful of African Americans jumped into the pool at Monson's Motor Lodge, the proprietor ran to a storage closet to pull out what he claimed was a container of acid. He began pouring, and the crowd dispersed, but not before one man was physically assaulted in the swimming pool by a police officer. After thirty days of these kinds of protests, segregationists were becoming more brazen in their attacks and police more vicious in their punishment, and the marchers ever wearier. On July 2, when President Johnson signed the Civil Rights Act into law, King and the SCLC called off the demonstrations. But white resistance and resentment did not end with their departure, and many white businesses quickly returned to an aggressive de facto segregation.[55]

Racial tensions in the city were made worse by the ongoing public presence of Klan groups and right-wing extremists such as J. B. Stoner, Connie Lynch, and Holstead "Hoss" Manucy, who regularly led counterdemonstrations and rallies and seized every opportunity to condemn Communists and "nigger lovers." Manucy was the head of the Ancient City Gun Club, a white supremacist group that overlapped in membership with the Klan and collaborated in harassing civil rights demonstrators. In August 1964 *Time* magazine reported that he and his men had been enjoined from picketing in front of more than a dozen motels and restaurants with signs reading "Niggers Eat Here. Would You?" White proprietors reported that they had been cowed into resegregating their establishments. St. Augustine's black citizens, emboldened by the Civil Rights Act, did not hesitate to take them to court.[56] Although Manucy was from a small town north of St. Augustine, Stoner and Lynch were itinerant segregationist activists who had devoted the past several years to visiting civil rights hotspots and organizing white resistance in local communities. J. B. Stoner had served as the chairman of the anti-Semitic, segregationist, anti-Communist, and nativist National States' Rights Party since the group's founding in 1958. Rev. Charles Conley "Connie" Lynch was a self-styled fundamentalist preacher whose career consisted of denouncing race mixing and godless communism. In St. Augustine, the three received almost daily press coverage in their attacks against the civil rights "invasion," and their inflammatory words helped set the tone for the battle over integration.

The eyes of the nation were on the small historic Florida city that lay two hundred miles from the state capital, and on the man viewed by most segregationists as the movement's most notorious subversive. The assistant special counsel on civil rights under Kennedy and Johnson, Lee White, had been dispatched to the city in the spring of 1964 to keep Johnson apprised of the situation. And as the crisis escalated over the summer,

Farris Bryant ordered hundreds of special police officers and highway patrolmen into St. Augustine. Local police and the St. John's County Sheriff's
Office were also monitoring every move made by civil rights activists.

FBI agents from nearby Jacksonville were there to keep tabs on both
sides as well. Since the March on Washington the previous August, the
bureau had stepped up its campaign to discredit the movement in general, and King in particular, as Communist-tainted. The historian Kenneth O'Reilly maintains that the massive demonstration in the nation's
capital marked a critical turning point in the FBI's treatment of King and
civil rights activists. He cites J. Edgar Hoover's "belief that blacks had
gone too far with their protests and now posed an imminent threat to
the established order" and his inability to contain the civil rights movement through "a relatively passive surveillance policy on the intelligence
front."[57] O'Reilly went on to document the full-scale assault by the FBI
on King's private life and associations, reflecting both the pragmatism
of a social conservative and a highly personal racist, sexualized animosity. But the connections drawn between perversion and subversion were
not simply the product of one man's imagination. By 1963, they had been
etched into the political landscape. O'Reilly claims that the "ease with
which the FBI slid from the communist issue to the morality issue indicates that the director and his aides were looking for something—anything—that might work to discredit King." But it indicates much more,
namely, that the Cold War had shaped ways of thinking about political
enemies as morally degenerate and sexually perverse. Coupled with enduring notions of black sexual licentiousness, the FBI's search was neither
desperate nor grasping.[58] Hoover's targeting of King's extramarital affairs
was more than a convenient ploy or a cheap attempt at character defama-
tion. It was also an expression of an anti-Communist ethos that equated
or linked—and sometimes did both—sexual immorality with radicalism
and un-Americanism.

In mid-August 1964, the FBI sent out copies of an intelligence analysis
report on "communist plans" for the upcoming St. Augustine march to
more than forty government offices. Agents identified eight close associates of King and the SCLC as having Communist links, and in the fall
of 1963, Hoover ordered a wiretap on King's home and office in Atlanta
and compiled voluminous reports on the civil rights leader's extramarital
affairs and contacts with accused subversives such as Stanley Levinson,
Jack O'Dell, and Bayard Rustin, who was further demonized for being a

homosexual. Hoover, who in one infamous memo called King a "tomcat," increasingly criticized the civil rights movement for attracting "Communists and moral degenerates."[59] And in the summer of 1964 the FBI had followed King to St. Augustine. Mayor Joseph Shelley, citing J. Edgar Hoover in a speech to a local civic club, reported on "how deeply the civil rights movement has become involved with communism. A lot of people think what has happened in St. Augustine in the past year is a simple matter of segregation and integration," but "that's just a coverup, just a pattern of what is happening all over the United States. It is part of an American revolution."[60]

Instead of sending investigators or hiring informants, the FLIC issued a fifteen-page account of J. B. Stoner, Connie Lynch, and their organization, the National States' Rights Party. Perhaps in an attempt at fair-mindedness, John Evans launched a public campaign to discredit the NSRP and to keep its candidates off the ballot in Florida for the 1964 election. He and the committee vice chairman told reporters that the men were "hawkers of hate" who had stirred up racial animosities in St. Augustine, and that their behavior was inimical to wholesome citizenship. The public statement had little effect, other than angering Stoner, who in turn charged that the Johns Committee "failed to place any blame whatever on Martin Luther King and the NAACP for the trouble that occurred in St. Augustine."[61] Although Stoner was a fringe character and easy to dismiss, his public taunts surely bothered Evans and the rest of the committee, who would never have dreamed of sympathizing with Martin Luther King.

*　　*　　*

Rather than actually insert themselves into the integration battles raging in St. Augustine, committee members continued to observe Florida's white university students, who were joining various liberal causes, chiefly civil rights, in growing numbers. In Gainesville, the Student Group for Equal Rights (SGER) took part in sit-ins and picketing at drugstores, restaurants, and movie theaters beginning in the summer of 1963. One member, anthropology graduate student Dan Harmeling, also attended regional SNCC meetings and was a founding member of the Southern Student Organizing Committee (SSOC), an offshoot of SNCC founded in 1964 and intended to mobilize white support for the civil rights movement. One of R. J. Strickland's last duties on behalf of the committee in July 1963, after he had resigned, was to confront SGER picketers in an attempt to coerce them into abandoning their protests, proving that some habits do die hard.[62] The Johns Committee files on SGER consisted mostly of the group's literature and newspaper clippings. At the same time, in Tallahassee, Board of Control member Charles Forman accused Florida State University president Gordon Blackwell of coddling the Young People's Socialist League, a subversive group that showed a "communist pattern." Because Blackwell had refused to ban the group (although he did try to "restrict" its activities), Forman claimed that he had fostered an "ultra-liberal" attitude on campus. At the end of July, Blackwell resigned to become the president of Furman University.[63] The issue became a running theme in the governor's race, as segregationist Jacksonville mayor Haydon Burns blustered on the campaign trail about the number of "pinks and commies" in the state's universities.[64] He went on to win the election.

The FLIC also spent the summer of 1964 monitoring a group of peace activists who, under the auspices of the Committee for Nonviolent Action (CNVA), were journeying from Canada to Cuba in support of nuclear disarmament. The CNVA was founded in 1958, emerging from a loosely organized series of protests against nuclear testing in the Nevada desert. Early sponsors included the War Resisters League and the Women's International League for Peace and Freedom, and members included such well-known pacifists as A. J. Muste, Bayard Rustin, Barbara Deming, and Albert Bigelow. During the late 1950s and early 1960s CNVA activists picketed the White House, sailed into restricted Pacific waters where the United States conducted nuclear tests, and protested against the construction of Polaris nuclear submarines. It was one of several organizations that made up a reinvigorated peace movement in the mid to late 1950s, spurred by growing fears of nuclear testing, the dangers of nuclear fallout, and Soviet expansion, and influenced by Gandhi's nonviolent revolution in India as well as the American civil rights movement's use of Gandhian tactics at home. The most visible of these was the Committee for a Sane Nuclear Policy (SANE), founded in 1957. SANE's membership grew in state and local chapters concentrated largely in the cities of the Northeast, Midwest, and western United States. Although by the early 1960s it was splintering along tactical lines—pacifists and direct-action radicals—the group organized many high-profile marches and rallies against nuclear testing and arms proliferation.[65]

In 1960 the CNVA had launched a six-thousand-mile, eleven-month "Walk for Peace" from San Francisco to Moscow. The group's second walk for peace began in the spring of 1963, originating in Quebec City and concluding prematurely in Miami. (U.S. government travel restrictions made it impossible for them to reach their original destination, Guantánamo Bay, Cuba.) In September 1963, as the marchers prepared to venture below the Mason-Dixon Line, the CNVA Walk Team issued guidelines stressing the need for propriety in their public behavior—most important among them, prohibiting drug use, advising limited and discreet alcohol consumption, and urging that "displays of affection" be kept within "the bounds of good taste."[66] The admonition proved irrelevant; the interracial male and female peace walkers could have been as decorous as Puritans and many conservative white southerners still would have loathed them. In Georgia, the group met with cattle prods, harassment, and imprisonment in Macon, Griffin, and Albany in late 1963 and early 1964. The peace walkers were in Macon when Kennedy was assassinated, and they suspended all protests and traveled to Atlanta, with the intention of resuming after the funeral. But police there "ordered them to leave the city" and threatened them with arrest if they stayed or "in the event of any demonstration."[67]

White southern conservatives saw the CNVA as a group of integrationist beatniks, and were infuriated as they monitored the march though their region. As A. J. Muste put it, the "fact that white girls and Negro men walked side by side tended, for many Southerners, to blot out everything else." He also noted that in Georgia, "the fact that 'peace' people, 'peaceniks' were beaten and reacted nonviolently" established "a link of common action and suffering that has made the 'cause' of peace and the 'cause' of civil rights one in a way that could hardly have been accomplished otherwise."[68]

Florida was no exception, especially since the group was slated to depart from Miami to reach Castro's Cuba. In 1964, the trek became an obsession for the Johns Committee, whose members watched as the civil rights movement exploded and St. Augustine became a flashpoint during the summer, until news of the violence there was supplanted by the story of three civil rights workers who had disappeared in Philadelphia, Mississippi. The first sign of trouble for Florida came with the news that ten FSU students, members of Students Act for Peace (SAP), had traveled to Albany to pressure officials there to release jailed CNVA walkers. When Chief Pritchett released the walkers, the Florida State delegation drove them to Koinonia Farm, the interracial Christian community in nearby

Americus. Steve Baum, the head of the Florida State University chapter of SAP, told the student newspaper, the *Florida Flambeau*, that the marchers had decided to alter their Florida route to go through Tallahassee and Gainesville, the state's most important college towns and sites of frequent demonstrations.[69]

The Johns Committee tabulated the racial and gender breakdown of the CNVA marchers and followed their southward progress daily. In one report, the committee noted that there were thirteen white males, five white females, three "colored" males, and three who were unidentified. From diverse backgrounds—San Francisco and Portland, Boulder and Chicago, Atlanta and Washington, D.C.—the marchers had attended or were attending some of the nation's best universities: Massachusetts Institute of Technology, Stanford, Rutgers, Wisconsin, Oberlin, and Morehouse. Most of them had also been active in the civil rights movement.[70] Although the CNVA had its share of detractors, Florida law enforcement officials made no attempt to arrest or otherwise pester the walkers. The FLIC reported in April, however, that two of the Negro marchers visited the apartment of two white women when the group reached Jacksonville. The foursome then went to Jacksonville Beach, "where they camped on a blanket and proceeded to engage in some heavy petting." When a crowd started gathering, police escorted the four off the beach. A few miles down the road, "several car loads of whites swooped down on the car carrying the Peace Marchers, stoned out its windows, shot out its tires and caused it to crash."[71] While in Jacksonville, the CNVA held demonstrations at three different naval bases, the Naval Air Station, Mayport, and Cecil Field. Some of the marchers stayed with members of the Florida Council on Human Relations, but the local branch of the NAACP made it clear that it would have nothing to do with the group because of its support for Cuba.[72]

After making protest stops at the Cape Kennedy Space Center and Patrick Air Force Base just south of Cocoa Beach, at the end of May the peace walkers arrived in Miami, where angry Cuban exiles shattered the relative calm that had surrounded the march thus far in Florida. The first assault on the marchers occurred as the group walked through Miami Beach, when people from passing cars began splattering them with red paint, spitting on them, and calling them "dirty Communists." The walk concluded with an antiwar demonstration at Bayfront Park, where again Cubans hurled insults at the protesters and ripped picket signs and pamphlets from their hands as the march coordinator called for peace between the U.S. and Cuban governments. The riot police stepped in just as the two opposing sides began trying to outsing each other, the exiles belting out the Cuban national anthem and the peace walkers breaking into choruses of "We Shall Overcome."[73] The CNVA elicited a similar outcry from Cubans and local police when they reached Key West in late June. This time they were arrested, however, and spent two days in the city jail.

Some marchers stayed behind to set up a permanent CNVA chapter in Miami. Steve Baum, the Florida State student, became a full-time worker there, serving as a coordinator. The Johns Committee enlisted a University of Miami student to infiltrate meetings and gather CNVA literature, just as it had relied on members of Young Americans for Freedom to spy on the Student Group for Equal Rights at the University of Florida. The surveillance ultimately accomplished little of substance, but it is worth noting that the Johns Committee continued to view civil rights and peace advocacy in the first half of the 1960s as subversive. As for the Quebec to Guantánamo Peace Walk, the marchers made several unsuccessful attempts to sail their boat, the *Spirit of Freedom*, to Cuba. Their final try, on October 27, 1964, landed them in jail.[74]

In September 1964, while keeping a watchful eye on the peace marchers in south Florida and student activists at FSU and UF, Johns Committee member George Stallings criticized Farris Bryant for caving in to the integrationists in St. Augustine and allegedly creating a biracial committee, even though Bryant refused to name a single member of the committee and it never actually met. The FLIC, Stallings said, had decided to investigate Bryant's handling of the entire crisis in St. Augustine. Rumormongers around Tallahassee whispered that the committee wanted to "use the St. Augustine investigation to build up sentiment in the state for presidential nominee Barry Goldwater." Many lifelong conservative Democrats, disappointed over their national party's liberalism, defected to the Republican ticket in the 1964 election. Goldwater, in part because of his vote against the Civil Rights Act, won five Deep South states and lost by two points in Florida.

By this time, staff director John Evans and investigator Lawrence Rice had resigned from the Johns Committee, claiming a difference of opinion about tactics and targets. Neither man felt entirely comfortable investigating the governor and his special police force in St. Augustine. They were also concerned that some of the committee members, namely, Charley

Johns and Pinellas County representative Bill Young, were meeting in secret, away from the staff, and initiating their own investigations.[75] At the end of September, however, with less than six months remaining before the next legislative session, Johns and Vice Chairman Robert Williams also resigned, frustrated by the committee's plummeting reputation, the absence of a functioning staff, and lack of a clear-cut target. Those left standing, Stallings, Young, Chairman Richard O. Mitchell (who had been sidelined by poor health for much of the past year), Bill Owens, and Leo Jones, refused to see the committee disbanded. "I disagree that there isn't much that could be accomplished," said George Stallings. Johns, on the other hand, told reporters that he probably ought to "close the office, lock up the records and save the taxpayers of Florida the remainder of the $155,000 appropriation."[76] That did not happen, and the remaining members spent the next several months putting together the promised report on St. Augustine. In October, just a month after Charley Johns left the antisubversive committee that had become synonymous with his name, Walter Jenkins, chief adviser to Lyndon Johnson, was apprehended in the men's room of a Washington, D.C., YMCA and charged with indecent exposure, caught by the police who had had the bathroom under surveillance.[77]

*   *   *

The FLIC released its final report, *Racial and Civil Disorders in St. Augustine*, in February 1965. Just as *Homosexuality and Citizenship in Florida* reinforced Cold War ideas about sexual deviance, so too did this report articulate segregationists' obsessions with communism, sex, and the outside agitator. The Johns Committee had stepped out on a limb with one report that told the public more than it seemingly cared to know about perversion. Now it retreated to more familiar representations that would be less shocking: black men as oversexed and a local movement exhorted to violence and disorder by trouble-making Communist outsiders.

Published almost six months after the events it described, *Racial and Civil Disorders in St. Augustine* comprised little more than a synopsis of the way race relations, allegedly amicable "for two centuries," rapidly deteriorated when newcomer Robert Hayling began advocating armed self-defense and when King and the SCLC entered the town early in the summer of 1964. In retelling the story of the lunch counter sit-ins, the report focused on the "juveniles" and "teenagers" who carried them out. "When picketing and other forms of harassment continued," it stated, "those under seventeen were escorted home and their parents summoned to juvenile court." This subtle message about the criminality of blacks steadfastly refused to acknowledge nonviolent sit-ins as a legitimate form of protest and labeled them criminal harassment. The next paragraph, detailing episodes of interracial violence, did not mention white shootings, physical assaults, bombings, or arson. Instead it highlighted "threatening or obscene telephone calls to white women" and the case of a white woman being "robbed and raped at knifepoint by an unidentified Negro." The report addressed the Klan's presence in the city later, with the disclaimer that "very few of them could be identified as citizens of St. Augustine."[78]

The next section dealt at some length with the SCLC's Florida Spring Project, which drew college students from New England to St. Augustine to participate in civil disobedience. When the mother of the Massachusetts governor arrived to join the sit-ins, she, and the city of St. Augustine, garnered the national publicity the movement sought. In the Johns Committee report, this was framed as an explicitly subversive strategy: "The tactic of inducing socially prominent and elderly ladies to act as 'cats paws' in order to win sympathy and wide publicity has long been a Communist and radical technique." Throughout the twenty-four pages that made up the main body of the report, the authors regularly inserted a sentence, always italicized for emphasis, about how "*most St. Augustine Negroes are not taking part in the movement*" or that participants had to be "*brought in from other states.*" In tallying arrest figures, the report emphasized that many "*were juveniles as young as fourteen years who gave their home addresses as being a thousand or more*" miles from the city. The report's author punctuated this section with one of many sardonic references to King's "Non-violent Army."[79]

Racial and Civil Disorders in St. Augustine also featured short sections that included a time line of "racial incidents," a slanted biography of Martin Luther King, a set of twenty-five appendices ranging from local newspaper articles about blacks arming themselves to NAACP and SCLC letters to President Johnson and the U.S. Commission on Civil Rights, Farris Bryant's executive orders, and outrageously biased police reports on blacks' demonstrations. The facts about King dwelled, in shopworn form, on his ties to the Highlander Folk School and the Southern Conference Educational Fund, and the report contained lengthy quotes from the Louisiana Joint Legislative Committee, which claimed in 1964, "The infiltration of the Communist Party into the so-called 'Civil Rights' movement through the SCEF is shocking and highly dangerous to this state, and the nation." The report also revealed that one of King's closest associates, Bayard Rustin, had been a member of the Young Communist League and, even worse, was a homosexual. Then followed the litany of subversives with whom King had long surrounded himself, and whom segregationists had been trotting out for years: Jack O'Dell, Aubrey Williams, James Dombrowski, and Carl and Anne Braden, "all identified as Communists before the Senate Internal Security Subcommittee."[80] Taken together, these exhibits were intended to impart to the reader two familiar narratives: one about outsiders stirring up racial discord, chaos, and disorder to weaken American democracy, and the other showing integrationists as perverted race mixers.

Soon after the release of *Racial and Civil Disorders in St. Augustine*, the nation watched as thousands of blacks and whites joined together in a dramatic march from Selma to Montgomery, Alabama, to demand equal voting rights. On March 25, 1965, the triumphant procession made its way past Dexter Avenue Baptist Church to the steps of the capitol for an afternoon of freedom songs and political exhortations, including King's speech that famously asked, "How long?" and answered, "Not long." When the march ended, the ad hoc transportation committee that had worked for the previous five days shuttling volunteers and marchers along Highway 80 between Selma and Montgomery still had work left to do. Dozens of participants needed rides to the airport or back home. In one of the transport cars, a 1963 Oldsmobile with a Michigan license plate, sat Viola Liuzzo, a thirty-nine-year-old white woman who had come to Alabama after watching the harrowing television coverage of Bloody Sunday from the comfort of her middle-class Detroit living room. In the passenger seat was Leroy Moton, an African American twenty years her junior, from Selma. That night, an automobile carrying four Klansmen, one an FBI informant, pulled up next to the Oldsmobile and the passengers opened fire. Liuzzo was fatally shot in the head.

The killing elicited yet another round of nationwide shock and grief and lent new urgency to the voting rights bill, but it also provoked a brutal character assassination from the Ku Klux Klan and the FBI, which leaked misinformation to the public about how Liuzzo had been sitting "very

very close" to Moton in the car, giving "all the appearances of a neck-ing party," and had "puncture marks in her arms indicating recent use of a hypodermic needle."[81] The rumors confirmed many white southern-ers' assumptions about what sort of woman would forsake her husband and children to carouse with Negroes in an unseemly display disguised as a voting rights march. In historian Dan Carter's words, these "pam-phlets, press releases, and speeches by conservative Alabamians, includ-ing George Wallace, reveal an obsession with 'orgies' and 'fornication' and 'debauchery.'" They also, as he puts it, "foreshadowed the beginnings of the sexual culture wars that would resonate through American society in the 1960s and 1970s."[82] The Johns Committee, like other conservative and segregationist groups in the mid-1960s, served the same purpose, ce-menting the imagined links between sexual and political deviance within right-wing discourse.

Many smear campaigns emanated from Selma. In 1966, Selma sheriff Jim Clark published a memoir, *The Jim Clark Story*, artlessly subtitled *I Saw Selma Raped*. Robert M. Mikell, an Auburn graduate and a writer from Montgomery, penned a book at Clark's request called *Selma*, which he claimed to be a "comprehensive testimonial" about what really hap-pened—as opposed to the "distorted facts and slanted reports" on televi-sion. Instead it was an excuse to publish all of the rumors and accusations that had circulated among angry Alabama whites during the most recent invasion of integrationists: public drunkenness and urination, men and women masquerading as priests and nuns, straggly beatniks and grubby Communists, and rampant and promiscuous sex. According to the wit-nesses whose affidavits Mikell read (most of whom turned out to work in law enforcement or state government), the Selma marchers, black and white, simply could not stop having sex—sex in the streets, sex on front lawns, sex behind buildings, sex inside the SNCC office, and even sex on a church floor.[83]

The most provocative exposé appeared in *The True Selma Story: Sex and Civil Rights*, a tabloid-style magazine published in Birmingham in 1965. Its similarities to the Johns Committee's reports are worth noting in the context of the burgeoning conservative narrative of sexual, racial, and political subversion. The cover was an unremarkable cartoon illustration of the famous photograph of civil rights marchers bearing American flags, though in this representation they were marching under a Kremlin-red sky. The inside front cover featured a full-page photograph of white and black marchers standing near the state capitol in a large puddle with streams running down the street. It was nighttime, and the picture was in black and white, and according to the caption, moments before the photo was snapped, SNCC's James Forman yelled to the group, "Stand up and relieve yourself!" On the next page, along with the table of contents, was a biographical sketch about the author, Albert "Buck" Parsons. An image of Parsons, with a cigarette in his mouth, a tough-guy scowl on his face, and a military-style buzz cut, accompanied it. He was a stringer for *Life* magazine, managing editor for an unnamed weekly Birmingham newspaper, and a pilot who volunteered for the Bay of Pigs mission. Alabama congressman William L. Dickinson enlisted Parsons to investigate the Selma to Montgomery march, and *The True Selma Story* was the result of his efforts.

The first section, the requisite retelling of Martin Luther King's personal peccadilloes and dubious associates, was titled "Black Knight of the Civil Rights Movement." The next segment comprised the centerpiece of the report, addressing sex and civil rights. It contained "sworn" statements about a "skinny white girl" having sex with a black man and then turning over to have sex with another black man lying next to the couple, an inebriated black woman singing freedom songs and then violently attacking the police, and a white man who dressed up as a priest and had sex with young black girls. In one affidavit, a witness claimed to have seen James Forman and a "red-haired white girl" engaging in an "abnormal sex act which consisted of each of the two manipulating the other's private parts with their mouths simultaneously"—an act commonly associated with male homosexuality and legally classified as sodomy. An Alabama state trooper swore, "One of the white beatniks, with a goatee, told one of my troopers" that he was being paid and given free meals and "all the Negro p——he wanted."[84] A section devoted to "Bayard and Ralph: Just a Couple of the Boys" described Bayard Rustin as a "homosexual who solicits on city streets, whose life's work is the subversion of the moral fiber of the youth of America" and Ralph Abernathy as a hypocrite who seduced a fifteen-year-old girl in his congregation and performed "abnormal intercourse" with her.[85] This is the narrative that conservative white Alabamans, like conservative white Floridians, told themselves to make sense of a world in which their values were being threatened. It was a narrative rooted in a specific time and place, shaped by the anti-Communist conception of political subversion and sexual perversion and used to defend segregation against liberal federal encroachment.

∗   ∗   ∗

In the spring of 1965 the Florida legislature did not have to vote on renewing the Florida Legislative Investigation Committee, which disappeared quietly in the aftermath of its recent ignominy. The committee had little to show for the 1963–65 biennium other than a controversial report on homosexuality and a little-noticed report on the integration crisis in St. Augustine. It had done nothing to stem the tide of growing student activism across Florida's universities or the demonstrations against segregated restaurants, theaters, and beaches in communities throughout the state. It had backfired in its attempt to shock Floridians with *Homosexuality and Citizenship in Florida* and raised the ire of liberals and moderates by interfering in the curriculum, pedagogy, and policies of the University of South Florida. Even conservative Democratic governor Haydon Burns said of the Johns Committee in early 1965, two months before the legislative session was to begin, "I think it serves no purpose whatsoever."[86]

But many in Florida and elsewhere would have disagreed. The committee had served a purpose, not only for the previous two years, but for its entire duration. By the mid-1960s, there was a groundswell of opposition against what some saw as a dangerous liberalizing trend in American politics and culture. From the John Birch Society to Citizens for Decent Literature, from Young Americans for Freedom to supporters of George Wallace and Lester Maddox, the echoes of postwar anti-Communism and massive resistance could be heard in conservative attacks against the Civil Rights Act, welfare, the constitutional banning of prayer in school, the Free Speech Movement in Berkeley, the loosening gender and sexual mores across a broad swath of American life, and many other ominous signs of moral decline facilitated by the federal government.[87] In Florida, the Johns Committee came to serve the same purpose, as a sounding board for, but also a symbol of, conservative and segregationist values. The committee's purview and methods may have come into question, but the larger weight of its mission did not. Even state agencies such as the Board of Control and the Department of Education appropriated some of the FLIC's ideology and duties, taking responsibility for keeping homosexuals and controversial books and speakers out of Florida's classrooms. School integration lagged for years, and the course on Americanism and communism continued to be taught in Florida's public schools into the 1970s. Political, sexual, and racial subversion, increasingly vilified under the umbrella of liberalism over the course of the decade, became a staple of the New Right. Conservatives in Florida who had found a champion in the committee so closely associated with Charley Johns did not disappear along with it in 1965.

Epilogue

Anita Bryant and Florida's Culture Wars

I have just been notified that the blacklisting of Anita Bryant has begun.
I have been blacklisted for exercising the right of a mother to defend her
children and all children, against their being recruited by homosexuals.

Anita Bryant, 1977

"We're not going to take this sitting down," Anita Bryant told the *New York Times* on January 18, 1977. Florida's Dade County Commission had just approved an ordinance banning discrimination in employment and housing on the basis of "sexual or affectional preference."[1] Bryant had moved to Miami Beach in 1960 after marrying Bob Green, a local disc jockey. It was the same year the Johns Committee and Duane Barker's unit were investigating male prostitution and pornography rings in Miami. In addition to performing and recording both popular and inspirational Christian music, Anita Bryant began serving as a spokesperson for the Florida Citrus Commission in 1968, appearing in television and print advertisements for Florida orange juice. The tagline, "A day without orange juice is like a day without sunshine," became her catchphrase, synonymous with the former Miss Oklahoma in the popular culture of the day.[2]

She became involved in civic affairs in 1969, when Jim Morrison, lead singer of the Doors and a Florida native, was arrested and charged with indecent exposure and public drunkenness during a performance at the Dinner Key Auditorium in Miami. Three weeks later, an estimated thirty thousand people packed Miami's Orange Bowl for a "Rally for Decency." Conceived by a local high school senior in response to Morrison's performance, the event featured Anita Bryant, the veteran comic actor Jackie Gleason, and 1940s radio star Kate Smith, most famous for her rendition of "God Bless America." A series of teenage speakers also addressed the crowd on what they called the "five virtues": belief in God, love of country, love of family, "reverence of one's sexuality," and equality.[3]

In early 1977, within weeks of the county commission vote, Anita Bryant and her husband Bob Green joined Coral Gables city councilman Robert Brake and several local religious leaders to form Save Our Children to repeal the ordinance. The group asked the commission to simply void it, to no avail. Instead, the county's voters would decide the issue in a special election on June 7.[4] With that, Florida found itself at the epicenter of a national debate pitting gay rights advocates against those who rejected the very concept of acknowledging, much less protecting, homosexuals as a minority group. And Anita Bryant found herself thrust into the spotlight as the cover girl for a newly assertive evangelical Christian influence in Republican politics, an influence that would flourish in subsequent decades.

Even as the anti-ordinance campaign helped to usher in a new era of religiously based, family values conservatism, it echoed earlier calls for protecting children, families, and schools from liberal intrusions and predatory homosexuals, and it politicized parents' right to do the same. It was a reframing of older notions of subversion and sexual deviance through religiously informed critiques of liberalism, and in particular liberal schools' imposing toxic secular values on America's children with the blessing of the Supreme Court. At the same time, as well, decades of opposition to what was perceived as overreaching federal power continued to ring loud and reverberate within the Christian Right.

Sociologist Sara Diamond has written that the "major social issues of the 1970s caused right-wing evangelicals to feel threatened about their ability to promote the supremacy of the traditional family."[5] To be sure, gay liberation, the Equal Rights Amendment, and the legalization of abortion can be credited with stirring up fears about traditional values, but the mobilization of conservatives around the issues of homosexual teachers and gay rights was not solely reactive. It had deeper roots, which lay in anti-Communist politics and, in Florida and the rest of the South, massive resistance. The wheels of mobilization in the 1970s had been greased by an earlier generation of cold warriors and segregationists consumed by anxieties about liberalism, sexuality, the federal government, and public schools—and the role each potentially played in precipitating or preventing the nation's moral decline. A worldview, a vocabulary, and a recent historical memory were all firmly in place, and the Dade County

ordinance became the issue around which a movement—on both sides—
went national.

* * *

By the time Save Our Children activists took to Miami's streets and
churches in a petition drive during the winter of 1977, reapportionment
and constitutional revision had dramatically transformed Florida's government. In 1967, the U.S. Supreme Court ruled in *Swann v. Adams* that
the Florida legislature's effort to reapportion itself was unconstitutional,
falling short of the one-man, one-vote standard. A federal district court
panel oversaw reapportionment, which, for the first time, created a pro-
portionally representative legislature in Florida.[6] The following year, under Claude Kirk, Florida's first Republican governor since Reconstruction,
legislators rewrote the state's 1885 constitution. The office of lieutenant
governor was established, the governor could now serve two consecutive
terms, state agencies were streamlined and consolidated, and the legislature was to convene every year rather than biannually. In addition, the
governor's cabinet was to be made up of appointed rather than elected
officials.[7]

The power of northern rural counties shrank. But the cumulative effect
of decades of indifference and outright hostility to urban interests became
glaringly apparent as the modern state government grappled with Florida's ongoing, skyrocketing growth. In 1964, political scientists William
Havard and Loren Beth had warned that the malapportioned, part-time
legislature, ruled by an ethos of low taxes and pork-barrel politics, was
alarmingly ill equipped to manage the state's rapid growth and urbanization. "Much of the opportunity to prepare in advance for the coming of
these new patterns of living has been lost, and the price of lack of foresight
probably will continue to mount," they wrote. "These problems naturally
spill over into practically all aspects of the state's activity—schools, highways, public health, conservation, state parks and recreation areas, and
revenue and taxation are closely related to the process of planning for
the future of urbanism." Or as a later scholar put it, "There was little indication that Florida had either the desire or the means to come to grips
with the great changes engulfing the state."[8] Having doubled between 1950
and 1960, Florida's population approached seven million in 1970.[9] Urban
metropolitan regions were expanding even faster, bearing out Havard and
Beth's predictions. The Miami–Ft. Lauderdale and Tampa–St. Petersburg

areas, respectively, were the first and third most populous metropolitan centers in the South at the end of the 1960s. Orlando soon followed, its growth ignited and its identity indelibly stamped by the opening of Walt Disney World in 1971.[10]

The steady stream of newcomers acutely affected Florida's schools, particularly in urban areas. In the late 1960s, this translated into a need for an estimated six to eleven thousand new teachers each year, a need that proved difficult to fill, given the legislature's persistent unwillingness to increase spending on education. In 1968, Florida had the ninth largest population and public school enrollment in the country, and was ranked tenth in total personal income. Yet it was twenty-sixth in teacher salaries and thirty-fourth in per student spending.[11] Similar problems plagued state colleges and universities, where the bulk of expenditures went to capital projects, modernizing facilities, and building new schools.[12] These disparities resulted from years of legislators favoring low or nonexistent taxes to enhance the state's attractiveness as a place to do business and to live. As contemporary observers noted, "Rural legislators and their urban partners who had similar ideological viewpoints or personal interests served well the conservative financial and industrial interests in Florida. Their expressed goal was to hold down taxes."[13] According to the Florida Development Commission, in 1968, corporations paid less than 8 percent of all taxes collected in the state, compared to 16 percent in the South and 18 percent nationally.[14]

The state's schools and universities remained battlegrounds on many fronts after the Johns Committee disappeared. Opposition to public school integration continued in Florida, as elsewhere. In 1970, Governor Kirk attempted to prevent the implementation of court-ordered busing in Manatee County, just south of the Tampa Bay area. He was also running for reelection that year, against liberal Democrat Reubin Askew, who supported busing as a temporary solution to the ongoing problem of de facto segregation in the state's schools. During the campaign, Kirk impugned his foe as a "momma's boy" and a "permissive liberal."[15]

Although Kirk ended up losing the election, busing was generally an unpopular proposition in Florida, and in 1972 George Wallace focused considerable attention on the issue while campaigning for his third presidential run. On Florida's ballot during the primary election was a nonbinding referendum on a constitutional ban against busing. Askew repeated the liberal mantra that it was a temporary measure, a necessary evil, and the law of the land. Still, the measure won overwhelmingly, by a count of 74 percent to 26 percent, and George Wallace won the Democratic primary in Florida with 42 percent of the vote.[16]

That summer, the Democratic National Convention took place in Miami Beach. Jim Foster, delegate from California and the political chairman of the Society for Individual Rights, was one of the speakers. The group, which Foster called "the Nation's largest gay rights organization," had formed in San Francisco in 1964, and claimed twelve hundred members. Foster was there to make the case for including gay rights in the Democratic platform, and his approach marked a dramatic shift from earlier attempts to articulate the rights of homosexuals: "We do not come to you pleading for your understanding or begging for your tolerance. We come to you affirming our pride in our life styles, affirming the validity of our right to seek and maintain meaningful emotional relationships and affirming our right to participate in the life of this country on an equal basis with every other citizen."[17] He concluded by urging the Democratic Party to "enact this gay rights plank. To our millions of gay brothers and sisters, as well as the Democratic Party, we say: We are here, we will not be still. We will not go away until the ultimate goal of gay liberation is realized, that goal being that all people can live in the peace, the freedom, the dignity of what they are."[18] He was followed by Madeline Davis, a lesbian from Buffalo, New York, reiterating the request to include Minority Report No. 8 in the Democratic platform with an appeal to the "basic civil rights of all human beings" as something that is "inherent in the American tradition," arguing that a "government that interferes with the private lives of its people is a government that is alien to the American tradition and the American dream." The plank in question would support the repeal of all state and federal laws prohibiting consensual, private sex, as well as those regulating gender-appropriate "attire." One delegate from Ohio opposed it because it failed to distinguish between "sexual acts between adults and those between adults and children."[19]

In the end, Minority Report No. 8 was not adopted. When it came time for delegates to cast their votes for the presidential nominee, George Wallace was chosen by seventy-five of Florida's eighty-one delegates. Hubert Humphrey, Shirley Chisholm, and George McGovern received two votes apiece.[20] The social issues brought to the convention floor by minority delegates only exacerbated some white Democrats' increasing sense of alienation from a party they were beginning not to recognize. Wallace

supporters in Miami Beach were openly dismissive of the minority reports and the time devoted to abortion, women's rights, and gay rights.
One called it "a disgrace," saying, "If I had known this kind of thing was
going to happen, I never would have come to the convention. I'm very,
very disgusted." Others said the Democratic Party was "finished" and had
"committed suicide."[21] As the historian Dan Carter later explained, "In
chastened form it might be possible to continue the social welfare tra-
ditions of the old Democratic Party, but the party had to stop scolding
Americans about the Bill of Rights and take a tough line opposing crime
in the streets, campus disruptions, drugs, and pornography. Above all else
... the party had to disentangle these issues from that of race."[22] The following month, Republicans held their national convention in Miami, and
gay and lesbian activists protested alongside Vietnam War opponents and
Richard Nixon critics.[23]

In the late 1960s and early 1970s, in Florida and many other parts of
the country, another major school-related social issue was sex education. Conservatives accused sex educators, and in particular the Sexuality
Information and Education Council of the United States (SIECUS), of
secretly trying to foist communism and perversion upon students under the guise of teaching them about sex. One of the group's core beliefs
was that childhood sexuality was healthy and normal and that parents,
schools, and churches should not teach them to feel shame and guilt about
sexual feelings, nor should they, in the words of sociologist Janice Irvine,
be "shielded from straightforward information about sexuality." In so doing, SIECUS "became the target of a movement that found itself able to
politically capitalize on the ideal of childhood innocence."[24] Just as important, it capitalized on the popular belief that children and teenagers were
impressionable to messages about sex, and discussing it with them would
encourage wide-ranging and dangerous experimentation.

In 1968 and 1969, nearly forty states experienced public controversy
and debate over sex education, and it was the subject of proposed legislation in half of them.[25] Groups such as the John Birch Society and the
Christian Crusade linked sex education to communism, homosexuality,
and interracial sex. Pamphlets and books such as *Is the Schoolhouse the
Place to Teach Raw Sex?* and *SIECUS: Corruptor of Youth* proliferated.[26] In
Florida, the state coordinator of the Ku Klux Klan articulated the group's
updated agenda, which was designed to take advantage of the "new conservatism of America" to increase membership. The Klan's list of enemies

of Americanism now included fluoridation, the United Nations, gun control, and sex education, a "Communist-backed effort to promote promiscuity and interracial sex."[27] Local chapters of the John Birch Society targeted specific programs and schools in Orlando, Cape Kennedy, and Seminole County. Activists from Citizens for Moral Education (CME) accused them of "following the Communist conspiracy right down the line." A Presbyterian minister and CME member from Orlando called sex education "purely and simply pornography and filth. It's degrading. It's unfit to be in our public schools."[28] During the 1970 legislative session, the state house passed a bill that would prohibit the use of SIECUS materials in Florida's schools, as well as the teaching of violence, "unpatriotic activities, and morals against a wholesome society." The bill never made it out of the senate's Education Committee.[29]

In addition to busing and sex education, homosexuality continued to be a political issue in Florida, though it was not explicitly tied to schools. In 1964 in Miami, Richard Inman founded the Atheneum Society of America—the state's and, according to some, the South's first homophile organization.[30] Inman, a cab driver, had a near-obsessive desire to fight back against the Johns Committee and other "heterosexuals who masquerade behind the guise of 'justice' and 'decency.'"[31] At the urging of a friend in the Washington, D.C., chapter of the Mattachine Society, Inman changed the name of his group to reflect an affiliation with the better-known, national group. Still, membership remained limited largely to Inman himself, though scholar James Sears noted that the Mattachine Society of Florida's newsletter, *Viewpoint*, had a wider audience.[32] In 1965, Inman appeared on a local Miami television show, *FYI*, in an episode titled "The Homosexual." Duane Barker, former investigator for the Johns Committee, also appeared as an expert on the problems and dangers associated with homosexuality, especially for young people.[33]

The Stonewall riots in Manhattan's West Village in June 1969 launched the gay liberation movement, which quickly caught fire throughout the country. In Florida, chapters of the Gay Liberation Front, the organization founded in response to police harassment of gay men and lesbians at the Stonewall Inn, were established in Gainesville and Tallahassee, and in early 1971 student members petitioned for official recognition from the University of Florida and Florida State University, respectively.[34] During the first half of the 1970s, various gay rights groups appeared in Florida's cities, among them the People's Coalition for Gay Rights and the Alliance for Gay Awareness in Tallahassee, the Suncoast Gay Alliance based in Clearwater, and the Florida Coalition of Gay Organizations in Miami.[35] Members sought protection from discrimination and recognition as equal citizens, a far cry from the homophile movement's politics of respectability in the 1950s and 1960s. In 1976, the People's Coalition for Gay Rights sent a questionnaire to 160 of Florida's representatives and senators, asking if they would support nondiscrimination legislation on behalf of gays and lesbians. According to one source, ten responded, five favorably. One Republican from St. Petersburg was public in his adamant rejection of the idea. "Of course they are discriminated against," he told a Daytona newspaper. "So are murderers, rapists and criminals. It's a disease. It's not a natural condition." He added, "Are you willing to ram more laws down the throats of millions of Floridians which pertain to only your selfish interests—interests outside the mainstream of Western civilization?"[36]

* * *

In 1975, a handful of Dade County gay activists, building on the increasing national attention to gay issues, crafted nondiscrimination legislation that would protect homosexuals in housing and employment. Nearly three dozen municipalities around the country had such laws in place, among them Ann Arbor, Minneapolis, Seattle, Wichita, and Washington, D.C.[37] In the fall of 1976, these activists mobilized around supporting pro-gay candidates for state and county offices, most of whom ended up winning. Bob Basker, a former encyclopedia salesman, worked with University of Miami law professor Bruce Winnick to draft the ordinance. The Florida Coalition of Gay Organizations approached county commissioner Ruth Shack for her support, and she agreed to sponsor the bill.[38]

Anita Bryant, Reverend William Chapman, and Coral Gables city councilman Robert Brake huddled after the Dade County Commission passed the ordinance on January 18, 1977. They discussed strategies for repealing the measure, finally concluding that a petition drive would be the most effective means of circumventing what they saw as the commission's favoring of an aberrant minority against the will of the majority.[39] By early March, Save Our Children had gathered more than sixty thousand signatures on a petition to overturn the ordinance or put it to a public vote. A week later, the commission voted for the latter.[40]

For the next three months, on both sides, the ordinance fight generated headlines, cash donations, and heightened emotions. During this time, many of the arguments put forward by Anita Bryant and Save Our Children were ideas that had first entered the political discourse during the Cold War and been brought to their logical conclusions in the work of the Johns Committee. Ordinance opponents maintained that homosexuality was a lifestyle choice and not biologically determined, homosexuals recruited young people, they sought to deceive the public and the state into believing that homosexuality was normal and acceptable, schools were the most dangerous places for homosexuals to work, parents' rights were being stripped away by a liberal, secular government, and the resulting moral decay would sap the nation's defenses against enemies foreign and domestic.

Anita Bryant's celebrity guaranteed a whirlwind of publicity, and she proved adept at staying on message. While getting her makeup done before an appearance on the *Phil Donahue Show*, she told a reporter, "Parents have a right to protect their children and provide a wholesome atmosphere for them so that they will not be given an alternative to God's law and the law of the land." She painted a sordid and conspiratorial picture, claiming that a group of male hustlers in Miami's high schools in 1966 "are grown up today and these are the militant homosexuals who have become a political bloc and are trying to pass these things. They are financed by a lesbian task force of the National Organization of [sic] Women. Now that's pretty frightening."[41] When a group of gay rights activists met with a presidential aide at the White House in March 1977, Save Our Children issued an indignant press release, claiming, "What these people really want hidden behind obscure lawyers' phrases is the legal right to propose to our children that there is an alternate way of life—that being a homosexual or a lesbian is not really wrong. . . . Behind the high-sounding appeal against discrimination in jobs and housing they are really asking to be blessed in their abnormal life-style by the office of the president of the United States."[42] That month, in a reaction against gay rights activists' claim that they were struggling for civil rights, Save Our Children placed a full-page ad in the *Miami Herald* that read, "The Civil Rights of Parents: To Save Their Children from Homosexual Influence." It called the ordinance an "Invitation to Recruit Our Children."[43]

The organization also invoked national security anxieties, recalling Cold War admonitions about the threat of moral laxity to the American way of life, and resuscitating the imagined links between homosexuality, criminality, and subversion. Following a county commission meeting in

April 1977, Bryant warned that the ordinance would signal not only to Miami but the nation that "moral character no longer counts. . . . All government jobs, even the most sensitive, must be thrown open to homosexuals, pimps, prostitutes and every other unsavory, unnatural sexual libertine." Republican presidential aspirant Ronald Reagan was a featured speaker at Bryant's thirty-seventh birthday celebration on March 25 hosted by the Florida Conservative Union.[44] In the weeks leading up to the vote, evangelical leader and later Moral Majority founder Jerry Falwell appeared at a rally against the ordinance at the Miami Beach Convention Center, featuring dozens of religious leaders and a crowd of more than nine thousand people. One minister warned that upholding the ordinance "could be the end of the United States of America."[45]

In her own account of the battle, published shortly after its conclusion, she included an excerpt from a report that Jesse Helms sent out to his constituents. The senator from North Carolina called Bryant a "concerned American—concerned about the erosion of moral principles in her country. She has spoken out against pornography and indecency in all of the forms spreading across America. She has warned that unless America returns to basic principles, our freedoms are in jeopardy." Max Rafferty was another conservative who penned a declaration of support for Bryant's book. Having served for much of the 1960s as superintendent of public instruction for the state of California and later as a syndicated columnist specializing in education, he wrote that children's reasoning "is stark in its simplicity and as certain as sunrise: 'If it's okay to hire a pervert to teach in a public institution and if it's okay to pay a pervert with tax money and if it's okay to put a pervert in charge of the educational destinies of school children, then it must be okay to be a pervert.' This, fellow Americans, we simply cannot have. We cannot have it because the actual survival of our country in the years ahead depends upon a generation which will be straight, not distorted."[46]

The arguments made by Save Our Children and Anita Bryant echoed those of the Johns Committee and earlier conservatives in other important ways as well, and the movement received the hearty endorsement of several anti-Communist and New Right luminaries and evangelicals. For her part, Bryant reached out to notable figures on the right who had been making the case for the impending decline of the United States at the hands of liberals. In addition to Reagan, Helms, and Falwell, she received the enthusiastic support from televangelists Jim Bakker and Pat

Robertson. Bryant appeared on Bakker's show, the *PTL Club*, twice during the Dade County fight, and accompanied by her husband Bob Green, she was a guest on Pat Robertson's television show, *700 Club*. A press release issued by Save Our Children in the spring of 1977 reminded the public of the conservative belief that homosexuality was "a choice, not a birthright," alluding to Phyllis Schlafly's influential conservative manifesto from 1964, *A Choice Not an Echo*.[47]

In *The Anita Bryant Story*, Bryant cited various experts to bolster her case against gay rights. Republican writer and activist George Gilder had published a critique of feminism in his 1973 book, *Sexual Suicide*, and Bryant quoted several passages in which he linked social disorder to homosexuality, arguing that "family breakdown is the chief cause of the problems that have come down with such force upon our country in recent years. The women's-liberation programs—many of them fostered by women with lesbian tendencies—have weakened family ties and worsened these problems." Recalling psychoanalytical theories about homosexuality from the postwar period, he also described homosexuality as a "flight from identity and love" and gay liberation as an "escape from sexual responsibility and its display a threat to millions of young men who have precarious masculine identities."[48]

Bryant employed other familiar postwar stereotypes of homosexuals by presenting the ideas of contemporary self-proclaimed experts. One of them, Murray Norris, wrote an article, "There Is Nothing Gay About Homosexuality," in which he argued, and Bryant quoted, "In homosexuals' own publications, in the writings of psychiatrists who treat them, in the words of the ministers who try to help them, there is this constant repetition of the loneliness of the homosexual life. This loneliness has led many homosexuals into drugs and alcoholism." Murray Norris was the president of Christian Family Renewal, founded in 1970 in California to "eliminate abortion and pornography and to fight satanism." By the 1980s, he was an advocate for home schooling, claiming that public schools were teaching humanism to children and encouraging sexual perversion, atheism, abortion, and euthanasia. Bryant also used the work of psychoanalyst Melvin Anchell, a conservative critic of sex education, to reiterate her case against accepting homosexuality, repeating his claim that "homosexuals are seldom satisfied with their relationships and are constantly seeking new thrills, or new forms of sexuality. They head into sadomasochism."[49]

*   *   *

Three weeks before the Dade County vote, liberal Democratic governor Reubin Askew weighed in on the issue. "I've never viewed the homosexual lifestyle as something that approached a constitutional right," he said, "so if I were in Miami I would find no difficulty in voting to repeal the ordinance."[50] By early June, Save Our Children was estimated to have raised almost two hundred thousand dollars, about a third of it coming from outside the state. Pro-ordinance forces raised three hundred thousand dollars, half of it from non-Floridians. Some polls indicated a slight advantage for ordinance supporters.[51]

On the day of the vote, the *New York Times* ran a piece by the coexecutive directors of the National Gay Task Force, Jean O'Leary and Bruce Voeller. They claimed that the controversy had benefited gay rights across the United States, and they quoted Anita Bryant from a recent television interview: "We're not going after their jobs, as long as they do their jobs and do not want to come out of the closet." The authors noted that ordinance opponents now wanted homosexuals to keep their sexuality private in order to be accepted, but that this was the very stricture that had kept gay men and lesbians feeling isolated, ashamed, sick, sinful, and criminal for decades. "So we believe that Anita Bryant is correct to put the focus right where it belongs: On children. And on morality," they argued. "We believe it is immoral to lie to children. We believe it is immoral to teach them to hate people whom they choose to love. We believe it is immoral to pretend to children that they don't have a variety of loving options in their own lives, or to force them to believe that they are the only ones in the world to have loving or sexual feelings for their own sex. We think it is immoral to foster prejudice and discrimination by pretending to children that there are no real people who are gay."[52]

By more than a two-to-one margin, roughly 202,000 to 90,000 votes, Dade County residents voted to repeal the ordinance. The *New York Times* reported that Bryant was "dancing a jig at her Miami Beach home" in celebration. In a statement to the press, she declared, "All America and the world will hear what the people have said, and with God's continued help, we will prevail in our fight to repeal similar laws throughout the nation which attempt to legitimize a life style that is both perverse and dangerous."[53]

Statewide, and across the country, the conversation about homosexuality and gay rights was shaped by the battle in Dade County. In Florida, state legislators seized the moment to pass legislation banning gay marriage and gay adoption. Governor Reubin Askew signed both bills on June 8, one day after voters repealed the ordinance. One senator declared that the legislation served as a message to gays and lesbians that "we are tired of you and wish that you would go back into the closet. The problem in Florida is that homosexuals are surfacing to such an extent that they are infringing on average, normal people who have a few rights, too."[54]

Later in June, gay pride events from San Francisco and New York to Atlanta and Miami were filled with signs and images pillorying Anita Bryant. The outrage was palpable, as it had been for months. She was so hated that one line of marchers in San Francisco displayed a series of enormous posters alongside one another with photographs of Adolf Hitler, Joseph Stalin, Idi Amin, the Ku Klux Klan, and Anita Bryant.[55] It became an iconic image. In spite of the anger and disappointment, some saw the ordinance vote as a positive, or at least potentially positive, force in transforming gay political consciousness. An editorial in the *Nation*, for example, called Bryant "the best thing ever to happen to American homosexuals" and claimed that "the country must now squarely face it as a political issue, uncomfortable though that may be." The *New York Times* reported that the Dade County vote had turned the issue of gay rights into a "nationwide debate and has made homosexual rights groups vow to undertake stronger political lobbying." A Gallup poll showed that 56 percent of Americans believed homosexuals should have equal job rights, unless they held positions of influence in churches and schools. In addition, 77 percent of respondents believed that gays and lesbians should not be allowed to adopt children. The perception, common during the postwar period, that the occurrence of homosexuality was increasing, also showed no signs of waning in 1977, as 66 percent said they believed that homosexuality was more prevalent at that point than twenty-five years earlier.[56]

If Bryant never succeeded in transforming Save Our Children into a truly national movement, she inspired the evangelical right to become increasingly focused on and vocal about homosexuality as a political issue. She also inspired one man to replicate her efforts on the state level, and her infamy and status as a target of gay rage only grew as a result. John Briggs, a Republican state senator from Orange County, California, was running for governor in 1978. He was also with Anita Bryant on June 7, 1977, when Dade County voters rejected the gay ordinance.

Briggs then returned to his home state, where a law banning sodomy had been repealed two years earlier. In August, he initiated a successful petition drive for a ballot measure that would make it illegal for public school teachers to engage in or advocate homosexual activity or identity. Proposition 6 energized the state's sizable gay population, while everyone from teachers' unions to conservatives like former governor Ronald Reagan were reluctant to support a measure that would impinge on First Amendment rights to free speech. Briggs's Cold War warnings that homosexuality was "a creeping disease, where it just continues to spread like a cancer creeping throughout the body," could not save the ballot initiative, which was defeated by a margin of 58 to 42 percent.[57]

Anita Bryant also, albeit unintentionally, inspired gay men and lesbians to reconceptualize their politics. Anger translated into activism in cities and towns across the country, and one man became the symbol of that change. Harvey Milk, an openly gay member of the San Francisco Board of Supervisors, responded to Briggs and Bryant with a speech on the steps of City Hall during the Gay Freedom Day Parade on June 25, 1978. He famously began by turning on its head a longstanding stereotype: "My name is Harvey Milk—and I want to recruit you." He followed it with an incendiary defense of the dignity of lesbians and gay men and an excoriation of what he viewed as right-wing slander. It was also a call to arms. "I ask my gay sisters and brothers to make the commitment to fight. For themselves. For their freedom. For their country," he declared. "I'm tired of the conspiracy of silence. . . . I'm tired of listening to the Anita Bryants twist the language and the meaning of the Bible to fit their own distorted outlook. . . . And I'm tired of John Briggs talking about false role models." Above all, he said, "I'm tired of the silence. So I'm going to talk about it. And I want *you* to talk about it."[58]

*   *   *

In the fall of 2008, Californians voted on a referendum that would overturn the state Supreme Court's ruling that same-sex couples have a constitutional right to marry. In the run-up to the vote, the figure of the predatory homosexual teacher appeared again, this time in the "Yes on 8" campaign. Television ads sponsored by the conservative profamily group Project Marriage were devoted mostly to the threat posed to children by gay marriage, through the conduit of public schools. In "It's Already Happened," a young girl ran into the kitchen excitedly telling her mother about her day at school: "I learned that a prince married a prince, and that I can marry a princess!" She handed her mother a book, *King and King*, which she examined with a mixture of horror and disgust. Suddenly, a law professor from Pepperdine University cut in and asked ominously, "Think it can't happen? It's already happened." He explained that when Massachusetts legalized gay marriage in 2004, "schools began teaching second graders that boys can marry boys." Moreover, courts determined that "parents had no right to object." Another ad, "Truth," informed viewers that a "public school took first-graders to a lesbian wedding, calling it a 'teachable moment.'" The spot ended with a closeup of a young blonde girl's downcast face, an unwilling guest at the unnatural nuptials. The idea that perverts corrupted children by convincing them that homosexuality was normal had been a staple of conservative ideology since the 1950s. That the referendum passed and gay marriage became illegal in California speaks to the resonance of such tactics in a state largely viewed as liberal, particularly on social issues. ·

The culture wars waged during the last half of the twentieth century, and into the twenty-first, were fought largely within a framework constructed during the post–World War II era. Conservatives came to power and held on to it in part by articulating a narrative of the social and national security threats of racial and sexual deviance, liberalism and secularism, and an intrusive federal government. Florida and the South helped to blaze a trail from Cold War politics to the ascendancy of social conservatism, a trail that wound its way from the Johns Committee to Anita Bryant, the Moral Majority, and Jesse Helms's assault on the National Endowment for the Arts, to name a few. The ideas that emerged from the confluence of anti-Communism, massive resistance, and the rise of the evangelical Right in the postwar years have displayed a breathtaking tenacity in American political culture.

When Harvey Milk exhorted the angry crowd at City Hall in 1978, it was a moment that transformed a movement, a clarion call that the closet was not only no longer viable but, in fact, detrimental for anyone with a stake in the struggle for equality. The irony was inescapable. For decades, conservatives in the Johns Committee and elsewhere had sought to expose homosexuals and had used the very concept of hidden homosexuals to paint a terrifying picture of national security threats, danger to children, and looming social decay. Now they wanted nothing more than to see gays and lesbians retreat into silence and invisibility. "Gay brothers and sisters, what are *you* going to do about it?" Harvey Milk asked. "You must *come out*. Come out . . . to your parents . . . *to your relatives . . . to your friends. . . . Come out* only to the people you know, *and who know you*. Not to anyone else. But once and for all, break down the myths, destroy the lies and distortions."[59]

Notes

Introduction

Epigraph source: Anne Braden, *House Un-American Activities Committee: Bulwark of Segregation* (Los Angeles: National Committee to Abolish the House Un-American Activities Committee, 1963), 37.

1. Michael Paterniti, "How Florida Became America," *New York Times Magazine*, April 21, 2002.

2. *Washington Post*, May 31, 2001.

3. *Gainesville Sun*, July 1, 1993; *St. Petersburg Times*, January 3, 1993; *Daytona Beach News-Journal*, July 1, 1993; and *Gainesville Sun*, July 6, 1993.

4. Gary R. Mormino, *Land of Sunshine, State of Dreams: A Social History of Modern Florida* (Gainesville: University Press of Florida, 2005).

5. Bruce J. Schulman, *From Cotton Belt to Sunbelt: Federal Policy, Economic Development, and the Transformation of the South, 1938–1980* (Durham, N.C.: Duke University Press, 1994), chap. 5; V. O. Key Jr., *Southern Politics in State and Nation* (New York: Alfred A. Knopf, 1949), 83.

6. See Jeff Woods, *Black Struggle, Red Scare: Segregation and Anti-Communism in the South, 1948–1968* (Baton Rouge: Louisiana State University Press, 2004).

7. K. A. Cuordileone, *Manhood and American Political Culture in the Cold War* (New York: Routledge, 2005), 40.

8. Robert D. Dean, *Imperial Brotherhood: Gender and the Making of Cold War Foreign Policy* (Amherst: University of Massachusetts Press, 2001), 66.

9. Numan V. Bartley, *The Rise of Massive Resistance: Race and Politics in the South During the 1950s* (Baton Rouge: Louisiana State University Press, 1969); Francis M. Wilhoit, *The Politics of Massive Resistance* (New York: George Braziller, 1973); Neil R. McMillen, *The Citizens' Council: Organized Resistance to the Second Reconstruction, 1954–1964* (Urbana: University of Illinois Press, 1971); Robert Sherrill, *Gothic Politics in the Deep South: Stars of the New Confederacy* (New York: Grossman Publishers, 1968); James W. Ely Jr., *The Crisis of Conservative Virginia: The Byrd Organization and the Politics of Massive Resistance* (Knoxville: University of Tennessee Press, 1976); and Earl Black, *Southern Governors and Civil Rights: Racial Segregation as a Campaign Issue in the Second Reconstruction* (Cambridge: Harvard University Press, 1976).

10. Numan V. Bartley, *The Rise of Massive Resistance: Race and Politics in the South During the 1950s,* 2nd ed. (Baton Rouge: Louisiana State University Press, 1997), 339.

11. Alan Brinkley, "The Problem of American Conservatism," *Journal of American History,* 99 no. 2 (April 1994): 409–29; John A. Andrew III, *The Other Side of the Sixties: Young Americans for Freedom and the Rise of Conservative Politics* (New Brunswick: Rutgers University Press, 1997); and Mary C. Brennan, *Turning Right in the Sixties: The Conservative Capture of the GOP* (Chapel Hill: University of North Carolina Press, 1995).

12. Dan T. Carter, *The Politics of Rage: George Wallace, the Origins of the New Conservatism, and the Transformation of American Politics* (New York: Simon and Schuster, 1995), 12.

13. Kevin M. Kruse, *White Flight: Atlanta and the Making of Southern Conservatism* (Princeton: Princeton University Press, 2005), 10–11.

14. Joseph H. Crespino, *In Search of Another Country: Mississippi and the Conservative Counterrevolution* (Princeton: Princeton University Press, 2007), 4.

15. Matthew D. Lassiter, *The Silent Majority: Suburban Politics in the Sunbelt South* (Princeton: Princeton University Press, 2007), 3.

16. Mary L. Dudziak, *Cold War Civil Rights: Race and the Image of American Democracy* (Princeton: Princeton University Press, 2000); and Brenda Gayle Plummer, *Rising Wind: Black Americans and U.S. Foreign Affairs, 1935–1960* (Chapel Hill: University of North Carolina Press, 1996).

17. Sarah Hart Brown, "Congressional Anti-Communism and the Segregationist South: From New Orleans to Atlanta, 1954–1958," *Georgia Historical Quarterly* 80, no. 4 (Winter 1996): 788–90. See also Sarah Hart Brown, *Standing Against Dragons: Three Southern Lawyers in an Era of Fear* (Baton Rouge: Louisiana State University Press, 1998).

18. Chris Myers Asch, *The Senator and the Sharecropper: The Freedom Struggles of James O. Eastland and Fannie Lou Hamer* (New York: New Press, 2008); and William A. Link, *Righteous Warrior: Jesse Helms and the Rise of Modern Conservatism* (New York: St. Martin's Press, 2008).

19. Yasuhiro Katagiri, *The Mississippi State Sovereignty Commission: Civil Rights and States' Rights* (Jackson: University Press of Mississippi, 2001), 87.

20. M. J. Heale, *McCarthy's Americans: Red Scare Politics in State and Nation, 1935–1965* (Athens: University of Georgia Press, 1998), 18–19, 25, 214.

21. Woods, *Black Struggle, Red Scare,* 5–6.

22. Ibid., 10–11.

23. George Lewis, *Massive Resistance: The White Response to the Civil Rights Movement* (New York: Oxford University Press, 2006), 185.

24. George Lewis, *The White South and the Red Menace: Segregationists, Anticommunism, and Massive Resistance, 1945–1965* (Gainesville: University Press of Florida, 2004).

25. Woods, *Black Struggle, Red Scare,* 4–5. See John Egerton, *Speak Now Against the Day: The Generation Before the Civil Rights Movement in the South* (Chapel Hill: University of North Carolina Press, 1994); Robin D. G. Kelley, *Hammer and Hoe: Alabama Communists during the Great Depression* (Chapel Hill: University of North Carolina Press, 1990); and Robert Rodgers Korstad, *Civil Rights Unionism: Tobacco Workers and the*

Struggle for Democracy in the Mid-Twentieth-Century South (Chapel Hill: University of North Carolina Press, 2003). Jacquelyn Dowd Hall credits Bayard Rustin with the term "classical" to describe the movement between *Brown* and the Voting Rights Act. See Hall, "The Long Civil Rights Movement and the Political Uses of the Past," *Journal of American History* 91, no. 4 (March 2005): 1233–63.

26. Glenda Elizabeth Gilmore, *Defying Dixie: The Radical Roots of Civil Rights, 1919–1950* (New York: W. W Norton, 2008), 4, 6.

27. Kari Frederickson, *The Dixiecrat Revolt and the End of the Solid South, 1932–1968* (Chapel Hill: University of North Carolina Press, 2000), 8–9.

28. John D'Emilio, "The Homosexual Menace: The Politics of Sexuality in Cold War America," in *Passion and Power: Sexuality in History,* ed. Kathy Peiss and Christina Simmons (Philadelphia: Temple University Press, 1989), 226–40; and John D'Emilio, *Sexual Politics, Sexual Communities: The Making of a Homosexual Minority in the United States, 1940–1970* (Chicago: University of Chicago Press, 1983); and Alan Bérubé, *Coming Out Under Fire: The History of Gay Men and Women in World War II* (New York: Free Press, 1990).

29. Dean, *Imperial Brotherhood,* 65.

30. David K. Johnson, *The Lavender Scare: The Cold War Persecution of Gays and Lesbians in the Federal Government* (Chicago: University of Chicago Press, 2006), 9.

31. Cuordileone, *Manhood and American Political Culture,* 39.

32. Clive Webb, ed., *Massive Resistance: Southern Opposition to the Second Reconstruction* (New York: Oxford University Press, 2005), 11. In her essay in Webb's volume, "The Theology of Massive Resistance: Sex, Segregation, and the Sacred after *Brown,*" Jane Dailey examines segregationists' theological defense of Jim Crow, but only within the religious context. My focus is on conservatives' secular invocations of miscegenation as a political issue in the fight against integration and subversion.

33. Michael Kazin and Joseph A. McCartin, *Americanism: New Perspectives on the History of an Ideal* (Chapel Hill: University of North Carolina Press, 2006).

34. Steven F. Lawson, "The Florida Legislative Investigation Committee and the Constitutional Readjustment of Race Relations, 1956–1963," in *An Uncertain Tradition: Constitutionalism and the History of the South,* ed. Kermit L. Hall and James W. Ely Jr. (Athens: University of Georgia Press, 1989); and Bonnie S. Stark, "McCarthyism in Florida: Charley Johns and the Florida Legislative Investigation Committee, July 1956 to July 1965" (master's thesis, University of South Florida, 1985).

35. *New York Times,* July 4, 1993; James A. Schnur, "Closet Crusaders: The Johns Committee and Homophobia, 1956–1965," in *Carryin' On in the Lesbian and Gay South,* ed. John Howard (New York: New York University Press, 1997), 156.

36. Dan Bertwell, "'A Veritable Refuge for Practicing Homosexuals': The Johns Committee and the University of South Florida," *Florida Historical Quarterly* 83, no. 4 (Spring 2005): 410–31; Karen L. Graves, "Doing the Public's Business: Florida's Purge of Gay and Lesbian Teachers, 1959–1964," *Educational Studies* 41, no. 1 (2007): 7–32; Gerard Sullivan, "Political Opportunism and the Harassment of Homosexuals in Florida, 1952–1965," *Journal of Homosexuality* 37, no. 4 (1999): 57–81; Karen L. Graves, *And They Were*

Wonderful Teachers: Florida's Purge of Gay and Lesbian Teachers (Urbana: University of Illinois Press, 2009); and James T. Sears, *Lonely Hunters: An Oral History of Lesbian and Gay Southern Life, 1948–1968* (Boulder, Colo.: Westview Press, 1997).

37. Bérubé, *Coming Out Under Fire*; Johnson, *Lavender Scare*; John Gerassi, *The Boys of Boise: Furor, Vice, and Folly in an American City* (New York: Macmillan, 1966); John Howard, "The Library, the Park, and the Pervert: Public Space and Homosexual Encounter in Post–World War II Atlanta," *Radical History Review* 62 (Spring 1995); and Barry Werth, *The Scarlet Professor: Newton Arvin, a Literary Life Shattered by Scandal* (New York: Anchor Books, 2001).

38. *Alabama Journal*, September 14, 1963, quoted in Carter, *Politics of Rage*, 163.

39. Victor S. Navasky, *Naming Names: The Social Costs of McCarthyism* (New York: Penguin, 1991), 3, 44.

Chapter 1. The NAACP and the Origins of the Johns Committee, 1956

Epigraph source: William D. Workman, *The Case for the South* (New York: Devin-Adair, 1960), 204.

1. Bureau of the Census, *Census of Population: 1950*, vol.2, *Characteristics of the Population*, pt. 10, Florida, Table 10 (Washington, D.C.: Government Printing Office, 1952); Bureau of the Census, *Census of Population: 1960*, vol.1, *Characteristics of the Population*, pt. 11, Florida, Table 13 (Washington, D.C.: Government Printing Office, 1963).

2. David R. Colburn and Richard K. Scher, *Florida's Gubernatorial Politics in the Twentieth Century* (Tallahassee: University Presses of Florida, 1980), 16–17.

3. Ibid., 12–13, 20.

4. Kevin N. Klein, "The Pork Chop Gang: Florida's Bourbon Legacy" (master's thesis, Florida State University, 1993), 4–8.

5. Ibid., 127.

6. Key, *Southern Politics*, 92; Arthur L. Goldberg, "The Statistics of Malapportionment," *Yale Law Journal*, 72, no. 1 (November 1962): 91.

7. Helen L. Jacobstein, *The Segregation Factor in the Florida Democratic Gubernatorial Primary of 1956* (Gainesville: University Press of Florida, 1956), 15.

8. H. D. Price, *The Negro and Southern Politics: A Chapter of Florida History* (New York: New York University Press, 1957), 98; James A. Schnur, unpublished manuscript on Thelma Brinson Johns (2009), in the author's possession.

9. Office of the Clerk, Florida House of Representatives, *The People of Lawmaking in Florida, 1822–1991* (Tallahassee: Florida House of Representatives, 1991), 50; James A. Schnur with author, personal correspondence, June 11, 2008.

10. *Ervin v. Collins*, 85 So. 2d 852; 1956 Fla., March 5, 1956.

11. Tom R. Wagy, *Governor LeRoy Collins of Florida: Spokesman of the New South* (Tuscaloosa: University of Alabama Press, 1985), 33–34; Martin A. Dyckman, *Floridian of His Century: The Courage of Governor LeRoy Collins* (Gainesville: University Press of Florida, 2006), 62–63.

12. Wagy, *Governor LeRoy Collins*, 36–37.

13. *What's the Story?* WTVJ-Miami, May 13, 1954, Florida Photographic Collection, State Archives of Florida, Tallahassee.

14. Price, *Negro and Southern Politics*, 98.

15. Nicholas Lemann, *The Promised Land: The Great Black Migration and How It Changed America* (New York: Alfred A. Knopf, 1991), chaps. 1 and 2; Neil R. McMillen, ed., *Remaking Dixie: The Impact of World War II on the American South* (Jackson: University Press of Mississippi, 1997); and R. Douglas Hurt, ed., *The Rural South Since World War II* (Baton Rouge: Louisiana State University Press, 1998).

16. See Glenn Feldman, ed., *Before Brown: Civil Rights and White Backlash in the Modern South* (Tuscaloosa: University of Alabama Press, 2004).

17. James R. McGovern, *Anatomy of a Lynching: The Killing of Claude Neal* (Baton Rouge: Louisiana State University Press, 1982); Steven F. Lawson, David R. Colburn, and Darryl Paulson, "Groveland: Florida's Little Scottsboro," in *The African American Heritage of Florida*, ed. David R. Colburn and Jane L. Landers (Gainesville: University Press of Florida, 1995), 298–325; Caroline Emmons, "'Somebody Has Got to Do That Work': Harry T. Moore and the Struggle for African-American Voting Rights in Florida," *Journal of Negro History* 82, no. 2 (Spring 1997): 232–43; and Raymond A. Mohl, "The Pattern of Race Relations in Miami since the 1920s," in *The African American Heritage of Florida*, ed. David R. Colburn and Jane L. Landers (Gainesville: University Press of Florida, 1995), 326–65.

18. David L. Chappell, *Inside Agitators: White Southerners in the Civil Rights Movement* (Baltimore: Johns Hopkins University Press, 1994), 86.

19. See Bartley, *Rise of Massive Resistance* (1969); McMillen, *Citizens' Council*; and Michael J. Klarman, *From Jim Crow to Civil Rights: The Supreme Court and the Struggle for Racial Equality* (New York: Oxford University Press, 2004).

20. Heale, *McCarthy's Americans*, 7–8.

21. Woods, *Black Struggle, Red Scare*, 97–99; Crespino, *In Search of Another Country*, 26.

22. Congressman E. C. Gathings in *Congressional Record*, 84th Cong., 2nd sess., 1956, vol. 102, pt. 2:3215–59, quoted in Woods, *Black Struggle, Red Scare*, 63. See also Lewis, *White South and the Red Menace*, chaps. 1 and 2.

23. Martha Hodes, *White Women, Black Men: Illicit Sex in the Nineteenth-Century South* (New Haven: Yale University Press, 1997), 172–73. See also Hodes, *White Women, Black Men*, chap. 7; and Joel Williamson, *New People: Miscegenation and Mulattoes in the United States* (Baton Rouge: Louisiana State University Press, 1995).

24. Hodes, *White Women, Black Men*, chap. 8; Jacquelyn Hall, "'The Mind that Burns in Each Body': Women, Rape, and Racial Violence," in *Powers of Desire: The Politics of Sexuality*, ed. Ann Snitow, Christine Stansell, and Sharon Thompson (New York: Monthly Review Press, 1983), 328–49; Gail Bederman, *Manliness and Civilization: A Cultural History of Gender and Race in the United States, 1880–1917* (Chicago: University of Chicago Press, 1995). See also Renee C. Romano, *Race Mixing: Black-White Marriage in Postwar America* (Cambridge: Harvard University Press, 2003); and Susan K. Cahn, *Sexual Reckonings: Southern Girls in a Troubling Age* (Cambridge: Harvard University Press, 2007).

25. Herman E. Talmadge, *You and Segregation* (Birmingham, Ala.: Vulcan Press, 1955), 14.

26. Stanley Rowland Jr., "Legal War on the NAACP," *Nation* 184, no. 6 (February 9, 1957): 115.

27. Ralph McGill, "The Angry South," *Atlantic Monthly* 197 (April 1956): 34.

28. Herbert Ravenel Sass, "Mixed Schools and Mixed Blood," *Atlantic Monthly* 198 (November 1956): 48–49.

29. Walter F. Murphy, "The South Counterattacks: The Anti-NAACP Laws," *Western Political Quarterly* 12, no. 2 (June 1959): 379–80. Florida is not mentioned in the article, despite the fact that it was, in Thurgood Marshall's words, one of the five most "intransigent" states, in which there was little justification for "even the faintest ray of hope that the present political leadership . . . will ever voluntarily respect the Fourteenth Amendment." Thurgood Marshall, "Keynote Address at the 47th Annual Convention," San Francisco, June 26, 1956, Group III, Series A, Box A-3, Records of the NAACP: Supplement to Part I, 1956–1960, Manuscript Division, Library of Congress, Washington, D.C.

30. Robert Jerome Glennon, "The Jurisdictional Legacy of the Civil Rights Movement," *Tennessee Law Review*, Spring 1994, 891.

31. *NAACP v. Alabama* ex rel. Patterson, 357 U.S. (1958).

32. *NAACP v. Alabama* ex rel. Flowers, 377 U.S. (1964). See also Murphy, "South Counterattacks," 378–79; and Lawson, "Florida Legislative Investigation Committee," 296–325.

33. Joseph Tomberlin, "Florida Whites and the *Brown* Decision of 1954," *Florida Historical Quarterly* 51, no. 1 (July 1972): 22–23.

34. Ibid., 25–29.

35. Richard W. Ervin, *Amicus Curiae Brief of the Attorney General of Florida, in the Supreme Court of the United States*, October Term, 1954, quoted in R. W. Puryear, "Desegregation of Public Education in Florida—One Year Afterward," *Journal of Negro Education* 24, no. 3 (Summer 1955): 219.

36. Darryl Paulson and Paul Hawkes, "Desegregating the University of Florida Law School: *Virgil Hawkins v. the Florida Board of Control*," *Florida State University Law Review* 12 (Spring 1984): 64.

37. *Florida Times-Union*, March 14, 1956.

38. *St. Petersburg Times*, May 9, 1955, and September 11, 1956.

39. Bartley, *Rise of Massive Resistance* (1997), 77–78.

40. *Congressional Record*, 84th Cong. 2nd sess., March 12, 1956, vol. 102, pt. 4:4459–60 (Washington, D.C.: Governmental Printing Office, 1956).

41. Numan V. Bartley, *The New South, 1945–1980* (Baton Rouge: Louisiana State University Press, 1995), 188–89; Bartley, *Rise of Massive Resistance* (1997), 131.

42. *Tallahassee Democrat*, January 1, 1956; Florida Board of Control, *Study on Desegregation*, May 1956, 2, Box 140, LeRoy Collins Papers, Special Collections, University of South Florida Library, Tampa (hereafter cited as Collins Papers).

43. Ibid., 3, 4–7, 13, 27.

44. David R. Colburn and Lance deHaven-Smith, *Government in the Sunshine State: Florida Since Statehood* (Gainesville: University Press of Florida, 1999), 60.

45. Bryant quoted in the *Tallahassee Democrat*, January 26, 1956.

46. *Florida Times-Union*, March 16, 1956; Jacobstein, *Segregation Factor*, 21–22, 40.

47. Lowry for governor pamphlet, n.d., Box 92, Collins Papers.

48. *Brooksville Journal*, February 9, 1956.

49. A. J. Musselman to LeRoy Collins, June 14, 1956, Box 33, LeRoy Collins Administrative Correspondence, State Archives of Florida, Tallahassee (hereafter cited as Collins Administrative Correspondence).

50. Ibid.

51. Allen Morris, *Our Florida Government* (Chicago: Lyons and Carnahan, 1961), 69; Dyckman, *Floridian of His Century*, 128.

52. S.B. 10 (56), *Journal of the Senate, State of Florida*, July 23, 1956, 5.

53. Senate Concurrent Resolution 17 (56), *Journal of the Senate, State of Florida*, July 23, 1956, 7, 9.

54. S.B. 38 (56), *Journal of the Senate, State of Florida*, July 24, 1956, 27.

55. *St. Petersburg Times*, February 24, 1957; Office of the Clerk, Florida House of Representatives, *People of Lawmaking in Florida*, 25.

56. *Journal of the House of Representatives, State of Florida*, July 30, 1956, 105, and July 31, 1956, 137. House speaker Ted David voted against the bill.

57. Stark, "McCarthyism in Florida," 6–9.

58. Ney M. Gore Jr. to LeRoy Collins, August 10, 1956, SCR ID 99-40-0-117-1-1-1, Mississippi Sovereignty Commission Files, Mississippi State Archives, Jackson (hereafter cited as Sovereignty Commission Files).

59. *Tallahassee Democrat*, August 21, 1956.

60. *Tampa Tribune*, August 22, 1956.

61. *Journal of the Senate, State of Florida* (1955), 182; quoted in Joseph A. Tomberlin, "Florida and the School Desegregation Issue, 1954–1959: A Summary View," *Journal of Negro Education* 43, no. 4 (Autumn 1974): 461.

62. *Tallahassee Democrat*, August 21, 1956.

63. Sumter L. Lowry to LeRoy Collins, August 8, 1956, Box 3, Collins Administrative Correspondence.

64. Mark Hawes, confidential progress report, January 17, 1957, 2, Box 1, Records of the Florida Legislative Investigation Committee, State Archives of Florida, Tallahassee (hereafter cited as FLIC Records).

65. Marshall, "Keynote Address."

66. *Tallahassee Democrat*, August 1, 1956.

67. Florida Legislative Investigation Committee, minutes (hereafter cited as FLIC, minutes), September 11, 1956, Box 1, FLIC Records; *St. Petersburg Times*, September 11, 1956.

68. Joe T. Patterson to Henry W. Land, September 26, 1956, SCR ID 99-40-0-99-1-1-1, Sovereignty Commission Files.

69. FLIC, minutes, October 10, 1956, Box 1, FLIC Records.

70. FLIC, minutes, September 11, 1956, Box 1, FLIC Records.

71. See Wagy, *Governor LeRoy Collins*.

72. Gilbert L. Porter, "The Status of Educational Desegregation in Florida," *Journal of Negro Education* 25, no. 3 (Summer 1956): 246.

73. William L. Rivers, "Governor Collins of Florida: The Fine Art of Moderation," *Nation* 185, no. 21 (December 21, 1957): 471–72.

74. Mississippi House Bill 880, Laws of 1956, SCR ID 99-211-0-1-1-1-1, Sovereignty Commission Files.

75. Robert B. Patterson to Ney Gore, June 15, 1956, SCR ID 99-40-0-152-1-1-1, Sovereignty Commission Files.

76. *Tampa Tribune*, October 19, 1956.

77. Chappell, *Inside Agitators*, 84–87.

78. Gregory B. Padgett, "C. K. Steele, A Biography" (Ph.D. diss., Florida State University, 1994), chap. 1.

79. See Glenda Alice Rabby, *The Pain and the Promise: The Struggle for Civil Rights in Tallahassee, Florida* (Athens: University of Georgia Press, 1999).

80. *Tallahassee Democrat*, June 30, 1956.

81. Rabby, *Pain and the Promise*, 18.

82. R. J. Strickland, Tallahassee Police Department confidential report, n.d., 6, Box 139, Collins Papers.

83. Ibid., 14.

84. Ibid., 15.

85. *Tallahassee Democrat*, October 21 and 22, 1956.

86. *Tallahassee Democrat*, October 18, 1956.

87. Lucas A. Powe Jr., *The Warren Court and American Politics* (Cambridge: Harvard University Press, 2000), 73–74.

88. Rabby, *Pain and the Promise*, 49.

89. *St. Petersburg Times*, March 1, 1970.

90. *Tampa Tribune*, November 14, 1956.

91. Hawes confidential progress report, 5–6.

92. Ibid., 213–14; *Tallahassee Democrat*, June 12, 1956.

93. Taylor Branch, *Parting the Waters: America in the King Years 1954–1963* (New York: Simon and Schuster, 1988), 193–96.

94. Raymond A. Mohl, *South of the South: Jewish Activists and the Civil Rights Movement in Miami, 1945–1960* (Gainesville: University Press of Florida, 2004), 49.

Chapter 2. Racial and Sexual Perversion, 1957–1958

Epigraph source: W. Stuart Towns, *Public Address in the Twentieth-Century South: The Evolution of a Region* (Westport, Conn.: Praeger, 1999), 131.

1. *Tallahassee Democrat*, February 9, 1957.

2. *Tallahassee Democrat*, January 8, 1957, and February 1, 1957. See also Rabby, *Pain and the Promise*, chap. 3.

3. *St. Petersburg Times*, February 1, 1957.

4. Testimony, Virgil D. Hawkins, February 4, 1957, Box 2, Florida Bar FLIC Records, State Archives of Florida, Tallahassee.

5. Report quoted in William Andrew Fordham's testimony, February 4, 1957, 105–7, Box 2, Florida Bar FLIC Records.

6. Ibid.

7. Testimony, Francisco A. Rodriguez, February 19, 1957, 999, Box 1, Florida Bar FLIC Records.

8. Testimony, Horace E. Hill, February 4, 1957, 164, 166, Box 2, Florida Bar FLIC Records.

9. *St. Petersburg Times*, February 6, 1957.

10. Testimony, Horace E. Hill, February 7, 1957, 598, Box 1, Florida Bar FLIC Records; *St. Petersburg Times*, February 5, 1957.

11. Testimony, John Boardman, February 6, 1957, 399, 421, 438, Box 1, Florida Bar FLIC Records.

12. Governor's Advisory Commission on Bi-Racial Problems, minutes, January 29, 1957, 10, 14, Box 117, Collins Administrative Correspondence.

13. Ibid., 3. See Brian Ward, *Just My Soul Responding: Rhythm and Blues, Black Consciousness, and Race Relations* (Berkeley and Los Angeles: University of California Press, 1998), chap. 2.

14. Governor's Advisory Commission on Bi-Racial Problems, minutes, 11.

15. *Tallahassee Democrat*, February 6, 1957.

16. *St. Petersburg Times*, February 7, 1957. Before World War II, the NAACP had targeted antimiscegenation laws but shifted its focus to desegregating education and public accommodations. See Peggy Pascoe, *What Comes Naturally: Miscegenation Law and the Making of Race in America* (New York: Oxford University Press, 2009), esp. 201–4.

17. *Tallahassee Democrat*, February 7 and 8, 1957; *St. Petersburg Times*, February 8, 1957.

18. *Tampa Tribune*, February 9, 1957.

19. Charley Johns press release, February 7, 1957, Box 1, FLIC Records.

20. Testimony, Emmett Bashful, February 18, 1957, 767, Box 4, FLIC Records.

21. *St. Petersburg Times*, February 19, 1957.

22. Testimony, Joseph Spagna, February 18, 1957, 825, 841, 865, Box 1, Florida Bar FLIC Records.

23. Testimony, Leonard Speed, February 18, 1957, 902, Box 1, Florida Bar FLIC Records.

24. Testimony, Harold Owens, February 18, 1957, 529, Box 1, Florida Bar FLIC Records.

25. Testimony before the Florida Legislative Investigation Committee, February 19, 1957, 919, Box 4, FLIC Records; *Tallahassee Democrat*, February 19, 1957; *St. Petersburg Times*, February 20, 1957.

26. *Tallahassee Democrat*, February 26, 1957; *St. Petersburg Times*, February 26, 1957.

27. Statement of the Attorney General on the Proposed Civil Rights Legislation Before the Subcommittee on Constitutional Rights of the Senate Judiciary Committee, press release, February 14, 1957, 1, "Civil Rights—Civil Rights Act of 1957," Digital Documents Project, Dwight D. Eisenhower Library, Abilene, Kans.

28. *St. Petersburg Times*, February 8, 1957.

29. Brian Lewis Crispell, *Testing the Limits: George Armistead Smathers and Cold War America* (Athens: University of Georgia Press, 1999), 121–25.

30. "Report of the Florida Legislative Investigation Committee to the 1959 Session

of the Legislature," n.d., 3, Box 9, Records of the Clerk of the House of Representatives, 1955–1965, State Archives of Florida, Tallahassee (hereafter cited as CHOR).

31. Ibid., 4, 10.

32. Ibid., 13.

33. *St. Petersburg Times*, February 10, 1957.

34. *Journal of the Senate, State of Florida*, April 15, 1957, 123, and May 10, 1957; *Tampa Tribune*, May 1, 1957.

35. House Concurrent Resolution 174, May 2, 1957, Acts of the Territorial Legislature and Acts of the Legislature, 1822–Present, Series S 222, State Archives of Florida, Tallahassee; William C. Havard and Loren P. Beth, *The Politics of Mis-Representation: Rural-Urban Conflict in the Florida Legislature* (Baton Rouge: Louisiana State University Press, 1962), 31.

36. *Tampa Tribune*, May 2 and 3, 1957.

37. *St. Petersburg Times*, June 1, 1957.

38. *St. Petersburg Times*, April 7, 1957.

39. *Tampa Tribune*, January 29, 1957.

40. Richard T. Jones, "Sodomy—Crime or Sin?" *University of Florida Law Review* 12 (1959): 83–91. The statute is quoted on 85.

41. *Tallahassee Democrat*, February 22, 1957. See also Jones, "Sodomy—Crime or Sin?"

42. Police report, L. J. Van Buskirk and M. Bromley, January 30, 1957, Box 1, FLIC Records.

43. Ibid.; report, M. Bromley, February 12, 1957, Box 13, FLIC Records.

44. Florida Sheriff's Bureau, Investigative Report, June 3, 1957, 1, Box 1, FLIC Records; Don McLeod to Ross Anderson, memo, May 23, 1957, Box 1, FLIC Records.

45. Florida Sheriff's Bureau, Investigative Report, June 3, 1957, 9.

46. Testimony, February 6, 1959, 9, Box 7, FLIC Records.

47. Ibid., 12–13.

48. Mohl, *South of the South*.

49. Woods, *Black Struggle, Red Scare*, 2004, 77.

50. Quoted in Mark Solomon, *The Cry Was Unity: Communists and African Americans, 1917–1936* (Jackson: University Press of Mississippi, 1998), chap. 1. See also Woods, *Black Struggle, Red Scare*; and Gilmore, *Defying Dixie*.

51. Kelley, *Hammer and Hoe*; Gilmore, *Defying Dixie*; and Korstad, *Civil Rights Unionism*.

52. Kelley, *Hammer and Hoe*, 220.

53. Testimony, Sylvia Crouch, January 7, 1958, Box 4, FLIC Records.

54. Thomas A. Krueger, *And Promises to Keep: The Southern Conference on Human Welfare* (Nashville: Vanderbilt University Press, 1967), 14–23.

55. Quoted in Krueger, *And Promises to Keep*, 167.

56. J. P. Coleman, Mississippi Sovereignty Commission memo, August 12, 1958, SCR ID 99-10-0-3-1-1-1; "Unmasking the Deceiver," SCR ID 1-85-0-7-1-1-1; and Senator John McLaurin testimony, July 31, 1963, 5, SCR ID 99-94-01-5-1-1, all in Sovereignty Commission Files.

57. Navasky, *Naming Names*, 86.

58. Robert Justin Goldstein, "Prelude to McCarthyism: The Making of a Blacklist," *Prologue* 38, no. 3 (Fall 2006).

59. Woods, *Black Struggle, Red Scare*, 26, 43–44, 57, 63.

60. J. B. Matthews, *Communism and the NAACP* (Atlanta: Georgia Commission on Education, 1958), 5, 8; Gilmore, *Defying Dixie*, 64.

61. Matthews, *Communism and the NAACP*, 9.

62. Mohl, *South of the South*, 3.

63. Ibid., 27–28.

64. Testimony, February 26, 1958, 181, Box 4, FLIC Records.

65. "Witnesses Who Have Been Subpoenaed to Appear February 26, 1958," 5, Box 13, FLIC Records.

66. Testimony, February 26, 1958, 190, 194, Box 4, FLIC Records.

67. Testimony, February 26, 1958, 223, 225–26, 229–30, 263, Box 4, FLIC Records.

68. Ibid., 310.

69. Testimony, February 26, 1958, 326, Box 4, FLIC Records.

70. Alex Lichtenstein, "Putting Labor's House in Order: Anticommunism and Miami's Transport Workers' Union, 1945–1949," *Labor History* 39, no. 4 (Winter 1998): 7–23.

71. Eric Tscheschlok, "'So Goes the Negro': Race and Labor in Miami, 1940–1963," *Florida Historical Quarterly* 76, no. 1 (Summer 1997): 49.

72. Gerald Horne, *Communist Front? The Civil Rights Congress, 1946–1956* (Rutherford, N.J.: Fairleigh Dickenson University Press, 1988), 13–14, 354–55; Mohl, *South of the South*, 42, 46, Bobbi Graff quoted on 47.

73. Testimony, February 27, 1958, 372–73, 379–80.

74. *Courier*, n.d., Box 1, Ruth Perry Papers, University of South Florida Special Collections, Tampa; Judith G. Poucher, "Raising Her Voice: Ruth Perry, Activist and Journalist for the Miami NAACP," *Florida Historical Quarterly* 84, no. 4 (Spring 2006): 517–40.

75. Testimony, February 27, 1958, 393–94, Box 4, FLIC Records.

76. Marvin Dunn, *Black Miami in the Twentieth Century* (Gainesville: University Press of Florida, 1997), 191.

77. Testimony, Theodore Gibson, February 27, 1958, 433–34, Box 4, FLIC Records.

78. Ibid., 434–35.

79. FLIC hearing, February 28, 1958, 435, Box 3, FLIC Records.

80. Lawson, "Florida Legislative Investigation Committee," 307–14; *Gibson v. Florida Legislative Investigation Committee*, 372 U.S. 539 (1963).

81. John D'Emilio, "The Homosexual Menace," in *Making Trouble: Essays on Gay History, Politics, and the University*, by John D'Emilio (New York: Routledge, 1992), 63.

82. George R. Bentley to J. Wayne Reitz, January 11, 1956, Box 12, Records of the American Association of University Professors, Florida Chapter, University of Florida Archives, Gainesville.

83. *St. Petersburg Times*, February 17, 1957.

84. Havard and Beth, *Politics of Mis-Representation*, 158–59.

85. Schnur, "Closet Crusaders," 134.

86. Charley E. Johns, "Homosexuality and Public Education" (Report of the FLIC,

1959), 1, Box 101, Collins Administrative Correspondence; Strickland quoted in Stark, "McCarthyism in Florida," 93.

87. Testimony, January 22, 1959, 1500, Box 7, FLIC Records.

88. Minutes of Florida Legislative Investigation Committee meeting, October 2, 1957, Box 9, CHOR.

89. John Tileston, interview with author, August 2, 1997, Alachua, Fla.

90. Witness statement, January 7, 1959, 661, Box 7, FLIC Records.

91. Minutes of Florida Legislative Investigation Committee meeting, September 27, 1958, 1–2, CHOR.

92. Laud Humphreys, *Tearoom Trade: Impersonal Sex in Public Places* (Chicago: Aldine Publishing, 1970), 41.

93. Ibid., 111–29.

94. Dean, *Imperial Brotherhood,* 65.

95. Deposition, October 1, 1958, Box 6, FLIC Records.

96. Deposition, October 13, 1958, Box 6, FLIC Records.

97. Deposition, October 20, 1958, Box 6, FLIC Records.

98. Deposition, November 20, 1958, Box 6, FLIC Records.

99. Statement of facts, December 12, 1958, Box 6, FLIC Records.

100. Clyde Miller to Gene Baro, December 6, 1958, Gene Baro Papers, Box 2, Special and Area Studies Collections, George A. Smathers Libraries, University of Florida, Gainesville (hereafter cited as Baro Papers).

101. Clyde Miller to Gene Baro, February 5, 1959, Baro Papers.

Chapter 3. Surveillance and Exposure, 1959–1960

Epigraph source: *Time*, December 7, 1953.

1. Testimony, January 5, 1959, 229, Box 6, FLIC Records.

2. Testimony, November 19, 1959, Box 7, FLIC Records.

3. Ellen W. Schrecker, *No Ivory Tower: McCarthyism and the Universities* (New York: Oxford University Press, 1986), 5, 68.

4. Witness statement, January 5, 1959, 35, 62–63, Box 6, FLIC Records.

5. Ibid., 68–75.

6. Cuordileone, *Manhood and American Political Culture*, 146.

7. Witness statement, January 5, 1959, 233, Box 6, FLIC Records.

8. Ibid., 249.

9. Ibid., 304.

10. Ibid., 340.

11. Ibid., 343.

12. Ibid., 354–55.

13. *Florida Alligator*, February 17, 1959.

14. J. Wayne Reitz to Harris G. Sims, February 3, 1959, J. Wayne Reitz Administrative Records, Box 26, University of Florida Archives, Gainesville (hereafter cited as Reitz Administrative Records).

15. *Tampa Tribune*, February 18, 1959.

16. Cuordileone, *Manhood and American Political Culture*, 147–49. See also Robert

Hofler, *The Man Who Invented Rock Hudson: The Pretty Boys and Dirty Deals of Henry Wilson* (New York: Da Capo Press, 2005); and Andrea Friedman, "The Smearing of Joe McCarthy: The Lavender Scare, Gossip, and Cold War Politics," *American Quarterly* 57, no. 4 (December 2005): 1105–29.

17. Erdman Palmore, "Published Reactions to the Kinsey Report," *Social Forces* 31, no. 2 (December 1952): 165–72. See James H. Jones, *Alfred C. Kinsey* (New York: Norton, 1997).

18. Edward Alwood, *Straight News: Gays, Lesbians, and the News Media* (New York: Columbia University Press, 1996), 23–26.

19. *Florida Alligator*, April 17, 1959, February 19, 1960.

20. Sears, *Lonely Hunters*, 21.

21. Fred Fejes, "Murder, Perversion, and Moral Panic: The 1954 Media Campaign Against Miami's Homosexuals and the Discourse of Civic Betterment," *Journal of the History of Sexuality*, 9, no. 3 (July 2000): 305–47; Sears, *Lonely Hunters*, 23.

22. Lyn Pederson, "Miami's New Type Witchhunt," *ONE* 4, no. 4 (April–May 1956): 12.

23. Estelle B. Freedman, "'Uncontrolled Desires': The Response to the Sexual Psychopath, 1920–1960," *Journal of American History* 74, no. 1 (June 1987): 83–106.

24. Philip Jenkins, *Moral Panic: Changing Concepts of the Child Molester in Modern America* (New Haven: Yale University Press, 1998), 57–58.

25. Irving Bieber, *Homosexuality: A Psychoanalytic Study* (Northvale, NJ: Jason Aronson, 1962), 47–53, and 114.

26. Albert Ellis, *Homosexuality: Its Causes and Cure* (New York: Lyle Stuart, 1965), 62.

27. Clifford Allen, *The Sexual Perversions and Abnormalities: A Study in the Psychology of Paraphilia* (New York: Oxford University Press, 1949), 134.

28. Eugene D. Williams, introduction to *The Sexual Criminal: A Psychoanalytic Study*, by J. Paul de River (Springfield, Ill.: Charles C. Thomas, 1950), xii.

29. *Atlanta Constitution*, October 11, 1953.

30. *Idaho Daily Statesman*, November 20, 1955, quoted in Gerassi, *Boys of Boise*, 17.

31. *Greensboro News and Record*, September 17, 2006.

32. Arthur Guy Mathews, *Is Homosexuality a Menace?* (New York: Robert M. McBride, 1957), 8–9. See also Geoffrey S. Smith, "National Security and Personal Isolation: Sex, Gender, and Disease in the Cold-War United States," *International History Review*, May 2, 1992.

33. J. Paul de River, *The Sexual Criminal: A Psychoanalytic Study* (Springfield, Ill.: Charles C. Thomas, 1950), 269; James Melvin Reinhardt, *Sex Perversions and Sex Crimes* (Springfield, Ill.: Charles C. Thomas, 1957), 21.

34. Graves, "Doing the Public's Business," 13–14.

35. Ellen Herman, *The Romance of American Psychology: Political Culture in the Age of Experts* (Berkeley and Los Angeles: University of California Press, 1995), 87–89.

36. Ibid., 92.

37. Bérubé, *Coming Out Under Fire*, 137.

38. Johnson, *Lavender Scare*, 17, 73, 166.

39. Ibid., 137; Bérubé, *Coming Out Under Fire*, 265–70; D'Emilio, "Homosexual

Menace," in Peiss and Simmons, *Passion and Power*, 59–60. See also D'Emilio, *Sexual Politics, Sexual Communities.*

40. FLIC Report, 1959, 4, Box 101, Collins Administrative Correspondence (hereafter cited as FLIC Report, 1959); *St. Petersburg Times*, April 30, 1959.

41. FLIC Report, 1959, 6–7.

42. *Florida Alligator*, May 12, 1959.

43. *Florida Alligator*, May 15, 1959.

44. *Florida Alligator*, May 8, 1959.

45. *Florida Alligator*, May 12, 1959.

46. Harrison L. Friese to J. Wayne Reitz, May 16, 1959, and Reitz to Friese, May 26, 1959, Reitz Administrative Records.

47. "Report of the Florida Legislative Investigation Committee to the 1959 Session of the Legislature," Part II, 12–13, 18, 22, Box 9, CHOR.

48. *Journal of the Senate, State of Florida*, June 2, 1959, 1233; June 5, 1959, 1675, 1687.

49. Office memoranda, State Department of Education, June 15, 1959, Box 13, Thomas D. Bailey Subject Files, State Archives of Florida, Tallahassee (hereafter cited as Bailey Subject Files).

50. FLIC, minutes, June 24, 1959, 1–7, Box 1, FLIC Records.

51. Unnamed to Charley Johns, August 18, 1959, Box 3, FLIC Records.

52. R. J. Strickland to Cliff Herrell, July 16, 1959, Box 3, FLIC Records.

53. Testimony, August 18, 1959, 10, 17, 22, Box 7, FLIC Records.

54. Ibid., 35–36, 39.

55. Testimony, August 19, 1959, 103–7, Box 7, FLIC Records.

56. R. J. Strickland to H. A. Poole, June 18, 1959, Box 3, FLIC Records.

57. R. J. Strickland to Cliff Herrell, July 1, 1959, Box 3, FLIC Records.

58. Irwin Klibaner, "The Travail of Southern Radicals: The Southern Conference Educational Fund, 1946–1976," *Journal of Southern History* 49, no. 2 (May 1983): 183.

59. Oral history interview with Virginia Foster Durr and Clifford Durr, March 1, 1975, 37, LBJ Ranch, Stonewall, Texas, Virginia Foster Durr Papers, Carton 1, Schlesinger Library, Harvard University.

60. Strickland to Herrell, December 15, 1959, Box 3, FLIC Records.

61. Murphy, "South Counterattacks," 378–79; Lawson, "Florida Legislative Investigation Committee," 307–11; *Gibson v. Florida Legislative Investigation Committee.*

62. *Atlanta Journal*, December 6, 1959.

63. Testimony, August 18, 1959, 54, Box 7, FLIC Records.

64. Testimony, January 13, 1960, 10, 13, Box 7, FLIC Records.

65. *St. Petersburg Times*, March 18, 1960.

66. Testimony, May 9, 1960, 2–3, 8, Box 8, FLIC Records.

67. Ibid., 13–14, 24–25.

68. Testimony, May 19, 1960, 14.

69. Testimony, October 14, 1960, 8, Box 8, FLIC Records.

70. Testimony, October 10, 1960, 15, Box 8, FLIC Records.

71. Testimony, October 19, 1960, 2, Box 8, FLIC Records.

72. Floyd T. Christian to J. T. Kelley, December 6, 1960, Box 13, Bailey Subject Files.

73. Dade County police report, December 10, 1960, 3, Box 13, FLIC Records.

74. Werth, *Scarlet Professor*.

75. Ellis, *Homosexuality*, 67–77.

76. Mathews, *Is Homosexuality a Menace?* 20–21 and 121.

77. Elizabeth Lapovsky Kennedy and Madeline D. Davis, *Boots of Leather, Slippers of Gold: The History of a Lesbian Community* (New York: Routledge, 1993).

78. Rabby, *Pain and the Promise*, 82–83.

79. Ibid., 88–89, 93–96; *Tallahassee Democrat*, March 13, 1960, and March 18, 1960; *Memphis Commercial Appeal*, March 18, 1960.

80. Testimony, Mary Mueller, March 21, 1960, 2, 8, 33–34, Box 8, FLIC Records.

81. Quoted in Adam Nossiter, *Of Long Memory: Mississippi and the Murder of Medgar Evers* (Reading, Mass.: Addison-Wesley, 1994), 101.

82. Quoted in John Howard, *Men Like That: A Southern Queer History* (Chicago: University of Chicago Press, 1999), 146, 148.

83. Mueller testimony, March 21, 1960, 38–39.

84. "Report of the Florida Legislative Investigation Committee to the 1961 Session of the Legislature," SCR ID 13-0-3-31-2-1-1, Sovereignty Commission Files.

85. *Tampa Tribune*, March 16, 1960.

86. Remarks by Governor LeRoy Collins, March 20, 1960, Box 96, Collins Papers.

87. Mrs. Carroll B. Austin to Collins, April 1, 1960; Mrs. Carole Bevan to Collins, April 5, 1960; J. A. Henderson to Collins, April 2, 1960; E. S. Holland to Collins, March 24, 1960; Sumter Lowry to Collins, March 21, 1960, all in Box 47, Collins Papers.

88. *Gibson v. Florida Legislative Investigation Committee*.

89. Ibid.; *New Orleans Times-Picayune*, August 31, 1960.

90. Strickland to Hawes, August 22, 1960, Box 3, FLIC Records; *Tampa Tribune*, August 17, 1960.

91. Florida Council on Human Relations, Report on the Jacksonville Riot, September 1960, Box 17, FLIC Records.

92. Dyckman, *Floridian of His Century*, 198–200.

Chapter 4. Subversion and Indecency, 1961–1962

Epigraph source: J. Edgar Hoover, *Masters of Deceit: The Story of Communism in America and How to Fight It* (New York: Henry Holt, 1958), 107–8.

1. Report, December 10, 1960, 2–3, Box 13, FLIC Records.

2. Testimony, 1961, 2, 4, Box 8, FLIC Records.

3. Testimony, April 3, 1961, 3, Box 8, FLIC Records.

4. Testimony, ca. June 1961, 13–14, Box 9, FLIC Records.

5. Testimony, January 6, 1961, 5, Box 9, FLIC Records.

6. Farris Bryant letter, April 9, 1961, Box 57, Farris Bryant Administrative Correspondence, Florida State Archives, Tallahassee (hereafter cited as Bryant Administrative Correspondence).

7. Report of the Governor's Advisory Committee on Decent Literature, March 15, 1961, 3, Box 80, Bryant Administrative Correspondence.

8. *Journal of the Senate, State of Florida*, April 5, 1961, 21; April 12, 1961, 111.

9. James Gilbert, *A Cycle of Outrage: America's Reaction to the Juvenile Delinquent in the 1950s* (New York: Oxford University Press, 1986), 3, 18–19.

10. Christopher M. Finan, *From the Palmer Raids to the Patriot Act: A History of the Fight for Free Speech in America* (Boston: Beacon Press, 2007), 175–77. See also Andrea Friedman, "Sadists and Sissies: Anti-pornography Campaigns in Cold War America," *Gender & History* 15, no. 2 (August 2003): 201–27.

11. *Comic Books and Juvenile Delinquency: Interim Report of the Committee on the Judiciary*, 84th Cong., 1st sess., Report No. 62, 7, 32. See also David Hajdu, *The Ten-Cent Plague: The Great Comic-Book Scare and How It Changed America* (New York: Farrar, Straus and Giroux, 2008).

12. William Murray, "Books Are Burning: The Spreading Censorship," *Nation*, May 2, 1953, 367–68; Thomas B. Leary and J. Roger Noall, "Public Pressures and the Law: Official and Unofficial Control of the Content and Distribution of Motion Pictures and Magazines," *Harvard Law Review* 71, no. 2 (December 1957): 326–67.

13. William J. Hempel and Patrick M. Wall, "Extralegal Censorship of Literature," *New York University Law Review* 33 (1958): 992–93.

14. *New York Times*, September 26, 1955, and May 6, 1959; *Time*, September 19, 1955; Jim Kepner, *Rough News, Daring Views: 1950s' Pioneer Gay Press Journalism* (New York: Routledge, 1997), 216–19; and Benjamin DeMott, "The Sad Tale of Newton Arvin," *New York Review of Books* 48, no. 19 (November 29, 2001).

15. *Rome News-Tribune*, May 31, 1953; Gregory C. Lisby, "'Trying to Define What May Be Indefinable': The Georgia Literature Commission, 1953–1973," *Georgia Historical Quarterly* 84 (Spring 2000): 72–97.

16. G. H. W. Schmidt to Hubert L. Dyer, February 2, 1961; and Mrs. Joe Popp to James Wesbury [*sic*], February 3, 1961, Box 3, Administrative Files, State Literature Commission of Georgia, Georgia Archives, Athens.

17. James Pickett Wesberry, *Every Citizen Has a Right to Know: A Report of the Georgia Literature Commission to the Governor, the General Assembly, and the People of Georgia* (Atlanta: Commission, 1954), 2, 9–10.

18. Ibid., 12, 19. See Lisby, "Trying to Define What May Be Indefinable."

19. Whitney Strub, "Perversion for Profit: Citizens for Decent Literature and the Arousal of an Antiporn Public in the 1960s," *Journal of the History of Sexuality* 15, no. 2 (May 2006): 258–91. Charles Keating gained notoriety as a key figure in the savings and loan scandal of the late 1980s.

20. Grant S. McClellan, ed., *Censorship in the United States* (New York: H. W. Wilson, 1967), 56–57.

21. John D'Emilio and Estelle B. Freedman, *Intimate Matters: A History of Sexuality in America* (New York: Harper & Row, 1988); Henry E. Scott, *Shocking True Story: The Rise and Fall of Confidential, "America's Most Scandalous Scandal Magazine"* (New York: Pantheon, 2010), chap. 1; and Kenneth C. Davis, *Two-Bit Culture: The Paperbacking of America* (Boston: Houghton Mifflin, 1984), 147.

22. Richard Kyle-Keith, *The High Price of Pornography* (Washington, D.C.: Public Affairs Press, 1961), 45–46, 48, and 57.

23. Ibid., 61–62.

24. Testimony, February 9, 1961,279–80, Box 5, FLIC Records.

25. R. J. Strickland to A. L. Hopkins, June 28, 1961 (including FLIC Report), SCR ID 3-6A-2-13-1-1-1, Sovereignty Commission Files.

26. Woods, *Black Struggle, Red Scare*, 213; Howard Zinn, *SNCC: The New Abolitionists* (Boston: South End Press, 2002), 172.

27. "Meeting of State Officials of several Southern and Western States at Atlanta, Georgia, for the purpose of discussing Communism, racial agitators, the Black Muslim Cult, and subversion in general," June 9, 1961, 1, 6, SRC ID 1-8-0-16-1-1-1, Sovereignty Commission Files; Barbara Ransby, *Ella Baker and the Black Freedom Movement: A Radical Democratic Vision* (Chapel Hill: University of North Carolina Press, 2002), 248.

28. Graves, "Doing the Public's Business"; Bailey quoted on 16.

29. Strickland to Hopkins, June 28, 1961; Florida Legislature, *Laws of Florida*, vol. 1, pt. 1, chap. 61–62, Tallahassee.

30. Graves, "Doing the Public's Business," 18; Thomas D. Bailey report, "Education in Florida," 1961, Box 11, Education in Florida Subject Files, 1947–1978, P. K. Yonge Library of Florida History, University of Florida.

31. Graves, "Doing the Public's Business," 19.

32. *New York Times*, May 21, 1961.

33. *New York Times*, September 24, 1961.

34. "American Bar Association Report of the Conference Committee on Need for Education as to Aims and Threat of Communism," February 9, 1961, 2, sent to Thomas Bailey by Northeast High School principal John Sexton, April 4, 1961, Box 5, Bailey Subject Files.

35. James Graham Cook, *The Segregationists* (New York: Appleton-Century-Crofts, 1962), 19.

36. *Florida's Children* 12 (November 1961): 2.

37. Ibid; quotation from Kenneth Goff, ed., *Brain-Washing: A Synthesis of the Russian Textbook on Psychopolitics* (Englewood, Colo.: Kenneth Goff, 1955), 26–27.

38. *Tallahassee Democrat*, January 17, 1962.

39. Report, Tom Scarbrough, November 17, 1961, 4–5, SCR ID 3-6A-2-20-1-1-1, Sovereignty Commission Files; *New York Times*, November 26, 1961.

40. Report, A. L. Hopkins, June 30, 1961, SCR ID 2-55-3-29-1-1-1, Sovereignty Commission Files; *New York Times*, May 26, 1961; and Raymond Arsenault, *Freedom Riders: 1961 and the Struggle for Racial Justice* (New York: Oxford University Press, 2006), 280, 346.

41. Rudd quoted in Arsenault, *Freedom Riders*, 324.

42. Testimony, Yvonne Ross, July 15, 1961, 5, 18–19, Box 9, FLIC Records.

43. Bureau of the Census, *Census of Population: 1960*, vol. 1, *Characteristics of the Population*, pt. 11, Florida, Table 120 (Washington, D.C.: Government Printing Office, 1963).

44. Donna Penn, "The Meanings of Lesbianism in Post-War America," *Gender & History* 3 (Summer 1991): 201.

45. Lillian Faderman, *Odd Girls and Twilight Lovers: A History of Lesbian Life in*

Twentieth-Century America (New York: Penguin, 1991), 145–47; D'Emilio, "Homosexual Menace," in D'Emilio, *Making Trouble*, 57–73.

46. Mathews, *Is Homosexuality a Menace?*, 20.

47. Florida School for Boys, pamphlet, n.d., 1–2, Box 3, Records of the Florida Children's Commission, Florida State Archives, Tallahassee (hereafter cited as FCC Records); Jerrell H. Shofner, *Jackson County, Florida: A History* (Marianna: Jackson County Heritage Association, 1985), 397.

48. "Suggestions to Staff Members for Working with Children," Marianna, 1957, Box 3, FCC Records.

49. Testimony, Robert L. Currie, n.d., 6, Box 9, FLIC Records.

50. "Report of the Florida Legislative Investigation Committee to the 1961 Session of the Legislature," Box 1, FLIC Records.

51. Currie testimony, 7, 10.

52. Ibid., 19, 33.

53. Florida Sheriff's Bureau, "Summary of Homosexual Activities Conferences," n.d., 1, Box 57, Bryant Administrative Correspondence.

54. *Tampa Tribune*, March 22, 1962.

55. *Tampa Tribune*, March 19, 1962.

56. *Florida Times-Union*, March 6, 1962; *Florida's Children* 13 (April 1962): 1.

57. *Florida's Children* 13 (February 1962): 6.

58. Ibid., 4.

59. *Tampa Tribune*, January 6, 1962.

60. E. Wilson Purdy to Farris Bryant, March 15, 1962, Box 18, Bryant Administrative Correspondence.

61. Report, Florida Children's Commission advisory committee, January 22, 1962, 3–4, 7, and 13, Box 1, FLIC Records.

62. *Lakeland Ledger*, October 16, 1961.

63. *Tampa Tribune*, January 17, 1962.

64. *Tallahassee Democrat*, April 27, 1962.

65. Testimony, April 17, 1962, 348–49, Box 9, FLIC Records.

66. Wayne Yeager to the Florida Children's Commission's Advisory Committee on Homosexuality, memo, June 4, 1962, 1–2, Box 57, Bryant Administrative Correspondence.

67. Russell M. Cooper and Margaret B. Fisher, *The Vision of a Contemporary University: A Case Study of Expansion and Development in American Higher Education, 1950–1975* (Gainesville: University Presses of Florida, 1982), xi–13.

68. George B. Stallings to Charley Johns, November 28, 1961, Box 2, FLIC Records.

69. Charley Johns to R. J. Strickland, December 4, 1961, Box 2, FLIC Records.

70. Michael J. Hansinger to Farris Bryant, November 24, 1961, Box 26, Bryant Administrative Correspondence.

71. Testimony, Thomas Wenner, June 7, 1962, Box 5, FLIC Records.

72. FLIC report of telephone conversation with Thomas Wenner, n.d., Box 9, FLIC Records.

73. Judith Ann Schiff, "Firing the Firebrand," *Yale Alumni Magazine* (May/June 2005); *New York Times*, October 24, 1979.

74. Testimony, Joe McClain, June 5, 1962, Box 5, FLIC Records.

75. John Allen to Winston W. Ehrmann, Staff Associate, American Association of University Professors, December 17, 1962, John Allen Papers, Box 3, Special Collections, University of South Florida, Tampa (hereafter cited as Allen Papers).

76. Report, n.d., written by Mrs. Smith (hereafter cited as Smith report), 1, Box 1, John Egerton Papers, Special Collections, University of South Florida, Tampa (hereafter cited as Egerton Papers); testimony, Jane Smith, June 4, 1962, 1639, Box 5, FLIC Records.

77. Smith report, 2.

78. Testimony, Sidney French, May 30, 1962, 966–67, Box 5, FLIC Records.

79. Smith report, 3.

80. Ibid., 3–4.

81. Florida Legislative Investigation Committee, memo, April 18, 1962, Box 1, FLIC Records.

82. Testimony, May 8, 1962, 1–2, Box 10, FLIC Records.

83. See Bertwell, "Veritable Refuge for Practicing Homosexuals," 419–20.

84. Testimony, May 9, 1962, 4–6, Box 10, FLIC Records.

85. Testimony, May 10, 1962, 2, Box 10, FLIC Records.

86. Ibid., 1–5.

87. Testimony, May 15, 1962, 1–2, Box 10, FLIC Records.

88. Testimony, May 10, 1962, 6, Box 10, FLIC Records.

89. Testimony, May 18, 1962, Box 10, FLIC Records.

90. Testimony, May 10, 1962, 6, Box 10, FLIC Records; testimony, May 15, 1962, 2, 6, Box 10, FLIC Records.

91. John Allen address, May 21, 1962, Box 1, Egerton Papers.

92. Cooper and Fisher, *Vision of a Contemporary University*, 94.

93. Testimony, May 23, 1962, 197–98, Box 5, FLIC Records; Cooper and Fisher, *Vision of a Contemporary University*, 23.

94. Cooper and Fisher, *Vision of a Contemporary University*, 224.

95. Ibid., 230–31, 247.

96. Testimony, May 24, 1962, 62–63, Box 5, FLIC Records.

97. Testimony, May 25, 1962, 358–59, Box 5, FLIC Records.

98. Testimony, May 23, 1962, Box 5, FLIC Records.

99. Testimony, May 30, 1962, 960, Box 5, FLIC Records.

100. Ibid., 1122–23.

101. Ibid., 1142–44.

102. Ibid., 1184.

103. A. L. Hopkins, investigative report, June 20, 1962, 2, SCR ID 3-16A-2-104-1-1-1, Sovereignty Commission Files.

104. Howard, *Men Like That*, 150–51.

105. Katagiri, *Mississippi State Sovereignty Commission*, 73; Howard, *Men Like That*, 158.

106. Statement of William McKindley Daywalt, February 10, 1963, 33, 42–43, SCR ID 1-76-0-55-11-1-1, Sovereignty Commission Files.

107. Ibid., 84.

108. Florida Board of Control, memorandum, July 17, 1962, 2–3, Box 1, Papers of J. B. Culpepper, Florida State Archives, Tallahassee (hereafter cited as Culpepper Papers).

109. Ibid.

110. Statements of position submitted by the Presidents of the State Universities, September 1962, 1, Box 1, Culpepper Papers.

111. Ibid., 1–2.

112. Report of the Special Committee of the Board of Control, September 14, 1962, 2, 5, Box 1, FLIC Records.

113. "Implementations of the Recommendations Approved by the Board of Control on September 14, 1962," Gainesville, October 19, 1962, Box 1, Culpepper Papers.

114. Norman Podhoretz, "The Know-Nothing Bohemians," *Partisan Review* (Spring 1958): 7.

115. *Tampa Times*, December 4, 1962.

116. Statement by Charles R. Forman, Ft. Lauderdale, December 7, 1962, 1, Box 26, Bryant Administrative Correspondence.

117. Executive Committee of the USF chapter of the American Association of University Professors to the Florida Board of Control, November 7, 1962, 1, Allen Papers.

118. American Association of University Women report, n.d., Allen Papers.

119. Florida Board of Control, Statement of Policy on Academic Freedom and Responsibilities, December 7, 1962, 1–3, Box 1, FLIC Records.

120. "Parent" to John Allen, August 1962, Allen Papers.

121. Orva Lee Ice to Farris Bryant, August 28, 1962; Bryant to Ice, September 4, 1962, both in Box 148, Bryant Administrative Correspondence.

122. *Tampa Tribune*, August 31, 1962.

123. "Resolution Unanimously Adopted by Membership of Florida State Chamber of Commerce," November 20, 1962, Box 1, Culpepper Papers.

Chapter 5. Sex and Civil Rights, 1963–1965

Epigraph source: *New York Times*, April 26, 1965.

1. *Tampa Times*, December 4, 1962.

2. Testimony, February 1963, Box 11, FLIC Records.

3. Schnur, "Closet Crusaders," 146–48. The story appeared three months later in numerous papers, including the *Pittsburgh Courier* on May 4, 1963; the SCEF distributed copies of this article, which was bitingly critical of the Johns Committee "Witch-Hunters."

4. Duane Barker to R. J. Strickland, February 28, 1963, Box 2, FLIC Records.

5. Floyd T. Christian to J. T. Kelley, March 21, 1963, Box 13, Bailey Subject Files; *Neal v. Bryant*, 149 So. 2d 529 (Fla. 1962); Schnur, "Closet Crusaders," 147.

6. *Gibson v. Florida Legislative Investigation Committee*; *New York Times*, March 26, 1963.

7. *Florida Alligator*, November 4, 1962; WTVT editorial, April 19, 1963, Allen Papers;

Women's Republican Club of St. Petersburg, Florida, resolution, April 10, 1963, Box 2, FLIC Records.

8. "Report of the Florida Legislative Investigation Committee to the Florida Legislature," April 18, 1963, 3, 12, 21, Box 1, Egerton Papers.

9. Ibid., 28–29.

10. John S. Allen, address to the state legislature, April 24, 1963, 2–6, Allen Papers.

11. Schrecker, *No Ivory Tower*, chap. 2.

12. Ibid., 105–6, 218.

13. C. Vann Woodward, "The Unreported Crisis in the Southern Colleges," *Harper's*, October 1962, 82–89; Stanley H. Smith, "Academic Freedom in Higher Education in the Deep South," *Journal of Educational Sociology* 32, no. 6 (February 1959): 297–308.

14. William J. Billingsley, *Communists on Campus: Race, Politics, and the Public University in Sixties North Carolina* (Athens: University of Georgia Press, 1999), 3–4.

15. Ibid., 62.

16. David R. Colburn, *Racial Change and Community Crisis: St. Augustine, Florida, 1877–1980* (Gainesville: University Press of Florida, 1991), 29–34; Taylor Branch, *Pillar of Fire: America in the King Years, 1963–65* (New York: Simon and Schuster, 1998), 35–40.

17. Branch, *Pillar of Fire*, 111.

18. Colburn, *Racial Change and Community Crisis*, 36–60.

19. R. J. Strickland letter, June 24, 1963, Box 2, FLIC Records.

20. *Florida Times-Union*, November 28, 1963.

21. Rabby, *Pain and the Promise*, 145–59.

22. Testimony, June 13, 1963, Box 11, FLIC Records; testimony, June 25, 1963, Box 11, FLIC Records.

23. Robert Dallek, *An Unfinished Life: John F. Kennedy, 1917–1963* (Boston: Little, Brown, 2003), chap. 17; Branch, *Parting the Waters*, chap. 20.

24. *St. Petersburg Times*, June 4, 1963, and June 19, 1963.

25. *Miami Herald*, January 12, 1964; Florida Legislative Investigation Committee, Staff Report 8, February 7, 1964, Box 1, FLIC Records; *Florida Flambeau*, February 12, 1964; John Evans to Francis J. McNamara, January 22, 1964, Box 1, FLIC Records; and Florida Legislative Investigation Committee, Staff Report 12, March 6, 1964, and Staff Report 15, April 3, 1964, Box 1, FLIC Records.

26. John E. Evans to Thomas D. Bailey, February 11, 1964; Bailey to Evans, February 25, 1964, Box 2, FLIC Records.

27. Florida Children's Commission, advisory meeting report, January 22, 1962, 11, Box 1, FLIC Records.

28. *Florida Times-Union*, March 6, 1962.

29. Yeager memo.

30. John E. Evans to Robert L. Shevin, July 13, 1964, 2, Box 2, FLIC Records.

31. Florida Legislative Investigation Committee, minutes, January 29, 1964, 7, Box 82, Bryant Administrative Correspondence.

32. Florida Legislative Investigation Committee, *Homosexuality and Citizenship in Florida*, Tallahassee, January 1964.

33. Ibid.

34. Robert H. Williams, "Sex, Tallahassee," *New Republic*, May 23, 1964, 5.

35. *Tallahassee Democrat*, March 20, 1964.

36. Florida Legislative Investigation Committee, *Homosexuality and Citizenship in Florida*.

37. Norman Mark, "Censorship: Fanatics and Fallacies: The Anonymous Smut Hunters," *Nation*, July 5, 1965, 5.

38. Citizens for Decent Literature, *Perversion for Profit* (1964), prod. Citizens for Decent Literature, Prelinger Archives.

39. Florida Legislative Investigation Committee, *Homosexuality and Citizenship in Florida*.

40. Williams, "Sex, Tallahassee," 5.

41. Bill Baggs to Harry Ashmore, June 8, 1964, Box 1, William C. Baggs Papers, Archives and Special Collections, Otto G. Richter Library, University of Miami.

42. *Life*, June 26, 1964, 74.

43. Hal Call, "1964 Open Letter to the Florida Legislature's 'Johns Committee,'" in *Speaking for Our Lives: Historic Speeches and Rhetoric for Gay and Lesbian Rights, 1892–2000*, ed. Robert B. Ridinger (Binghamton, N.Y.: Harrington Park Press, 2004), 86–87.

44. Anonymous to Richard Mitchell, March 19, 1964, Box 2, FLIC Records.

45. "A Voter and a Good Citizen" to Richard Mitchell, n.d., Box 2, FLIC Records.

46. "Another Mister X" to Florida Legislative Investigation Committee, June 28, 1964, Box 2, FLIC Records.

47. *Tallahassee Democrat*, March 20, 1964.

48. Hobart Coffey to John Evans, April 17, 1964, Box 2, FLIC Records.

49. Professor Anonymous, "Perverts Under the Palms," *Confidential* 12, no. 2 (February 1964): 32–33.

50. *Tallahassee Democrat*, March 20, 1964.

51. Andrew E. Kroha to Florida Legislative Investigation Committee, March 18, 1964; Harold S. Dalton to Florida Legislative Investigation Committee, March 18, 1964; Mrs. A. B. Sawyer to Florida Legislative Investigation Committee, March 18, 1964; Anonymous to John Evans, May 13, 1964, all in Box 2, FLIC Records.

52. Evans to Shevin, July 13, 1964, 2.

53. Colburn, *Racial Change and Community Crisis*, 61–70; Milton A. Oman to Mrs. Malcolm Peabody, April 2, 1964, Box 114, Bryant Administrative Correspondence.

54. Colburn, *Racial Change and Community Crisis*, chap. 4.

55. Ibid.

56. Michael Newton, *The Invisible Empire: The Ku Klux Klan in Florida* (Gainesville: University Press of Florida, 2001), 163; *Time*, August 14, 1964.

57. Kenneth O'Reilly, *"Racial Matters": The FBI's Secret File on Black America, 1960–1972* (New York: Free Press, 1989), 131–32.

58. Ibid., 141.

59. Ibid., chap. 4.

60. *St. Augustine Record*, July 31, 1964.

61. *St. Petersburg Times*, August 1, 1964; *Florida Times-Union*, August 3, 1964.

62. Gregg L. Michel, *Struggle for a Better South: The Southern Student Organizing Committee, 1964–1969* (New York: Palgrave Macmillan, 2004), chap. 1; "Calendar of Events Connected with the Establishment of the Student Group for Equal Rights," n.d., University of Florida Student Organizational Files, Box 1, University of Florida Archives, Gainesville.

63. *St. Petersburg Times*, July 26, 1964, and July 31, 1964; *Florida Flambeau*, July 31, 1964.

64. *Tampa Tribune*, September 11, 1964.

65. Robert Kleidman, *Organizing for Peace: Neutrality, the Test Ban, and the Freeze* (Syracuse: Syracuse University Press, 1993), 91–113.

66. CNVA Walk Team, memo, September 18, 1963, Box 9, Barbara Deming Papers, Schlesinger Library, Harvard University (hereafter cited as Deming Papers).

67. Neil Haworth memo, November 26, 1963, Deming Papers.

68. A. J. Muste, "The Meaning of Albany," n.d., Deming Papers.

69. *Florida Flambeau*, February 24, 1964.

70. Florida Legislative Investigation Committee, "Background Information on Walk for Peace," report, February 1, 1964, Box 1, FLIC Records.

71. Florida Legislative Investigation Committee, Staff Report 16, April 10, 1964, Box 1, FLIC Records.

72. Lawrence Rice to John Evans, April 3, 1964, Box 1, FLIC Records.

73. *Orlando Sentinel*, May 30, 1964.

74. Brad Lyttle to CNVA membership, October 30, 1964; Van Gosse, *Where the Boys Are: Cuba, Cold War America and the Making of a New Left* (New York: Verso, 1993), 234–40.

75. *Tampa Tribune*, September 11, 1964.

76. Paul Willis, Associated Press, September 30, 1964.

77. *Washington Post*, October 16, 1964.

78. Florida Legislative Investigation Committee, *Racial and Civil Disorders in St. Augustine* (Tallahassee: State of Florida, February 1965), 1–4.

79. Ibid., 8, 13, 15–16.

80. "Martin Luther King," in Florida Legislative Investigation Committee, *Racial and Civil Disorders in St. Augustine*, 3, 5.

81. Mary Stanton, *From Selma to Sorrow: The Life and Death of Viola Liuzzo* (Athens: University of Georgia Press, 1998), 53, 55.

82. Carter, *Politics of Rage*, 259.

83. Robert M. Mikell, *Selma* (Charlotte, N.C.: Citadel Press, 1965).

84. Albert C. Persons, *The True Selma Story: Sex and Civil Rights* (Birmingham, Ala.: Esco Publishers, 1965), 2–11.

85. Ibid., 15, 27.

86. *St. Petersburg Times*, February 26, 1965.

87. David Farber and Jeff Roche, introduction to *The Conservative Sixties*, ed. David Farber and Jeff Roche (New York: Peter Lang, 2003).

Epilogue

Epigraph source: Anita Bryant, *The Anita Bryant Story: The Survival of Our Nation's Families and the Threat of Militant Homosexuality* (Old Tappan, N.J.: Revell, 1977), 61.

1. Bruce J. Winick, "The Dade County Human Rights Ordinance of 1977: Testimony Revisited in Commemoration of Its Twenty-Fifth Anniversary," *Law & Sexuality: A Review of Lesbian, Gay, Bisexual, and Transgender Legal Issues* 11 (2002): 2–3; *New York Times*, January 19, 1977.

2. Fred Fejes, *Gay Rights and Moral Panic: The Origins of America's Debate on Homosexuality* (New York: Palgrave Macmillan, 2008), 78–79.

3. *New York Times*, March 24, 1969.

4. *New York Times*, April 20, 1977.

5. Sara Diamond, *Roads to Dominion: Right-Wing Movements and Political Power in the United States* (New York: Guilford Press, 1995), 161.

6. *St. Petersburg Evening Independent*, January 9, 1967; David R. Colburn, *From Yellow Dog Democrats to Red State Republicans: Florida and Its Politics since 1940* (Gainesville: University Press of Florida, 2007), 61; *Miami News*, April 3, 1967.

7. Neal R. Peirce, *The Deep South States: People, Politics, and Power in the Seven Deep South States* (New York: W. W. Norton, 1974), 456.

8. Havard and Beth, *Politics of Mis-Representation,* 46–47; Edmund F. Kallina Jr., *Claude Kirk and the Politics of Confrontation* (Gainesville: University Press of Florida, 1993), 206.

9. Mormino, *Land of Sunshine, State of Dreams,* 12–13.

10. Ibid., 19.

11. James Cass, "Politics and Education in the Sunshine State: The Florida Story," *Theory into Practice* 7, no. 2 (April 1968): 91; Parke B. Loren and Ira A. England, "Florida Education: Running a Political Obstacle Course," *Phi Delta Kappan* 50, no. 1 (September 1968): 27.

12. *New York Times*, September 7, 1961.

13. Loren and England, "Florida Education," 28.

14. Cass, "Politics and Education in the Sunshine State," 91.

15. Gordon E. Harvey, *A Question of Justice: New South Governors and Education, 1968–1976* (Tuscaloosa: University of Alabama Press, 2002), 6–7.

16. *St. Petersburg Evening Independent*, February 18, 1972; Harvey, *Question of Justice*, 78, 83.

17. Sheila Hixson and Ruth Rose, *The Official Proceedings of the 1972 Democratic National Convention* (Washington, DC, 1972), 328.

18. Ibid., 330.

19. Ibid., 331–32.

20. Ibid., 385.

21. *Sarasota Herald-Tribune*, July 13, 1972.

22. Carter, *Politics of Rage*, 378.

23. Fejes, *Gay Rights and Moral Panic*, 65.

24. Janice M. Irvine, *Talk about Sex: The Battles over Sex Education in the United States* (Berkeley and Los Angeles: University of California Press, 2002), 33.

25. Ibid., 35.

26. Ibid., 50–51.

27. *St. Petersburg Times*, November 16, 1969.

28. *St. Petersburg Evening Independent*, April 24, 1969.

29. *Sarasota Herald-Tribune*, April 17, 1970; *St. Petersburg Times*, April 17, 1970; *St. Petersburg Times*, May 6, 1970.

30. Sears, *Lonely Hunters,* 213; Vern L. Bullough, ed., *Before Stonewall: Activists for Gay and Lesbian Rights in Historical Context* (New York: Harrington Press, 2002), 198.

31. Sears, *Lonely Hunters*, 213.

32. Bullough, *Before Stonewall*, 294; Sears, *Lonely Hunters*, 214.

33. Fejes, *Gay Rights and Moral Panic*, 64.

34. *St. Petersburg Times*, February 6, 1971.

35. *Daytona Beach Morning Journal*, June 22, 1976; *St. Petersburg Times*, June 21, 1976; *Miami News*, November 16, 1976; and *Lakeland Ledger*, March 26, 1977.

36. *Daytona Beach Morning Journal*, June 22, 1976.

37. *Miami News*, March 23, 1977; Fejes, *Gay Rights and Moral Panic*, 67, 70.

38. Fejes, *Gay Rights and Moral Panic*, 67–69; *Miami News*, November 16, 1976.

39. Fejes, *Gay Rights and Moral Panic*, 82.

40. *Miami News*, March 23, 1977.

41. *St. Petersburg Evening Independent*, March 19, 1977.

42. *New York Times*, March 28, 1977; Bryant, *Anita Bryant Story*, 59.

43. Quoted in Fejes, *Gay Rights and Moral Panic*, 120–21.

44. Quoted in ibid., 113; ibid., 122.

45. *Newsweek*, June 6, 1977. Bryant quoted in Fejes, *Gay Rights and Moral Panic*, 134.

46. Bryant, *Anita Bryant Story*, 101, 142.

47. Ibid., 41–43, 59.

48. Ibid., 53–55.

49. *Nevada Daily Mail*, June 7, 1985; Bryant, *Anita Bryant Story,* 97.

50. *St. Petersburg Evening Independent*, May 14, 1977.

51. *New York Times*, June 5, 1977.

52. *New York Times*, June 7, 1977.

53. *New York Times*, June 8, 1977.

54. *Daytona Beach Morning Journal*, June 9, 1977.

55. Randy Shilts, *The Mayor of Castro Street: The Life and Times of Harvey Milk* (New York: St. Martin's Press, 1982), 164.

56. *Nation*, July 9, 1977, 34; *New York Times*, July 19, 1977.

57. Fejes, *Gay Rights and Moral Panic*, 181–83, 186, 205–9.

58. Quoted in Shilts, *Mayor of Castro Street*, 364–66.

59. Ibid., 368.

Bibliography

Archival Collections

Allen, John. Papers. Special Collections. University of South Florida, Tampa.

Baggs, William C. Papers. Special Collections, Otto G. Richter Library. University of Miami, Coral Gables, Fla.

Bryant, Farris. Correspondence. State Archives of Florida, Tallahassee.

Clerk of the House of Representatives. Records. State Archives of Florida, Tallahassee.

Collins, LeRoy. Correspondence. State Archives of Florida, Tallahassee.

———. Papers. Special Collections. University of South Florida Library, Tampa.

Deming, Barbara. Papers. Schlesinger Library, Harvard University.

Durr, Virginia Foster. Papers. Schlesinger Library, Harvard University.

Egergton, John. Papers. Special Collections. University of South Florida, Tampa.

Florida Children's Commission. Records State Archives of Florida, Tallahassee.

Florida Department of Education. Records. State Archives of Florida, Tallahassee.

Florida Legislative Investigation Committee. Records. State Archives of Florida, Tallahassee.

Mississippi Sovereignty Commission. Files. Mississippi State Archives, Jackson.

National Association for the Advancement of Colored People Records, 1842–1999. Manuscript Division. Library of Congress, Washington, D.C.

State Literature Commission of Georgia. Administrative Files. Georgia Archives, Athens.

Superintendent of Public Instruction. Records. State Archives of Florida, Tallahassee.

Books and Articles

Adams, J. Frank. *Unearthing Seeds of Fire: The Idea of Highlander*. Winston-Salem, N.C.: John F. Blair, 1975.

Alwood, Edward. *Straight News: Gays, Lesbians, and the News Media*. New York: Columbia University Press, 1996.

Andrew, John A., III. *The Other Side of the Sixties: Young Americans for Freedom and the Rise of Conservative Politics*. New Brunswick: Rutgers University Press, 1997.

Arsenault, Raymond. *Freedom Riders: 1961 and the Struggle for Racial Justice*. New York: Oxford University Press, 2006.

Asch, Chris Myers. *The Senator and the Sharecropper: The Freedom Struggles of James O. Eastland and Fannie Lou Hamer*. New York: New Press, 2008.

Bartley, Numan V. *The Rise of Massive Resistance: Race and Politics in the South During the 1950s*. Baton Rouge: Louisiana State University Press, 1969.

———. *The New South, 1945–1980*. Baton Rouge: Louisiana State University Press, 1995.

Bederman, Gail. *Manliness and Civilization: A Cultural History of Gender and Race in the United States, 1880–1917*. Chicago: University of Chicago Press, 1995.

Bentley, Eric, ed. *Thirty Years of Treason: Excerpts from Hearings before the House Committee on Un-American Activities, 1938–1968*. New York: Viking Press, 1971.

Bertwell, Dan. "'A Veritable Refuge for Practicing Homosexuals': The Johns Committee and the University of South Florida." *Florida Historical Quarterly* 83, no. 4 (Spring 2005): 410–31.

Bérubé, Allan. *Coming Out Under Fire: The History of Gay Men and Women in World War II*. New York: Free Press, 1990.

Billingsley, William J. *Communists on Campus: Race, Politics, and the Public University in Sixties North Carolina*. Athens: University of Georgia Press, 1999.

Black, Earl. *Southern Governors and Civil Rights: Racial Segregation as a Campaign Issue in the Second Reconstruction*. Cambridge: Harvard University Press, 1976.

Black, Earl, and Merle Black. *The Rise of Southern Republicans*. Cambridge: Harvard University Press, 2003.

Blount, Jackie M. *Fit to Teach: Same-sex Desire, Gender, and School Work in the Twentieth Century*. Albany: State University of New York Press, 2004.

Braden, Anne. *The Wall Between*. New York: Monthly Review Press, 1958.

———. *House Un-American Activities Committee: Bulwark of Segregation*. Los Angeles: National Committee to Abolish the House Un-American Activities Committee, 1963.

Brady, Tom. *Black Monday*. Winona, Miss.: Association of Citizens' Councils, 1955.

Branch, Taylor. *Parting the Waters: America in the King Years, 1954–63*. New York: Simon and Schuster, 1988.

———. *Pillar of Fire: America in the King Years, 1963–65*. New York: Simon and Schuster, 1998.

———. *At Canaan's Edge: America in the King Years, 1965–68*. New York: Simon and Schuster, 2007.

Brennan, Mary C. *Turning Right in the Sixties: The Conservative Capture of the GOP*. Chapel Hill: University of North Carolina Press, 1995.

Brinkley, Alan. "The Problem of American Conservatism." *Journal of American History* 99, no. 2 (April 1994): 409–29.

Brown, Sarah Hart. "Congressional Anti-Communism and the Segregationist South: From New Orleans to Atlanta, 1954–1958." *Georgia Historical Quarterly* 80, no. 4 (Winter 1996): 785–816.

———. *Standing Against Dragons: Three Southern Lawyers in an Era of Fear*. Baton Rouge: Louisiana State University Press, 1998.

Bryant, Anita. *The Anita Bryant Story: The Survival of Our Nation's Families and the Threat of Militant Homosexuality*. Old Tappan, N.J.: Revell, 1977.

Bryant, Anita, and Bob Green. *At Any Cost*. Old Tappan, N.J.: Revell, 1978.

Matthews, J. B. *Communism and the NAACP*. Atlanta: Georgia Educational Commission, 1958.

May, Elaine Tyler. *Homeward Bound: American Families in the Cold War Era*. New York: Basic Books, 1988.

McClellan, Grant S., ed. *Censorship in the United States*. New York: H. W. Wilson, 1967.

McCreery, Patrick. "Save Our Children/Let Us Marry: Gay Activists Appropriate the Rhetoric of Child Protectionism." *Radical History Review* 100 (Winter 2008): 186–207.

McGirr, Lisa. *Suburban Warriors: The Origins of the New American Right*. Princeton: Princeton University Press, 2001.

McMillen, Neil R. *The Citizens' Council: Organized Resistance to the Second Reconstruction, 1954–1964*. Urbana: University of Illinois Press, 1971.

———, ed. *Remaking Dixie: The Impact of World War II on the American South*. Jackson: University Press of Mississippi, 1997.

Michel, Gregg L. *Struggle for a Better South: The Southern Student Organizing Committee, 1964–1969*. New York: Palgrave Macmillan, 2004.

Miller, Neil. *Sex-Crime Panic: A Journey to the Paranoid Heart of the 1950s*. New York: Alyson Books, 2002.

Mohl, Raymond A., with Matilda "Bobbi" Graff and Shirley M. Zoloth. *South of the South: Jewish Activists and the Civil Rights Movement in Miami, 1945–1960*. Gainesville: University Press of Florida, 2004.

Morris, Allen. *Our Florida Government*. Chicago: Lyons and Carnahan, 1961.

Murphy, Walter F. "The South Counterattacks: The Anti-NAACP Laws." *Western Political Quarterly* 12 (June 1959): 371–90.

Navasky, Victor S. *Naming Names*. New York: Penguin, 1991.

Newton, Michael. *The Invisible Empire: The Ku Klux Klan in Florida*. Gainesville: University Press of Florida, 2001.

O'Reilly, Kenneth. *"Racial Matters": The FBI's Secret File on Black America, 1960–1972*. New York: Free Press, 1989.

Pascoe, Peggy. *What Comes Naturally: Miscegenation Law and the Making of Race in America*. New York: Oxford University Press, 2009.

Paulson, Darryl, and Paul Hawkes. "Desegregating the University of Florida Law School: Virgil Hawkins v. the Florida Board of Control." *Florida State University Law Review* 12 (Spring 1984): 59–71.

Peirce, Neal R. *The Deep South States of America: People, Politics, and Power in the Seven Deep South States*. New York: W. W. Norton, 1974.

Plummer, Brenda Gayle. *Rising Wind: Black Americans and U.S. Foreign Affairs, 1935–1960*. Chapel Hill: University of North Carolina Press, 1996.

Porter, Gilbert R. "The Status of Educational Desegregation in Florida." *Journal of Negro Education* 25, no. 3 (Summer 1956): 246–53.

Poucher, Judith G. "Raising Her Voice: Ruth Perry, Activist and Journalist for the Miami NAACP." *Florida Historical Quarterly* 84, no. 4 (Spring 2006): 517–40.

Powe, Lucas A., Jr. *The Warren Court and American Politics*. Cambridge: Harvard University Press, 2000.

Price, H. D. *The Negro and Southern Politics: A Chapter of Florida History.* New York: New York University Press, 1957.

Rabby, Glenda Alice. *The Pain and the Promise: The Struggle for Civil Rights in Tallahassee, Florida.* Athens: University of Georgia Press, 1999.

Record, Wilson. *Race and Radicalism: The NAACP and the Communist Party in Conflict.* Ithaca: Cornell University Press, 1966.

Ridinger, Robert B. *Speaking for Our Lives: Historic Speeches and Rhetoric for Gay and Lesbian Rights, 1892–2000.* New York: Routledge, 2004.

Rogin, Michael Paul. *Ronald Reagan, the Movie: And Other Episodes in Political Demonology.* Berkeley and Los Angeles: University of California Press, 1987.

Romano, Renee C. *Race Mixing: Black-White Marriage in Postwar America.* Cambridge: Harvard University Press, 2003.

Saunders, Robert W., Sr. *Bridging the Gap: Continuing the Florida NAACP Legacy of Harry T. Moore, 1952–1966.* Tampa: University of Tampa Press, 2000.

Schnur, James A. "Closet Crusaders: The Johns Committee and Homophobia, 1956–1965." In *Carryin' On in the Lesbian and Gay South,* ed. John Howard, 132–63. New York: New York University Press, 1997.

Schrecker, Ellen. *No Ivory Tower: McCarthyism and the Universities.* New York: Oxford University Press, 1986.

———. *Many Are the Crimes: McCarthyism in America.* New York: Little, Brown, 1998.

Schulman, Bruce J. *From Cotton Belt to Sunbelt: Federal Policy, Economic Development, and the Transformation of the South, 1938–1980.* Durham, N.C.: Duke University Press, 1994.

Scott, Henry E. *Shocking True Story: The Rise and Fall of Confidential, "America's Most Scandalous Scandal Magazine."* New York: Pantheon, 2010.

Sears, James T. *Lonely Hunters: An Oral History of Lesbian and Gay Southern Life, 1948–1968.* Boulder, Colo.: Westview Press, 1997.

Sherrill, Robert. *Gothic Politics in the Deep South: Stars of the New Confederacy.* New York: Grossman Publishers, 1968.

Shilts, Randy. *The Mayor of Castro Street: The Life and Times of Harvey Milk.* New York: St. Martin's Press, 1982.

Solomon, Mark. *The Cry Was Unity: Communists and African Americans, 1917–1936.* Jackson: University Press of Mississippi, 1998.

Strub, Whitney. "Perversion for Profit: Citizens for Decent Literature and the Arousal of an Antiporn Public in the 1960s." *Journal of the History of Sexuality* 15, no. 2 (May 2006): 258–91.

Sullivan, Gerard. "Political Opportunism and the Harassment of Homosexuals in Florida, 1952–1965." *Journal of Homosexuality* 37, no. 4 (1999): 57–81.

Talmadge, Herman E. *You and Segregation.* Birmingham, Ala.: Vulcan Press, 1955.

Tomberlin, Joseph A. "Florida and the School Desegregation Issue, 1954–1959: A Summary View." *Journal of Negro Education* 43, no. 4 (Autumn 1974): 457–67.

Tscheschlok, Eric. "'So Goes the Negro': Race and Labor in Miami, 1940–1963." *Florida Historical Quarterly* 76, no. 1 (Summer 1997): 43–68.

Wagy, Tom R. *Governor LeRoy Collins of Florida: Spokesman of the New South*. Tuscaloosa: University of Alabama Press, 1985.

Walker, Anders. *The Ghost of Jim Crow: How Southern Moderates Used* Brown v. Board of Education *to Stall Civil Rights*. New York: Oxford University Press, 2009.

Ward, Brian. *Just My Soul Responding: Rhythm and Blues, Black Consciousness, and Race Relations*. Berkeley and Los Angeles: University of California Press, 1998.

Webb, Clive, ed. *Massive Resistance: Southern Opposition to the Second Reconstruction*. New York: Oxford University Press, 2005.

Werth, Barry. *The Scarlet Professor: Newton Arvin, a Literary Life Shattered by Scandal*. New York: Anchor Books, 2001.

Wilhoit, Francis M. *The Politics of Massive Resistance*. New York: George Braziller, 1973.

Williamson, Joel. *New People: Miscegenation and Mulattoes in the United States*. Baton Rouge: Louisiana State University Press, 1995.

Winick, Bruce J. "The Dade County Human Rights Ordinance of 1977: Testimony Revisited in Commemoration of Its Twenty-Fifth Anniversary." *Law & Sexuality: A Review of Lesbian, Gay, Bisexual, and Transgender Legal Issues* 11 (2002): 1–9.

Woods, Jeff. *Black Struggle, Red Scare: Segregation and Anti-Communism in the South, 1948–1968*. Baton Rouge: Louisiana State University Press, 2004.

Unpublished Sources

Clark, Wayne Addison. "An Analysis of the Relationship Between Anti-Communism and Segregationist Thought in the Deep South, 1948–1964." Ph.D. diss., University of North Carolina, 1976.

Klein, Kevin N. "The Pork Chop Gang: Florida's Bourbon Legacy." Master's thesis, Florida State University, 1993.

Padgett, Gregory B. "C. K. Steele, A Biography." Ph.D. diss., Florida State University, 1994.

Schnur, James A. "Cold Warriors in the Hot Sunshine: The Johns Committee's Assault on Civil Liberties in Florida, 1956–1965." Master's thesis, University of South Florida, 1995.

Stark, Bonnie S. "McCarthyism in Florida: Charley Johns and the Florida Legislative Investigation Committee, July 1956 to July 1965." Master's thesis, University of South Florida, 1985.

Index

Stacy Braukman, an independent scholar, is the coauthor of *Gay and Lesbian Atlanta*.